# The Roots of Modern Psychology and Law

# The Roots of Modern Psychology and Law

*A Narrative History*

**EDITED BY**

**THOMAS GRISSO**

AND

**STANLEY L. BRODSKY**

Oxford University Press is a department of the University of Oxford. It furthers
the University's objective of excellence in research, scholarship, and education
by publishing worldwide. Oxford is a registered trade mark of Oxford University
Press in the UK and certain other countries.

Published in the United States of America by Oxford University Press
198 Madison Avenue, New York, NY 10016, United States of America.

CIP data is on file at the Library of Congress
ISBN 978–0–19–068870–7

9 8 7 6 5 4 3 2 1

Printed by Webcom, Inc., Canada

# CONTENTS

CONTRIBUTORS   VII

EDITORS' PROLOGUE   XIII
  *Stanley L. Brodsky and Thomas Grisso*

1. The Evolution of Psychology and Law   1
   *Thomas Grisso*

SECTION I **Psychological Science and Law**   29

2. Eyewitness Testimony: An Eyewitness Report   31
   *Elizabeth F. Loftus*

3. Applying Social Psychology to Law and the Legal Process   44
   *Michael J. Saks*

4. Jury Research   61
   *Shari Seidman Diamond*

5. Mental Health Law and the Seeds of Therapeutic Jurisprudence   78
   *David B. Wexler*

6. Mental Disability, Criminal Responsibility, and Civil Commitment   94
   *Stephen J. Morse*

7. Framing, Institutionalizing, and Nurturing Research
   in Psychology and Law   109
   *Bruce D. Sales*

SECTION II **Assessment, Interventions, and Practice in Legal Contexts** 125

8. Forensic Mental Health Services and Competence
   to Stand Trial   127
   *Ronald Roesch*

9. Predictions of Violence   143
   *John Monahan*

10. Developmental Psycholegal Capacities   158
    *Thomas Grisso*

11. Correctional Psychology   178
    *Stanley L. Brodsky*

12. The Founding and Early Years of the American Board
    of Forensic Psychology   195
    *Florence W. Kaslow*

13. Community Psychology, Public Policy, and Children   207
    *N. Dickon Reppucci*

EDITORS' EPILOGUE   223
   *Thomas Grisso and Stanley L. Brodsky*
INDEX   227

**Stanley L. Brodsky, PhD,** is professor emeritus and scholar-in-residence at the University of Alabama, where he was a faculty member from 1972 to 2016. He previously was chief psychologist at the U.S. Disciplinary Barracks, Fort Leavenworth, Kansas, and was with the Center for the Study of Crime, Delinquency, and Corrections at Southern Illinois University, Carbondale. He was a founding member of the American Psychology–Law Society and has received the awards for Outstanding Achievement from the American Psychology–Law Society and the American Association of Correctional Psychologists. He is the editor or author of 15 books and over 250 articles, mostly in the area of psychology applied to the law.

**Shari Seidman Diamond, PhD, JD,** is Howard J. Trienens Professor of Law and Professor of Psychology at Northwestern University, where she heads the JD/PhD program, and a research professor at the American Bar Foundation. She was president of the American Psychology–Law Society (1987–1988), editor of the *Law & Society Review* (1988–1991), and co-president of the Society for Empirical Legal Studies (2010–2011). She received the American Psychological Association's award for Distinguished Contributions to Research in Public Policy (1991) and the Law and Society Association's Harry Kalven Jr. award for Empirical Scholarship That Has Contributed Most Effectively to the Advancement of Research in Law and Society (2010). She was elected to the American Academy of Arts and Sciences (2012).

**Thomas Grisso, PhD,** is emeritus professor of psychiatry (clinical psychology) at the University of Massachusetts Medical School. Other primary academic appointments during his career included Ashland University (1969–1974) and Saint Louis University (1975–1987). He was president of the American Psychology–Law Society in 1990 and executive director of the American Board of Forensic Psychology from 2003 to 2017. He received the American Psychology–Law Society's award for Outstanding Contributions to Psychology and Law (2012), American Psychological Association awards for Distinguished Contributions to Research in Public Policy (1994) and Contributions to Applied Research (2014), the American Psychiatric Association's Isaac Ray Award (2005), and is an elected Fellow of the Royal College of Psychiatrists (UK).

**Florence W. Kaslow, PhD,** is Distinguished Visiting Professor of Psychology at Florida Institute of Technology, Melbourne, Florida. Prior academic appointments include adjunct professor of medical psychology, Duke University Medical Center (1982–2004), and professor and co-director of the PsyD/JD program at Hahnemann Medical College and Villanova Law School (1973–1980). She was the founding and first president of the American Board of Forensic Psychology and American Academy of Forensic Psychology and is a recipient of many awards from American Psychological Association, American Psychological Foundation, and American Board of Professional Psychology. She is board certified in forensic, clinical, and couple and family psychology.

**Elizabeth F. Loftus, PhD,** is distinguished professor at the University of California–Irvine. She holds faculty positions in two departments: psychology and social behavior and criminology, law, and society. She received her PhD in psychology from Stanford University and was formerly on faculty at University of Washington. She has published 22 books, including the award-winning *Eyewitness Testimony* (5th ed. LexisNexis, 2013), and over 500 scientific articles. Loftus's research of the last 40 years has focused on the malleability of human memory. She has been recognized for this research with seven honorary doctorates and election to the Royal Society of Edinburgh, the American Philosophical Society, and the

National Academy of Sciences. She is past president of the Association for Psychological Science, the Western Psychological Association, and the American Psychology–Law Society

**John Monahan, PhD,** is the John Shannon Distinguished Professor of Law at the University of Virginia, where he is also a professor of psychology and of psychiatry. He was on the faculty at the University of California–Irvine, from 1972 to 1980. He was the president of the American Psychology-Law Society (1978) and the founding president of the American Psychological Association's Division of Psychology and Law (1981) receiving that organization's Distinguished Contribution to Research in Public Policy Award. He also twice received the American Psychiatric Association's Manfred Guttmacher (1982 and 2002) and Isaac Ray Awards (1996). He was elected a Fellow of the American Academy of Arts and Sciences in 2016.

**Stephen J. Morse, JD, PhD,** is the Ferdinand Wakeman Hubbell Professor of Law and professor of psychology and law in psychiatry at the University of Pennsylvania since 1988. Previously he was the Orrin B. Evans Professor of Law, professor of psychology and of psychiatry and the behavioral sciences at the University of Southern California. He was president of the American Psychology–Law Society (1981–1982) and was president of Division 41/American Psychology–Law Society (1986–1987). He received the American Academy of Forensic Psychology's Distinguished Contribution to Forensic Psychology Award (1989) and the Isaac Ray Award from the American Psychiatric Association (2014) for distinguished contributions to forensic psychiatry and the psychiatric aspects of jurisprudence

**Nicholas Dickon Reppucci, PhD,** is emeritus professor of psychology at the University of Virginia Psychology Department. He was a lecturer at Harvard University (1967–1968), assistant and associate professor at Yale University (1968–1976) and professor at University of Virginia (1976–2017). He was president of Society for Community Research and Action (American Psychological Association's Division of Community Psychology; 1987) and received its Award for Distinguished Scientific and Theoretical Contributions (1998) and its Inaugural Award for Education and Training in Community Psychology (1999). He also received the American Psychology–Law Society's Award for Outstanding Contibutions to Teaching and Mentoring (2007) and Society for Research in Adolescence's Award for Outstanding Article on Adolescence and Social Policy (2008).

**Ronald Roesch, PhD,** is professor of psychology and director of the Mental Health, Law, and Policy Institute at Simon Fraser University. He received his PhD in clinical psychology from the University of Illinois in 1977. He was president of the American Psychology–Law Society in 1994. He was editor-in-chief of *Law and Human Behavior* and *Psychology, Public Policy, and Law*. Professor Roesch received the American Psychology–Law Society Outstanding Teaching and Mentoring in the Field of Psychology and Law Award in 2009 and its Outstanding Contributions to the Field of Psychology and Law Award in 2010. In 2011, he also received the Lifetime Achievement Award for Contributions to Psychology and Law from the European Association of Psychology and Law.

**Michael J. Saks, PhD, MSL,** is regents professor at the Arizona State University where he is on the faculties of the law school and psychology department and an affiliated professor at the University of Haifa (Israel). Previously, he was a faculty member at the University of Iowa and Boston College and taught in the University of Virginia Law School's LLM program for appellate judges. He was president of the American Psychology–Law Society (1989), and was the editor of *Law and Human Behavior* (1985–87). He received the American Psychological Association's award for Distinguished Contributions to Psychology in the Public Interest (1987) and the American Psychology–Law Society's Distinguished Contributions to Psychology and Law (2017).

**Bruce D. Sales, PhD, JD, DSc(hc),** is the Virginia L. Roberts Professor of Criminal Justice at Indiana University, Bloomington. He was previously a professor of psychology and law at the University of Nebraska–Lincoln (1973–1981) and of psychology, sociology, psychiatry and law at the University of Arizona (1981–2008). He was the first editor of the journals *Law and Human Behavior* and *Psychology, Public Policy, and Law.* He is a life member of the American Law Institute and twice served as president of the American Psychology–Law Society (1976–1977, 1985–1986). He received the American Psychology–Law Society Award for Distinguished Contributions to Psychology and Law (1992), and the American Psychological Association Award for Distinguished Professional Contributions to Public Service for having "pioneered the development of psychology and law as a field of research, teaching, and practice" (1995).

**David B. Wexler, JD,** is professor of law, University of Puerto Rico, and distinguished research professor of law emeritus, University of Arizona. He served on the full-time law faculty of the University of Arizona from 1967 until 1997. He is an honorary president of the newly formed International Society for Therapeutic Jurisprudence (since 2017) and is honorary president of the Iberoamerican Association of Therapeutic Jurisprudence (since 2012). He is an honorary distinguished member of the American Psychology–Law Society (2010), received the Manfred Guttmacher Forensic Psychiatry Award of the American Psychiatric Association (1972), and, for his work on therapeutic jurisprudence, was awarded the Distinguished Service Award of the National Center for State Courts (2000).

The impetus for this volume began several years ago. We recognized that the American Psychology–Law Society, inaugurated in 1969, would soon be celebrating its fiftieth anniversary. We had witnessed the Society's earliest years, and we found ourselves reflecting on the importance of capturing some of the essence of that formative time.

As an outgrowth of those reflections, we were among a group of senior scholars in a symposium at the annual meeting of the American Psychology–Law Society in 2015, all of us speaking about how our careers developed and the personal and professional trajectory of our lives. The full and overflowing audience signaled a deep and not necessarily predictable interest in the lived history of psychology and law in North America.

After all, it is easy to be ahistorical. Everything else equal, scholars value the newest studies in our field. When we review manuscripts in which the references are 20 or 30 years old, we frequently view the submissions with a skeptical eye. We similarly value highly the newest editions of tests, the newest books, and the most recent articles. Yet, there are compelling reasons to look at our history. This book addresses how modern psychology and law began.

Psychology and law as a scholarly and professional field did not appear spontaneously and fully formed. The leaves and branches are visible, but the roots are the elements from which everything grew. Knowing and understanding the roots and how our own tree of knowledge grew tells a lot about who we are and where we came from.

The historical record of our field is skimpy. This edited volume is the first book on the history of the modern field of psychology and law. It offers new perspectives on the origins of modern psychology and law, as written by those who lived and created it.

Many students of the history of psychology know that psychology's interaction with law emerged early in the 20th century. Yet that early start amounted to a premature fanfare after which the potential lay dormant for another 30 or 40 years.

The emergence of psychology and law as a modern field of scholarship was marked by the founding of the American Psychology–Law Society in 1969. The scientific foundation on which the modern field grew was established by a small group of psychological researchers, legal scholars, and clinicians who became widely known and respected. The contributors to this edited volume are among those groundbreakers. Their work led to the current burgeoning subfields and topics in psychology and law and forensic psychology. The contributors, appropriately considered among the founders of their field, are now nearing retirement yet are still remarkably vital, productive contributors to scholarly knowledge.

In a narrative voice, each of the contributors has described the key professional events in his or her career during the 1970s, the first decade of the American Psychology–Law Society. In some cases these events were their first major research studies using psychology applied to legal issues. In others, it was their development of seminal ideas, innovations, or experiences that had a later impact on the field's development. They were in their thirties, there was no coherent field of psychology and law, and they were imitating no one. Their projects became cornerstones in the foundation of modern psychology and law.

Each contributor's story covers a period of time, often just a decade or so, when the researcher developed the seminal effort that spawned subfields of research or gave birth to the organizational structure of the field. While telling their stories, they reflect on events and issues in U.S. law and policy in the 1960s and 1970s that stimulated their work, where they borrowed from then-current psychological science to further their efforts, and on their own needs, hopes, aspirations, and frustrations that drove them forward at that point in their personal and professional development. The last portion of each chapter describes the later evolution, up to the present, of the field for which their earliest work provided a foundation.

The book begins with our chapter about the evolution of psychology and law research and of forensic–clinical interactions with law. Starting with brief observations about early 20th-century interactions between psychology and law, it describes the conditions in which psychology and law took root in the 1970s when the 12 chapter authors were developing the field. It continues with a description of the enormous contributions of the American Psychology–Law Society in those early years, as well as the successes, conflicts, and challenges that arose as the Society matured into the 21st century. This is followed by our 12 contributors' chapters, arranged in two broad areas: (a) psychological science and law, and (b) assessment, interventions and practice in legal contexts.

By almost any measure the persons who have authored those chapters are among the early leaders in psychology and law. There were certainly others, and all 12 authors acknowledge and identify those who were beginning to do work similar to theirs during the 1970s. Enlisting these specific authors for this task was guided in part by our effort to represent the scope of topics that arose in the 1970s and to achieve balance by minimizing repetition across the whole enterprise. The social psychology of the law: check. Violence prediction: check. Memory: check. Professional credentialing: check. Juveniles: check. Community psychology: check. Mental disability law: check. And much more.

The last thing we wanted was for this book to be a dry, tired, and difficult read that covered ground already well-trodden. For that reason, we asked the authors of the chapters to write about their personal journeys. When occasionally we received a draft that was light on personal reflections, we asked them to reveal more about their own odysseys. And they did it, much more than we expected. We learned new things about people we have known for four decades. Who knew that John Monahan started out in a seminary? Or that so many barriers impeded the paths of our contributors?

The contributions fascinated us. At moments, we felt like leaping and clicking our heels, if clicking our heels were still within our modest leaping repertoires. We smiled. We often were moved. For the first time in one place, the life stories have been gathered of the people and the work that has shaped so much of psychology and law.

We truly did not know just what to expect in response to our invitations to the authors. The replies and chapters went well beyond our hopes. The process fit into the Japanese Zen notion of *mu*, in which the context of the question was too small for the breadth and truth of the answer.

In light of Beth Loftus's body of work on the malleability of memory, it is perhaps reasonable to ask whether these recollections and memories of the development of psychology and law are accurate. As exemplary as our contributors are, decades have gone by. We had asked everyone to go back to the 1970s and to trace where they were and how their paths led to where they are now. Are the memories dependable and accurate?

To one way of thinking, it may not make a difference. There are many articles and a book with similar themes asserting that there is no such thing as nonfiction (Brock, 2011; Kilgore, 2010). Tom Waits has declared that nonfiction does not exist (Maher, 2011, p. 424). Norman Mailer, in an award address, said that everything written is fiction, because the reality of any given moment is impossible to describe. Instead, he encouraged writers to aim to come close to what happened. In his chapter "Historical Text as Literary Artifact," Hayden White (2002) takes a more philosophical position, claiming that authors endow nonfiction stories with their own meanings and life metaphors and always offer biased details (p. 201). E. L Doctorow (1988) argued in a *New York Times* book review much the same conclusion, "There is no longer any such thing as fiction or nonfiction; there's only narrative."

All of us have had the experience of sharing memories of events with a person who was there, only to find that some element or statement of outcome was differently recalled. Yet a form of fact-checking is in place. These recollections are supported by references and publications or are narrated in considerable detail. We are excited to share them.

## REFERENCES

Brock, M. (2011). There's no such thing as a nonfiction novel! Retrieved from https://marciebrockbookmarketingmaven.wordpress.com/2011/08/06/theres-no-such-thing-as-a-nonfiction-novel/

Doctorow, E. L. (1988). *New York Times Book Review*, January 27, 1988.

Kilgore, C. (2010). *There's no such thing as non-fiction*. Morrisville, NC: Lulu.

Maher, P. (2011). *Tom Waits on Tom Waits: Interviews and encounters*. Chicago: Chicago Review.

White, H. (2002). The historical text as literary artifact. In H. Richardson (Ed.), *Narrative dynamics: Essays on time, plot, closure, and frames*. Columbus. OH: Ohio State University Press.

# The Evolution
# of Psychology and Law

THOMAS GRISSO

The 50th anniversary of the American Psychology–Law Society (AP–LS) in 2019 will occur about 110 years after Munsterberg's (1908) treatise on psychology's potential for application to legal issues. Munsterberg's overture was soundly rejected as premature by legal scholars of the time (Wigmore, 1909). Yet in the intervening years, the success of an applied science called *psychology and law* has been remarkable in its influence on the law, legal systems and procedures, and the provision of evidence in legal cases.

This chapter examines how the field of psychology and law evolved. This account does not describe fully what psychology and law is or what it has achieved. That can be found in psychology and law textbooks, more detailed histories (e.g., Bartol & Bartol, 2015; Brigham & Grisso, 2003), and in each of the other 12 chapters in this book. In contrast, the present chapter focuses on the important motives, forces, and social conditions that influenced how the field grew. It also examines the role of the AP–LS as one of the major forces in psychology and law's development. The evolution of the field seems to divide naturally into three major eras. The first two, the birth of legal psychology (1890–1930) and a dormant era (1930–1960), are described briefly. The chapter attends primarily to the third, modern era of psychology and law that blossomed in the 1970s and 1980s and continues to mature.

## THE EARLY ROOTS OF PSYCHOLOGY AND LAW

Before psychology and law as we know it came on the scene, legal psychology had flourished for about 30 years early in the 20th century and then slumbered for another 30 years. Some of that history is relevant for understanding the modern era.

### The Legal Psychology Era (1890–1930)

In the late 19th and early 20th centuries, laboratories like that of Wilhelm Wundt's began building a basic science of human behavior—mapping, classifying, and determining the structural and functional boundaries of memory, perception, sensation, and motor reactions. As basic data and principles emerged, Wundt's students began identifying how the principles might have practical use in business, military affairs, education, advertising, public health, and, of course, law.

The earliest descriptions of psychology's potential for application to law were largely speculative. For example, Munsterberg's (1908) treatise, *On the Witness Stand*, mostly contained visionary hypotheses. Some researchers took the next step, performing studies that used basic lab findings to predict behavior in experimental situations that approximated the circumstances of legal cases (e.g., Benussi, 1914; Marston, 1917; Stern, 1906, 1910). An early review by Slesinger and Pilpel (1929) found 11 of these hypothesis-testing articles pertaining to psychology of eyewitness testimony and 10 reports of applied studies for detection of deception, although there were many more on other topics (as reviewed by Burtt, 1931).

There is no record of an organized affiliation or association of psychologists engaged in those earliest studies. Indeed, the young, eager researchers who first explored psychology's applications to law seemed not to identify themselves as "forensic" or "legal" psychologists. They were simply applied psychologists. Any one of them was likely to be examining applications to industry, advertising, education, or the military at the same time.

A few of these applied psychologists, however, did come close to identifying legal psychology as their primary specialty. For example, William Marston obtained both a law degree and a PhD in psychology at Harvard in 1921 (studying with Munsterberg). He joined the faculty at American University in 1922 in what is believed to be the first position entitled "Professor of Legal Psychology" (Heilbrun, Grisso, & Goldstein, 2009). He studied errors in eyewitness accounts (Marston, 1924) and polygraphic detection of deception (Marston, 1917), testimony on the latter making him the focus of the *Frye v. United States* (1923) decision (Weiss, Watson, & Xuan, 2014).[1] Others were William Healy (a psychologically minded neurologist) and Grace Fernald (a psychologist). Together they founded the Juvenile Psychopathic Institute in 1909 to serve the first juvenile court in the United States (Cook County, Chicago, opened in 1899; Schetky & Benedek, 1992). This was the first court-related psychological clinic on record, breaking ground with comprehensive "studies of the child" to assist the court in dispositional decisions (Healy, 1915) and creating the first specialized psychological tests to evaluate delinquent youth (Domino & Domino, 2006).

Harold Burtt produced a book, *Legal Psychology* (Burtt, 1931) that best summarizes how far the field had come in its first 30 years. Born in 1890, Burtt trained with Munsterberg at Harvard and served in World

---

1. Even Marston, though, had other applied interests, including his consultation to an educational publishing company, leading to his invention of DC Comics' Wonder Woman (Lepore, 2014).

War I to apply psychology to the war effort. After the war he joined the faculty at Ohio State University in 1919.[2] His contributions were diverse including early attempts to select aviators, to detect lies and other forms of deception, to enhance advertising effectiveness, to avoid copyright/trademark infringement, and to improve street lighting ("Obituary," 1992). He was one of the founders in 1938 of the American Association for Applied Psychology, which broke away from the American Psychological Association (APA) because of APA's perceived lack of support or attention to applied psychology.

Burtt's *Legal Psychology* was a major work of 459 pages with 19 chapters. If the chapters had been clustered, their sections almost could serve as the outline for a modern text in psychology and law (e.g., four chapters on witness accuracy and testimony, two on court procedures and jury decision making, two on psychopathology and crime). Munsterberg's (1908) more famous book was actually a collection of previously published magazine articles largely without scholarly citations (Grisso & Brigham, 2013). In contrast, Burtt thoroughly referenced an impressive number and range of basic and applied studies from many labs, describing them in great detail together with published tables and graphs illustrating their results. He also cited over 120 legal cases, using their facts to illustrate psychology's relevance for law and legal process.

Taking note of what was *not* in Burtt's book provides some insight into the broader social context in which early legal psychology was evolving and how different that context was when compared to the rise of modern psychology and law in the 1970s. First, this new field appeared to have no interest in the parallel rise of forensic psychiatry. Isaac Ray, Bleuler and Kraepelin, Freud's and Jung's forays into legal questions, the relevance of mental disorder for criminal responsibility—none of that appeared in Burtt's *Legal Psychology*. Burtt seemed to presume that when legal psychology evolved a bit further, it would offer the law something entirely

---

2. Burtt's career actually spanned the years between Munsterberg and the modern era of psychology and law. He chaired the Psychology Department at Ohio State University until he retired in 1960. He died at age 101 in 1991, when the AP–LS was about 20 years old.

different than psychiatry and more far-reaching in "value to those who are interested in furthering justice and improving society" (Burtt, 1931, p. 459).

Second, the book suggests that "furthering justice and improving society" in those days had a different meaning than when modern psychology and law emerged in the 1970s. Burtt's book offers little research directed specifically at concerns about human rights or civil liberties, sometimes encouraging deprivation of rights of people with disabilities for their own and society's benefit. Early legal psychology reflected the times in which it evolved. Racial discrimination (*Plessy v. Ferguson*'s 1896 separate-but-equal policy) and sterilization of persons with hereditary intellectual impairments (*Buck v. Bell*, 1927) were constitutional.[3] Some leaders in biological science (e.g., Davenport, 1928) and applied sciences (e.g., Alexander Graham Bell, 1914) were promoting the eugenics movement to reduce the burden of "mental defectives" on society and to purify the nation's population. Burtt's chapter on heredity, character, and intelligence interpreted research to favor the eugenics movement, offering little evidence of discomfort regarding human rights.[4]

Finally, absent from Burtt's book were Munsterberg's (1908) uncompromising conclusions that psychologists had all the answers and lawyers were simply too stubborn to listen to them (Grisso & Brigham, 2013). In contrast, Burtt cautioned both lawyers and psychologists that "legal psychology is not a well-organized body of knowledge" (Burtt, 1931, p. 459), although certain areas had "nearly reached the stage" (p. 448) when they could qualify as evidence in legal cases. Legal psychology was poised to fulfill its potential.

3. The court in *Buck v. Bell* explained: "It is better for all the world if, instead of waiting to execute degenerate offspring for crime or to let them starve for their imbecility, society can prevent those who are manifestly unfit from continuing their kind . . . three generations of imbeciles is enough" (*Buck v. Bell*, 1927).

4. The United States was not alone in the use of applied psychology to promote such policies. Applied psychologists in South Africa were interpreting their research to support a racially separated social system. In the 1950s, this led to the government's formal apartheid policies drafted by Prime Minister Hendrik Verwoerd, an applied psychologist trained in pre-Nazi Germany.

## The Dormant Era (1930–1960)

Then nothing happened. Writing early in the modern era, June Louin Tapp (1976, p. 361) observed with puzzlement that after the 1930s: "Not until the late 1960s was the exchange between psychologists and lawyers on matters of justice and law anything more than sparse and sporadic." Tapp did not try to explain the hiatus, but several circumstances offer grounds for reasonable speculation. Moreover, much *did* happen that eventually would shape psychology and law when it blossomed in the third era.

One could blame Munsterberg's (1908) book and Wigmore's (1909) scathing response for legal psychology's failure take hold (Bersoff, 1999). Yet it was also likely that the law was not ready for psychology. While critiquing Munsterberg, Wigmore also chastised his own colleagues for taking so little interest in using what the sciences produced. During the 1920s and 1930s, the legal world was debating legal realism (e.g., Frank, 1930). Skepticism and disagreement surrounded the notion that scientific evidence about social implications of legal decisions should have a role in shaping judicial thinking. Also, at that time psychology, relative to psychiatry, had little legal standing as a profession for expert testimony on legal issues and mental disorder. In fact, clinical psychology as we know it barely existed (Compas & Gotlib, 2002). Finally, World War II offered great opportunities and demands for applying psychology to personnel selection, communications, and improving instrument panels for aircraft and other weapons. These alternatives may have contributed to a waning of applied psychologists' attention to applications in law.

While little was happening in legal psychology scholarship during the dormant years, two specialties in psychology—social and clinical—were developing in ways that set the stage for modern psychology and law. In the late 1930s, social psychology was beginning to do what Kurt Lewin called "action research": psychological studies in quasi-naturalistic settings that could bear on contemporary social problems and promote social change (Adelman, 1993). Thus arose a group devoted to policy-relevant research, the Society for the Psychological Study of Social Issues (Krech & Cartwright, 1956). Society members went beyond the laboratory to issue their own statements on political issues of the World War II era. At first antiwar, later they used their group-behavior research to demonstrate the destructive effects of totalitarian social systems. Postwar research of this type set the stage for a focus on policy-relevant research and human rights that would be a central motivation for psychology and law in the third era.

The dormant era also saw the formal recognition of clinical psychology. Psychologists were developing a new generation of psychological tests, including tests of psychopathology (e.g., MMPI; Hathaway & McKinley, 1942). The war created demands for treatment of soldiers that exceeded the capacity of the psychiatric workforce, offering opportunities for psychologists to take on new diagnostic and psychotherapeutic roles in medical and psychiatric settings (Benjamin, 2005; Watson, 1953). Between 1945 and 1950, the new field of clinical psychology acquired its own APA division, a *Journal of Clinical Psychology*, the development of the American Board of Professional Psychology in 1947 (Watson, 1953) and, in the 1950s, the first formal university programs in clinical psychology (Compas & Gotlib, 2002).

During the 1950s, clinical psychologists' new recognition led to an increase in their involvement in correctional settings (Bartol & Freeman, 2005; see Brodsky, this volume) and as experts in legal cases in which personality or mental disorder were the focus of civil and criminal litigation (Greenburg, 1956; Loh, 1981). The 1950s also brought an uptick in experimental, social, and developmental psychological testimony, marked notably by Kenneth Clark's appearance in *Brown v. Board of Education* (1954; which ruled that school racial segregation violated the Fourteenth Amendment). Yet the law clearly had not thrown open the door. As described at that time, "An important problem in psychology today is the legal status of the psychologist and his relationship to the courts. . . . The use of the [psychological] expert witness is a fairly modern innovation in the field of legal evidence" (McCary, 1956, p. 8).

Legal psychology may have advanced little in the dormant era. Yet the development of clinical and social psychology would play a key role in the field's reawakening.

## BIRTH OF THE MODERN ERA (1960–1990)

Scholarly signs of a new era appeared in two books of the 1960s: social psychologist Hans Toch's (1961) edited volume on *Legal and Criminal Psychology* and James Marshall's (1966) *Law and Psychology in Conflict*. Burtt's *Legal Psychology* in 1931 and Toch's book in 1961, marking the beginning and end of the dormant era, had titles and topics that matched remarkably well. Toch's authors identified a few new studies of the 1950s, yet the greatest number of their citations to empirical work were the 1920s and 1930s studies of Burtt and his contemporaries.

These books were essays speculating about the possibility of a future field. In Toch's book, a chapter by Robert Redmount (lawyer and clinical psychologist) titled simply "Psychology and Law" concluded:

> The psychologist . . . who confronts law in all its estate is bold indeed. In fact, he does not yet exist. That there is plenty of psychology in law . . . is plain to behold. But psychologists . . . have been rather more timorous in their infiltration into law than into medicine and education" (Redmount, 1961, pp. 37–38). Similarly, Marshall observed that "[P]articipation by lawyers and psychologists in empirical research into the processes of law . . . is practically non-existent, and it is curious in view of the common deductive approach of both science and the law. (Marshall, 1966, pp. 103–104)

Marshall and Redmount were the last authors to have reason to wonder about psychology's "timorous" and "curious" lack of interactions with law. So much began happening that only about a decade later the *Annual Review of Psychology* published Tapp's (1976) *Psychology and the Law: An Overture* describing the emergence of this new field. Explaining this blossoming is more hypothesis than history, but primary considerations are (a) an awakening of social conscience in American society in the 1950s and 1960s, (b) favorable federal support, and (c) the emergence of an organization that offered the field a group identity.

## Postwar Law and Human Rights

The 1950s and 1960s saw sweeping changes in U.S. society's consciousness regarding human rights, civil liberties, and social justice. They included a whirlwind of federal cases related to racial desegregation (e.g., *Brown v. Board of Education*, 1954), women's rights (e.g., *Griswold v. Connecticut*, 1965), criminal defendants' and prisoners' rights (e.g., *Dusky v. U.S.*, 1960; *Wyatt v. Stickney*, 1971), children's rights (e.g., *In re Gault*, 1967; *Tinker v. Des Moines*, 1969), the rights of persons with mental disorders (e.g., *Lake v. Cameron*, 1966), and informed consent (*Natanson v. Kline*, 1960). These reforms profited by the appearance of judges like David Bazelon and, a little later, Harry Blackmun who were disposed to listen to arguments promoting human rights in medical and psychiatric contexts. The law began listening to relevant empirical information about human behavior when shaping policy and law. The stage was set.

This zeitgeist also was preparing the lawyers and psychologists—among them, authors of the stories in this book—who would fuel the rise of modern psychology and law during the 1960s and 1970s. It had a socializing effect on their young lives, often forming their motivation to use their professions for social justice. This vision may have been the major difference between the modern era of psychology and law and the legal psychology of the early 1900s.

## Federal Support

A second factor in the rise of psychology and law was the convergence of law and federal initiatives offering support for psychology's interactions with law. *Jenkins v. U.S.* (1962) cleared the way for clinical psychologists' testimony in cases involving questions of mental illness, formerly the province of psychiatrists. Research that would build a scientific foundation for the field profited by establishment in 1968 of the Center for Studies of Crime and Delinquency at the National Institute of Mental Health (NIMH). NIMH funding for crime and delinquency research was not new, having been around for about 15 years before the Center was established (Voit, 1995). What made the difference was the new Center's director, Saleem Shah.

A clinical psychologist receiving his PhD in 1957, Shah had worked for several years as a court clinician in Washington, DC, before taking the Center position. He reoriented the Center's mission toward empirical work in law and mental health that would benefit persons in need who were socially marginalized. Shah was an "advocate for relevance" (Roth, 1995), not impressed with research that would provide *only* understanding; he favored projects allowing for fairly direct translation into policy or practice. He was staunchly against any discipline's special claim to authority; the Center funded psychologists, sociologists, psychiatrists, criminologists, and lawyers. In a special issue of *Law and Human Behavior* devoted to remembering Shah after his tragic death, the editors wrote, "No one else among us has had so significant an impact on the history of modern mental health law in policy and practice" (Grisso & Steadman, 1995, p. 2).

## The American Psychology-Law Society (AP-LS)

The third factor that helped modern psychology and law blossom was the birth of the AP–LS at a meeting of 13 psychologists, initiated by lawyer and psychologist Jay Ziskin, at the APA convention in San Francisco in 1968. AP–LS was launched in 1969 with 101 charter members, more than doubling within two years (Grisso, 1991). Beginning with assets of $202 (the $2 dues from its charter members) and a mimeographed newsletter, today it has over 3,500 members, significant financial assets, a multitude of specialty committees serving its members, a journal, a book series, websites, and conferences.

A detailed narrative of AP–LS's early history is beyond the limits of this chapter, but we have comprehensive descriptions of AP–LS's first 20 years (Grisso, 1991) and an update to the 21st century (Fulero, 1999). The most significant organizational change occurred in 1981when some of AP–LS's leaders called for the development of a new Division 41 of Psychology and

Law within the APA. AP–LS members were strongly divided on the prospect of merging with the new APA division. After three years of debate, they arrived at an amicable consensus to merge (in 1984) after APA agreed to accommodate to AP–LS's terms (Grisso, 1991). For example, AP–LS demanded that persons with law degrees but without psychology degrees could have Division membership even though they did not qualify for membership in APA.

The impact of AP–LS on the evolution of modern psychology and law during its 50 years is woven through various sections in the remainder of this chapter. AP–LS was only one of many organizations that played a major supportive role in psychology and law's growth (others will be noted later), but it has been the most influential. It provided what every field of science and practice requires to grow and strengthen: a sense of collective identity and an authoritative platform for social influence. Its key supports were (a) publication resources, (b) establishing standards, (c) promoting conferencing opportunities, and (d) stimulating training.

## PUBLICATION RESOURCES

A field of science and practice is defined by its peer-reviewed knowledge. AP–LS's journal, *Law and Human Behavior* (LHB), was launched in 1977 under the initiative of its first editor, Bruce Sales (see Sales, this volume).[5] LHB now ranks in the top echelon of journals in the categories "Psychology, social" and "Law."[6] LHB was preceded by American Association of Correctional Psychologists' *Criminal Justice and Behavior* (first appearing in 1974; see Brodsky, this volume). Eventually those two journals were joined by 11 more with distinct psychology-and-law identity, as well as about 17 journals in law–psychiatry and various criminal and civil law journals with social science specialization (Heilbrun, Grisso, & Goldstein,

5. Subsequent LHB editors to date were Michael Saks, Ronald Roesch, Richard Wiener, Brian Cutler, Margaret Bull Kovera, and, currently, Brad McAuliff.

6. According to the Social Science Citation Index from Clarivate Analytics' Journal Citation Reports, LHB recently had the thirteenth highest impact factor among 147 journals in the "Law" category.

2009). APA developed *Psychology, Public Policy and Law* in 1995 (also with Bruce Sales as founding editor). AP–LS's book series, Perspectives in Law and Psychology, helped jump-start a new wave of books for the field. In a 1979 national survey of university psychology courses that included law in their content, 85% of the 27 books used in those courses had been published in AP–LS's first decade (Grisso, Sales, & Bayless, 1982).

## STANDARDS

A field of science and practice is controlled, and its credibility enhanced, by its consensus regarding standards. The American Board of Forensic Psychology (ABFP), and its collaborative organization for psychologists it certified, the American Academy of Forensic Psychology (AAFP), began in 1987 with AP–LS assistance (see Kaslow, this volume). Through its certification of forensic psychological practitioners, ABFP identified and promoted advanced forensic practice standards. Together AP–LS and ABFP/AAFP developed the first *Specialty Guidelines for Forensic Psychologists* (Committee on Ethical Guidelines for Forensic Psychologists, 1991) and then its revision with APA sponsorship (APA, 2013). AAFP has annually provided a series of workshops for forensic practitioners that has elevated standards of practice.

## CONFERENCES

A field of science and practice is energized by its collective gatherings that provide face to face exchange and a relational sense of group identity. The first AP–LS conference in 1974 was followed in 1977 by the beginning of a biennial convention tradition when about 25 members met at Snowmass, Colorado, to present to each other for two days in one meeting room. The AP–LS merger with APA Division 41 led to APA annual convention programming, but AP–LS continued its biennial meetings until switching to annual meetings in 2002. By 2017, AP–LS conferences featured over 100 symposia, attended by about 1,000 members.

## TRAINING

A field of science and practice is sustained by its programs for training students of the field. Before the 1970s, no academic training centers existed pertaining specifically to psychology and law. By the end of the 1970s, however, about one-fourth of graduate psychology programs in the United States had courses in which at least 50% of their content pertained to psychology and law (Grisso Sales & Bayless, 1982). The 1970s also saw the start-up of the first five training programs with joint psychology and law degrees.[7] Legally or forensically specialized doctoral programs in psychology blossomed in the 1980s and 1990s, and Donald Bersoff managed the Villanova Training Conference in 1995, a three-day effort to sort out the needs and challenges of training programs for the growing field (Bersoff et al., 1997). Subsequently, two of the 1970s JD–PhD programs (University of Nebraska and Drexel University) survived to the present and have been joined by others, and 25 graduate psychology departments now offer specialized psychology doctoral degrees in the field (AP–LS, 2017b). Over 40 academic and hospital settings now offer postdoctoral training for psychology-and-law research or forensic psychological practice (AP-LS, 2017a).

## IDENTIFYING MODERN PSYCHOLOGY AND LAW

The maturation and identity of modern psychology and law from the 1990s forward can be defined by its *content*—the evolution of its research, its practice, and their impact on society—and by its *process*—the organized strivings of those who nurtured, promoted and controlled the field as it developed. The first definition—its content and accomplishments—is best left to other resources that review how far the field has come in its diverse areas of research, its forensic uses of that knowledge, and their impact on law, policy, and human rights and welfare (e.g., Carson & Bull, 2003; Cutler & Zapf, 2015; Goldstein, 2007; Heilbrun, DeMatteo, & Goldstein,

---

7. The JD–PhD programs at Stanford University in 1972, University of Nebraska–Lincoln in 1974 and, in 1979, Johns Hopkins University/University of Maryland, Hahnemann Medical School/Villanova University (now Drexel University), and the JD–PsyD program at University of Denver's Law School and School of Professional Psychology.

2016; Melton Petrila, Poythress, & Slobogin, 2007; Weiner & Otto, 2013). The other 12 chapters in this volume capture some of that identity in their chronicle of the evolution of key areas of research and practice from the 1970s to the present. The big picture is 50 years of ever-increasing, almost bewildering differentiation of subtopics within broader categories of research. Psychology and law has drawn from all of the behavioral, social, and biological sciences to explore complexities in diverse areas of criminal, civil, and juvenile law and legal process.

The second way to define the field—the process of its growth—requires examining recurrent themes in the strivings of those who sought to influence and use the field. The increasing diversity of the field's interests has often contributed to tension. As the field matured, its conflicting interests expanded and sometimes challenged its identity as a single field. Some of those challenges involved (a) relations between organizations, (b) demographic diversity of its contributors, and (c) problems of identity related to competing professional interests.

## Interorganizational Relations

During its overture in the 1970s, the field began with organizational support from AP–LS (Grisso, 1991) and the American Association of Correctional Psychologists (Brodsky, 2007). Many other organizations arose subsequently, notably the AAFP, ABFP, the International Association of Forensic Mental Health Services, and the International Academy of Law and Mental Health.[8]

These organizations have operated relatively independently, yet they have rarely been overtly competitive. After the rise of AP–LS and AACP, subsequent organizations did not form as alternatives but primarily to

---

8. In addition, the American Academy of Psychiatry and Law was founded just one year before AP–LS and has provided a venue for psychology and law research and practice. Other organizations developed mental health and forensic subsections and committees: for example, the Forensic division of the National Association for State Mental Health Program Directors; the Criminal Justice System–Mental Health Committee of the American Bar Association. AP–LS

focus on some subset of psychology's applications to law or, like ABFP's certification of forensic psychologists, to play some circumscribed role that AP–LS did not seek to fulfill. Even after ABFP's tense spin-off from AP–LS (see Kaslow, this volume), the two have maintained collaborative relations. Psychology and law's supportive network of organizations, therefore, has enjoyed predominantly friendly, laissez faire, and often mutually supportive relations.

AP–LS's relation with APA has been more complex. AP–LS's history includes important collaborative relations with APA that have benefited AP–LS and APA alike. APA's *Psychology, Public Policy and Law,* its Committee on Legal Issues, its legal office's amicus briefs to appellate courts, and its interest in collaborative initiatives with the American Bar Association have drawn heavily on the assistance of AP–LS scholars and provided the field with major avenues of influence on law and policy. Moreover, in the past 30 years, the careers of six of APA's presidents have included psychological contributions to legal, correctional, or forensic issues.[9] In 1988, a standing APA president joined a past APA president to publish an article in *Science* (Fowler & Matarazzo, 1988) in support of forensic psychology, in response to another *Science* article claiming that psychological research did not provide a sufficiently validated foundation to support the expert testimony of psychologists (Faust & Ziskin, 1988).

Yet the history of AP–LS and its relations with APA also has seen moments of conflict. For example, when AP–LS developed the *Specialty Guidelines for Forensic Psychologists* in 1991 (under the guidance of Stephen Golding), APA asserted that any division's published standards should be approved by APA, recognizing that the *Guidelines* could impact psychologists in other specialties who occasionally testified in court. AP–LS resisted because it feared that the *Guidelines* would be "watered down"

also has enjoyed relations with psychology and law organizations in other countries: for example, Australian and New Zealand Association of Psychiatry, Psychology and Law; European Association of Psychology and Law; European Association for Forensic Child and Adolescent Psychiatry and Psychology.

9. Theodore Blau (1977), Raymond Fowler (1988), Patrick DeLeon (2000), Philip Zimbardo (2002), Gerald Koocher (2006), and Donald Bersoff (2013).

to suit nonforensic practitioners' interests. AP–LS won that argument, but later it capitulated when APA began its 2002 revision of its ethics code with the intention of including a section on ethics in forensic cases. This led to AP–LS input on the forensic section of the APA ethics code and eventually, under Randy Otto's guidance, to APA's adoption of a revision of the AP–LS's *Specialty Guidelines for Forensic Psychology* (APA, 2013). The battle of the *Guidelines* also created tension among AP–LS members, as described later.

## Demographics and Degrees

The demographics of contributors to a field of study can influence how it develops: for example, what the field studies, who controls its progress, and how it is perceived by those outside the field. Psychology and law's demographics have shifted during its 50-year history in both beneficial and worrisome ways. Tracking demographics for the field of psychology and law is difficult, but data about AP–LS membership provide some approximation.

In 1969, only 9 of the 101 charter members of AP–LS were women (Grisso, 1991). This proportion shifted dramatically across the years, so that now women comprise well over one-half of the Society's membership (some estimate two-thirds). This is consistent with the growing proportion of women members of APA (about two-thirds; APA, 2015). This shifting gender demographic has fostered healthy dialogue and better attention to women's professional issues in psychology and law, and it has been reflected in AP–LS's leadership. The organization elected two women and eight men as presidents during its first 10 years. That proportion persisted until 2005, after which about one-half of AP–LS's presidents were women.

As in psychology generally, however, the increasing gender imbalance toward women raised concern about public perceptions of psychology and law. There is a tendency for fields in which women constitute the majority to suffer economic disadvantages (Millward & Woodland,

1995; Preston, 1999; Reskin & Roos, 1990). Others have noted the effects of gender-biased perceptions of psychologists' authority when presenting evidence in legal forums (Larson & Brodsky, 2014; Neal, Guadagno, Eno, & Brodsky, 2012). If the field's estimates are correct (APA, 2015), gender imbalance toward women in psychology generally and psychology and law is likely to increase beyond 75% in the future, as current graduate students (almost 80% women) enter the field and the field's oldest cohort (mostly men) retire.

Psychology and law as a field has always had only a small proportion of African-American, Hispanic, and Asian contributors. Specific estimates are difficult to determine, but they are probably less than in the psychology workforce in general, where only 16% of psychologists claim racial/ethnic minority status (APA, 2015). One must question the future health of a field in which the race/ethnicity of its contributors vastly underrepresents that of the public it serves, especially in light of projections that within 25 years, non-Hispanic whites will comprise the minority of the U.S. population (Colby & Ortman, 2015).

Regarding academic degrees, almost all of the founders of AP–LS were trained in clinical psychology (Grisso, 1991). The mid-1970s, however, saw increasing diversity as more nonclinical psychologists—largely cognitive, social, and developmental (hereinafter, experimental)—adopted AP–LS as their base for advancing their research on law, legal systems, and legal process. In addition, within the first two years after AP–LS's inauguration, a remarkable 40% of its members had law degrees (Grisso, 1991). During the organization's 50 years, its presidents have been clinical and experimental in nearly equal proportions, and about 35% have had law degrees (all but one with experimental or clinical psychology degrees as well).

Recent years, though, have raised concern about the field's lawyers. Their proportion within AP–LS ranks has decreased markedly, as has lawyers' leadership in AP–LS. For the organization's first 35 years, almost one-half of its presidents had law degrees. Yet there were none in the 12 succeeding years (2004–2015), and AP–LS conferences saw a dwindling presence of lawyers and legal scholarly contributions. In most recent years, AP–LS has initiated special efforts to revitalize law scholarship and lawyers' identification with the field, an effort characterized by a recent AP–LS president as "increasing the L in AP–LS" (DeMatteo, 2016, p. 1).

## Identity and Professional Interests

Perhaps no other issue has placed more stress on the field across its modern era than the basic questions, "What is psychology and law?" and "What is forensic psychology?"[10] Are they the same or different? The questions were first posed at the beginning of the modern era. When the founders of the new organization asked its membership to choose a name, members split 50–50 between names including the words "law/legal" and "forensic" (Grisso, 1991).

Although most of the charter members of AP–LS were clinically trained, about one-half were in private practice and one-half were doing research in academic settings (Grisso, 1991). This accounted in part for the group's fractious reaction when founder Jay Ziskin (1970), shortly after the organization began, announced that psychologists had no place in the courtroom until the field's researchers had done enough work to warrant the courts' faith in them (Grisso, 1991). By the mid-1970s, some practitioners were dubious about the Society's value. Researchers with less interest in clinical forensic practice took the executive reins of AP–LS, leaving many of the practicing clinicians to find means outside AP–LS to create an organization (i.e., ABFP) that would meet their needs (see Kaslow, this volume).

Events in the 1990s, though, raised the most serious identity tensions, threatening to fracture into smaller, specialized units. By that time, the range of specialized topics within the field had greatly diversified, as widely different as eyewitness testimony and therapeutic jurisprudence and psychopathy, addressing a growing array of topics across criminal,

10. Research for this section included a detailed review of AP–LS newsletters and executive minutes from the 1990s to the present, as well as personal communications solicited in 2017 from most of the presidents of AP–LS since the 1990s.

civil, and juvenile/family law. This challenged psychology and law's identity as a single field and the notion that a single organization could meet its disparate needs.

The decade of the 1990s was bracketed by efforts to define problems facing the expansion of forensic psychology (Grisso, 1987; Otto & Heilbrun, 2002), and by two AP–LS-initiated study-group retreats managed by AP–LS presidents Gary Melton in 1991 and James Ogloff in 1999 (Fulero, 1999; Roesch, Hart, & Ogloff, 1999). Yet as the field entered the 21st century, one AP–LS president warned that it was threatened by "balkanization": "The discipline is by now so large that we risk becoming victims of our own success, breaking up into sub-disciplines. It is now possible to attend the Biennial [AP–LS convention], go to a session in each time slot, and hear papers on a single topic. . . . If, indeed, we want Law and Psychology to be recognized as a distinct field of study, we need to find ways to slow and even reverse this trend" (Hart, 2002, p. 3).

Problems of diversity, though, were more complex than just the multiplication of special areas of research. A second dimension pertained to various academic degrees—experimental (e.g., social, developmental, cognitive), law, and clinical. And a third dimension cutting across those degree areas was identification with research versus practice. Some social and cognitive psychologists doing research (e.g., on eyewitness testimony or jury selection) were not only researchers; they also engaged in practice in the form of consultation to attorneys and courts. Similarly, while many clinical psychologists in the field were solely practitioners, others engaged in research to improve practice. Thus, as elaborated in the following discussion, understanding the field's professional conflicts during the 1990s required a complex three-dimensional analysis: subfields of research, experimental–clinical degrees, and research–practice interests.

Tensions about identity and specialty interests ran very high during the 1990s (Fulero, 1999). AP–LS's executive group manifested a growing dominance by clinicians throughout that decade. While AP–LS presidencies were equally balanced between clinical and experimental psychologists across the organization's 50 years, AP–LS members elected presidents with clinical degrees 11 out of the 15 years between 1989 and 2003. Many experimental psychologists felt that clinical and/or practitioner psychologists were "taking over," and a similar trend arose in APA at the same time. Some of psychology and law's experimental psychologists began transferring their allegiance from APA and AP–LS to APA's new rival, the American Psychological Society (now Association for Psychological Science, dedicated more substantially to research), further unbalancing the organization and weakening its experimental-research base.

Late in the 1990s, clinical psychologists within AP–LS petitioned APA to formally designate forensic psychology as a *practice* specialty. Many AP–LS researchers became concerned. Would all of psychology and law become a forensic practice specialty? After all, the *Specialty Guidelines for Forensic Psychologists* (Committee on Ethical Guidelines for Forensic Psychologists, 1991) were written to cover psychologists who "engaged regularly as experts . . . in an activity intended primarily to provide professional psychological expertise to the justice system" (p. 656). If this definition were used, would experimental researchers, who sometimes offered jury-selection consultation or testified about scientific findings on eyewitness accuracy, be required to meet training criteria as though they were forensic practitioners? Should the field split, distinguishing between forensic psychology (the practitioners) and legal psychology (the researchers)? AP–LS presidents of the 1990s describe polarized power struggles around these issues. Predictions about an organizational fracturing of the field were frequent and argumentative (Fulero, 1999).

In the end, most researchers decided that participating in shaping an APA forensic specialty through AP–LS involvement offered better prospects and fewer risks than leaving the task to forensic practitioners (e.g., through ABFP/AAFP). Forensic psychology received APA recognition as a formal specialty in 2001, with criteria that did not unduly burden researchers in the type of consultations and testimony that they provided.

Balance seems to have been restored after those years of tension. Since 2004, experimental and clinical psychologists once again have been elected to annual AP–LS presidencies in almost equal proportions. Only the naïve would conclude that questions about the field's legal and forensic identity have been resolved. Yet the field ends its first 50 years with a healthy tolerance for the ambiguity and recognition of the value of its diversity. The field has not fractured. The conclusion of this account of the field's evolution offers a speculation about what has held it together.

## THE HEART OF PSYCHOLOGY AND LAW

Is there something at the heart of psychology and law that connects all of the field's diversity, bonding it across time and its diversified subfields? Finding it would identify the field's resilience and energy. Yet this might also reveal the field's central tensions. Whatever is valued most creates both one's greatest joy and greatest source of anxiety.

The essence might lie in the field's dual commitments: science and advocacy. At its heart, *science* is neutral, blind to practical purposes, and devoted only to knowing what can be discovered objectively and reliably. Science has faith that what is discovered may be useful, but it recognizes that knowledge will be of no use if it is tainted by applied interests that might unduly influence its discovery. At its heart, *advocacy* is unlike science. It seeks only a beneficial end, be it social justice or personal gain. Advocacy is less concerned with truth or fact. It seeks a desired outcome that is justified and sought because of treasured values and ardent beliefs.

The dynamic interaction of science and advocacy is why psychology and law is both exciting and dangerous. Advocacy drives our scientific studies, shaping their purpose and design, yet always with the threat of contaminating scientific integrity. Scientific evidence gives advocacy power but always with the potential that facts will modulate or frustrate advocacy's deeply valued purposes. Science and advocacy are uncertain partners, going forward with faith that the collaboration will improve society yet always risking conflicts and disappointment.

The final, defining intersection of the partnership between science and advocacy is the *expert opinion*. It is the social psychologist's consultation to a legislature, a developmental psychological amicus brief to the U.S. Supreme Court, or the clinical psychologist's conclusion that a defendant lacks capacities relevant for competence to stand trial. The expert opinion is the purpose of psychology and law's strivings that unites it as a field.

This expert opinion is different than the opinion in other arenas where psychology is applied—the clinic, the school, industry. Psychology and law's expert opinions are shaped by the law's concepts, and the legal forum puts them in the glaring spotlight of public scrutiny and challenge. Our expert opinions create precedent and policies—gradually or in a single stroke—that can change society in ways that affect millions.

Despite essential differences between science and advocacy, there is no conflict when their intersection, the expert opinion, is driven by science reliably discovered and applied to a cause justly sought. The devil, though, is in the balance—deciding when the science is good enough and, when it is, deciding the manner in which to apply it to avoid advocacy damaging the opinion's credibility even when the scientific basis is sound.

Disagreements about that balance have been at the heart of most of psychology and law's struggles. It was there in the modern era's earliest debates about the readiness of our science for expert testimony (Bonnie & Slobogin, 1980; Ennis & Litwack, 1974; Faust & Ziskin, 1988; Monahan, 1981; Morse, 1982; Poythress, 1982; Ziskin, 1970), potential uses and misuses of our science (Saks & Baron, 1980), and later in our discussions of the ability of our science to meet *Daubert* standards (Groscup & Penrod, 2011; Shuman & Sales, 1999). It arose as we faced questions about the proper role of our science and advocacy in our amicus briefs (Grisso & Saks, 1991; Roesch, Golding, Hans, & Reppucci, 1991) and our efforts to perform advocacy-driven science in ways that minimize bias (Grisso & Steinberg, 2005).

Seeking the balance drove the development of our ethical guidelines that limit expert opinion, our training standards that sustain the field's integrity, and our debates about errors in testimony (e.g., Borum, Otto, & Golding, 1993; Dvoskin, 2007). It was the defining reason for our search for psycholegal and personality assessment methods that would provide an objective data base, increase legal relevance, and limit bias in our opinions (Grisso, 1986/2003; Heilbrun, 2001; Melton et al., 2007). As we near 50 years of vigilance to improve the balance, it continues to be challenged by new evidence about the questionable dependability of the research on which we base our opinions (Lilienfeld, 2012; Nosek & Bar-Anan, 2012) and the roles of cognitive bias in interpretation of our data (Dror, 2016; Murrie & Boccaccini, 2015; Murrie et al., 2013; Neal & Brodsky, 2016; Neal & Grisso, 2014).

Whether in the laboratory or the forensic evaluation clinic, the balance of science and advocacy is a common concern that unites the diversity within psychology and law. It creates the tension and energy that keeps us interested and moves us forward. May it continue to do so as the field matures beyond its first 50 years.

## REFERENCES

Adelman, C. (1993). Kurt Lewin and the origins of action research. *Educational Action Research*, *1*, 7–24.

American Psychological Association. (2013). Specialty guidelines for forensic psychology. *American Psychologist, 68*, 7–19.

American Psychological Association. (2015). *Demographics of the U.S. psychology workforce: Findings from the American Community Survey.* Washington, DC: APA.

American Psychology-Law Society (2017a). Training resources. http://www.apls-students.org/training.html

American Psychology–Law Society. (2017b). *Guide to graduate programs in forensic and legal psychology.* Retrieved from http://ap-ls.wildapricot.org/resources/Documents/2016_2017GuidetoGraduateProgramsinForensicPsych.pdf

Bartol, C., & Bartol, A. (2015). *Introduction to forensic psychology.* New York: Sage.

Bartol, C. R., & Freeman, N. J. (2005). History of the American Association of Correctional Psychology. *Criminal Justice and Behavior, 32*, 123–142.

Bell, A. (1914). How to improve the race. *Journal of Heredity, 5*, 1–7.

Benjamin, L. (2005). A history of clinical psychology as a profession in America (and a glimpse at its future). *Annual Review of Clinical Psychology, 1*, 1–30.

Benussi, V. (1914). Atmungssymptome der Lüge. *Archiv für die gesamte Psychologie, 31*, 244–273.

Bersoff, D. (1999). Preparing for two cultures: Education and training in psychology and law. In R. Roesch, S. Hart, & J. Ogloff (Eds.), *Psychology and law: State of the discipline* (pp. 375–401). New York: Plenum.

Bersoff, D., Goodman-Delahunty, J., Grisso, T., Hans, V., Poythress, N., & Roesch, R. (1997). Training in law and psychology: Models from the Villanova Conference. *American Psychologist, 52*, 1301–1310.

Bonnie, R., & Slobogin, C. (1980). The role of mental health professionals in the criminal process: The case for informed speculation. *Virginia Law Review 66*, 427–522.

Borum, R., Otto, K., & Golding, S. (1993). Improving clinical judgment and decision making in forensic evaluation. *Journal of Psychiatry and Law, 21*, 35–76.

Brigham, J., & Grisso, T. (2003). The history of forensic psychology. In D. K. Friedheim & I. B. Weiner (Eds.), *Comprehensive handbook of psychology:* Vol. 1. *The history of psychology* (pp. 391–411). New York: Wiley.

Brodsky, S. (2007). Correctional psychology and the American Association of Correctional Psychology: A revisionist history. *Criminal Justice and Behavior, 34*, 862–869.

*Brown v. Board of Education of Topeka*, 347 U.S. 483 (1954).

*Buck v. Bell*, 274 U.S.200, 207 (1927).

Burtt, H. (1931). *Legal psychology*. New York: Prentice-Hall.

Carson, D., & Bull, R. (Eds.). (2003). *Handbook of psychology in legal contexts*. New York: Wiley.

Colby, S., & Ortman, J. (2015). Projections of the size and composition of the U.S. Population: 2014 to 2060. Current population reports, P25-1143, United States Census BureauSize, Washington, D.C.

Committee on Ethical Guidelines for Forensic Psychologists. (1991). Specialty guidelines for forensic psychologists. *Law and Human Behavior, 15*, 655–665.

Compas, B., & Gotlib, I. (2002). *Introduction to clinical psychology*. New York: McGraw-Hill.

Cutler, B., & Zapf, P. (Eds.). (2015). *APA handbook of forensic psychology*. Washington, DC: American Psychological Association.

Davenport, C. B. (1928). Crime, heredity, and environment. *Journal of Heredity, 19*, 307–313.

DeMatteo, D. (2016). President's column. *AP–LS Newsletter*, October 1–2.

Domino, G., & Domino, M. (2006). *Psychological testing: An introduction* (2nd ed.). New York: Cambridge University Press.

Dror, I. (2016). A hierarchy of expert performance. *Journal of Applied Research in Memory and Cognition, 5*, 121–137.

*Dusky v. United States*, 362 U.S. 402 (1960).

Dvoskin, J. (2007). Presidential column. *AP–LS News, 27* (Winter), 2–3.

Ennis, B., & Litwack, T. (1974). Psychiatry and the presumption of expertise: Flipping coins in the courtroom. *California Law Review, 62*, 693–752.

Faust, D., & Ziskin, J. (1988). The expert witness in psychology and psychiatry. *Science, 241*, 31–35.

Fowler, R., & Matarazzo, J. (1988). Psychologists and psychiatrists as expert witnesses. *Science, 241*, 1143.

Frank, J. (1930). *Law and the modern mind*. New York: Brentano.

*Frye v. United States*, 293 F. 1013 (D.C. Cir. 1923).

Fulero, S. (1999). A history of Division 41 (American Psychology–Law Society): A rock and roll odyssey. In D. Dewsbury (Ed.), *Unification through division: Histories of the divisions of the American Psychological Association* (Vol. 4, pp. 109–127). Washington, DC: American Psychological Association.

Golding, S., & Roesch, R. (1984). Assessment and conceptualization of competency to stand trial: Preliminary data on the Interdisciplinary Fitness Interview. *Law and Human Behavior, 8*, 321–334.

Goldstein, A. (Ed.). (2007). *Forensic psychology: Emerging topics and expanding roles.* Hoboken, NJ: Wiley.

Greenburg, J. (1956). Social scientists take the stand: A review and appraisal of their testimony in litigation. *Michigan Law Review, 54,* 953–970.

Grisso, T. (1986, second edition 2003). *Evaluating competencies: Forensic assessments and instruments.* New York: Kluwer Academic/Plenum Publishers.

Grisso, T. (1987). The economic and scientific future of forensic psychology. *American Psychologist, 42,* 831–839.

Grisso, T. (1991). A developmental history of the American Psychology–Law Society. *Law and Human Behavior, 15,* 213–223.

Grisso, T., & Brigham, J. (2013). Forensic psychology. In D. Freedheim & I. Weiner (Eds.), *Handbook of psychology: Vol. 1: History of psychology* (second edition, pp. 429–447). Hoboken, N.J.: John Wiley and Sons.

Grisso, T., & Saks, M. (1991). Psychology's influence on constitutional interpretation: A comment on how to succeed. *Law and Human Behavior, 15,* 205–211.

Grisso, T., Sales, B., & Bayless, S. (1982). Law-related courses and programs in graduate psychology departments. *American Psychologist, 37,* 267–278.

Grisso, T., & Steadman, H. (1995). Saleem A. Shah: The man and his imperative. *Law and Human Behavior, 19,* 1–3.

Grisso, T., & Steinberg, L. (2005). Between a rock and a soft place: Developmental research and the child advocacy process. *Journal of Clinical Child and Adolescent Psychology, 34,* 619–627.

*Griswold v. Connecticut,* 381 U.S. 479 (1965).

Groscup, J., & Penrod, S. (2011). *Daubert's* meanings for admissibility of behavioral and social science evidence. *Seton Hall Law Review, 33,* 1141–1165.

Hart, S. (2002). President's column: The state of the division. *American Psychology-Law Society News, 22,* 3.

Heilbrun, K. (2001). *Principles of forensic mental health assessment.* New York: Kluwer Academic/Plenum.

Hathaway, S. R., & McKinley J. C. (1942). *Manual for the Minnesota Multiphasic Personality Inventory.* Minneapolis: University of Minnesota Press.

Heilbrun, K., DeMatteo, D., & Goldstein, N. (Eds.). (2016). *APA handbook of psychology and juvenile justice.* Washington, DC: American Psychological Association.

Heilbrun, K., Grisso, T., & Goldstein, A. (2009). *Foundations of forensic mental health assessment.* New York: Oxford University Press.

Healy, W. (1915). *The individual delinquent: A textbook of diagnosis and prognosis for all concerned in understanding offenders.* Boston: Little, Brown.

*In re Gault,* 387 U.S. 1 (1967).

*Jenkins v. U.S.,* 307 F.2d 637 (D.C. Cir. 1962).

Krech, D., & Cartwright, D. (1956). On SPSSI's first twenty years. *American Psychologist, 11,* 470–473.

*Lake v. Cameron,* 364 F.2d 657 (D.C. Cir. 1966).

Larson, B. S., & Brodsky, S. L. (2014). Assertive women as expert witnesses: A study of assertive and defensive responses in male and female experts. *Behavioral sciences and the Law, 32,* 149–163.

Lepore, J. (2014). The surprising origin story of Wonder Woman. *Smithsonian Magazine*, October. Retrieved from http://www.smithsonianmag.com/arts-culture/origin-story-wonder-woman-180952710/

Lilienfeld, S. (2012). Scientific utopia or scientific dystopia? *Psychological Inquiry, 23*, 277–280.

Loh, W. D. (1981). Perspectives on psychology and law. *Journal of Applied Social Psychology, 11*, 314–355.

Marshall, J. (1966). *Law and psychology in conflict.* New York: Bobbs-Merrill.

Marston, W. (1917). Systolic blood pressure symptoms of deception. *Journal of Experimental Psychology, 2*, 117–163.

Marston, W. (1924). Studies in testimony. *Journal of American Institute of Criminal Law, 15*, 5–31.

McCary, J. (1956). The psychologist as an expert witness in court. *American Psychologist, 11*, 8–13.

Melton, G., Petrila, J., Poythress, N., & Slobogin, C. (2007). *Psychological evaluations for the courts: A handbook for mental health professionals and lawyers* (3rd ed.). New York: Guilford.

Millward, N., & Woodland, S. (1995). Gender segregation and the male/female wage differences. *Gender, Work, and Organization, 2*, 125–139.

Monahan, J. (1981). *The clinical prediction of violent behavior.* Rockville, MD: National Institute of Mental Health.

Morse, S. (1982). Reforming expert testimony: An open response from the tower (and the trenches). *Law and Human Behavior, 6*, 45–47.

Munsterberg, H. (1908). *On the witness stand.* New York: Doubleday.

Murrie, D., & Boccaccini, C. (2015). Adversarial allegiance among expert witnesses. *Annual Review of Law and Social Science, 11*, 37–55.

Murrie, D., & Boccaccini, C., Guarnera, M., & Rufino, K. (2013). Are forensic experts biased by the side that retained them? *Psychological Science, 24*, 1889–1897.

*Natanson v. Kline*, 350 P.2d 1093 (1960).

Neal, T., & Brodsky, S. (2016). Forensic psychologists' perceptions of bias and potential correction strategies in forensic mental health evaluations. *Psychology, Public Policy, and Law, 22*, 58–76.

Neal, T., & Grisso, T. (2014). The cognitive underpinnings of bias in forensic mental health evaluations. *Psychology, Public Policy, and Law, 20*, 200–211.

Neal, T. M., Guadagno, R., Eno, C., & Brodsky, S. L. (2012). Warmth and competence on the witness stand: Implications for credibility of male and female expert witnesses. *Journal of American Academy of Psychiatry and Law, 40*, 488–497.

Nosek, B., & Bar-Anan, Y. (2012). Scientific utopia: I. Opening scientific communication. *Psychological Inquiry, 23*, 217–243.

Obituary: Harold E. Burtt. (1992). Retrieved from http://www.siop.org/Museum/TIP/Thayer%20_%20Austin%20(1992)%20Burtt%20Obituary.pdf

Otto, R., & Heilbrun, K. (2002). The practice of forensic psychology: A look toward the future in light of the past. *American Psychologist, 57*, 5–18.

*Plessy v. Ferguson*, 163 U.S. 537 (1896).

Poythress, N. (1982). Concerning reform in expert testimony: An open letter from a practicing psychologist. *Law and Human Behavior, 6,* 39–43.

Preston, J. (1999). Occupational gender segregation trends and explanations. *Quarterly Review of Economics and Finance, 39,* 611–624.

Redmount, R. (1961). Psychology and law. In H. Toch (Ed.), *Legal and criminal psychology* (pp. 22–50). New York: Holt, Rinehart and Winston.

Reskin, B. F., & Roos, P. A. (1990). *Job queues, gender queues: Explaining women's inroads into male occupations.* Philadelphia, PA: Temple University Press.

Roesch, R., Golding, G., Hans, V., & Reppucci, N. (1991). Social science and the courts: The role of amicus curiae briefs. *Law and Human Behavior, 15,* 1–11.

Roesch, R., Hart, S., & Ogloff, J. (Eds.). (1999). *Psychology and law: The state of the discipline.* New York: Kluwer Academic/Plenum.

Roth, L. (1995). Saleem Shah: His national and international contributions to forensic mental health systems. *Law and Human Behavior, 19,* 15–23.

Saks, M., & Baron, C. (Eds.). (1980). *The use/nonuse/misuse of applied social research in the courts.* Cambridge, MA: Abt.

Schetky, D., & Benedek, E. (1992). *Clinical handbook of child psychiatry and the law.* Baltimore, MD: Williams & Wilkins.

Shuman, D., & Sales, B. (1999). The impact of *Daubert* and its progeny on the admissibility of behavioral and social science evidence. *Psychology, Public Policy, and Law, 5,* 3–15.

Slesinger, D., & Pilpel, M. E. (1929). Legal psychology: A bibliography and a suggestion. *Psychological Bulletin, 12,* 677–692.

Stern, L. W. (1906). Zur psychologie der aussage. *Zeaschrift fur die qesamte Strafrechswissenschaft, 23,* 56–66.

Stern, L. W. (1910). Abstracts of lectures on the psychology of testimony. *American Journal of Psychology, 21,* 273–282.

Tapp, J. (1976). Psychology and the law: An overture. *Annual Review of Psychology, 27,* 359–404.

*Tinker v. Des Moines Independent Community School District,* 393 U.S. 503 (1969).

Toch, H. (Ed.). (1961). *Legal and criminal psychology.* New York: Holt, Rinehart and Winston. Retrieved from https://archive.org/details/legalcriminalpsy00toch

Voit, E. (1995). Developing a research program: Saleem Shah's leadership role at the National Institute of Mental Health. *Law and Human Behavior, 19,* 5–14.

Watson, R. (1953). A brief history of clinical psychology. *Psychological Bulletin, 50,* 321–346.

Weiner, I., & Otto, R. (Eds.). (2013). *The handbook of forensic psychology.* New York: Wiley.

Weiss, K., Watson, C., & Xuan, Y. (2014). *Frye's* backstory: A tale of murder, a retracted confession, and scientific hubris. *Journal of the American Academy of Psychiatry and the Law, 42,* 226–233.

Wigmore, J. (1909). Professor Munsterberg and the psychology of testimony being a report of the case of *Cokestone v. Munsterberg. Illinois Law Review, 3,* 399–445.

*Wyatt v. Stickney,* 325 F.Supp. 781 (M.D. Ala. 1971).

Ziskin, J. (1970). *Coping with psychiatric and psychological testimony.* Beverly Hills, CA: Law and Psychology.

# Psychological Science and Law

# 2

# Eyewitness Testimony

*An Eyewitness Report*

**ELIZABETH F. LOFTUS**

When asked by the editors to write a chapter on "eyewitness identification," my first decision was to change the title to "Eyewitness Testimony." I used that title in my first book on the subject (Loftus, 1979) for one simple reason: Eyewitness testimony arises in instances that deal not only with someone's ability to identify a person but also with the ability to accurately recall other kinds of details that were part of an important incident. So, of course, we are interested in whether an eyewitness accurately identified the perpetrator of the Oklahoma bombing as Timothy McVeigh or the inaccurate identification of Ronald Cotton by rape victim Jennifer Thompson (Thompson-Cannino & Cotton, 2009). But we are interested also in the accuracy with which people identify how an event occurred. For example, in the opening chapter of my first book on eyewitnesses, I provided a description of a plane crash about which one witness was certain that the plane had gone "right toward the ground—straight down" just before impact. The witness was apparently not aware that there were photographs of the crash that proved that the plane hit flat and at a low enough angle to skid for almost 1,000 feet.

## THE HISTORY OF EYEWITNESS TESTIMONY

The psychological study of witnesses had a long history by the time I decided to study it myself, although I didn't know about that history. I would only learn about it after I decided to write a *Psychological Bulletin*-type review article on the topic and then the eyewitness testimony book. I learned a great deal, for example, about Hugo Munsterberg and his seminal book *On the Witness Stand* (Munsterberg, 1908). Munsterberg was fond of staging incidents in his Harvard classroom and asking students to recount what they had seen. He documented their common mistakes. Munsterberg was highly controversial at the time, largely over his insistence that the legal field needed to pay more attention to psychology. Not long after his book was published, law professor John Henry Wigmore wrote a wonderfully satirical attack on the book, construed in the form of a trial in which the members of the bar sued Munsterberg for defamation. Of course, the trial never happened, and the satirical nature of the article was made clear when readers realized the case took place on April Fool's Day and Mr. X. Perry Ment was the name of one of Munsterberg's defense lawyers. Munsterberg's book was an important piece of history here; it introduced the public to many ideas that are still central to the field of eyewitness testimony. Through his helter-skelter "studies," he showed how error prone witnesses can be. He attacked the assumptions of the legal system about insufficient protections against witness error. He urged the legal field to listen to the messages that psychological science has to offer.

In the first quarter of the 20th century other psychologists contributed mightily to our understanding of witness testimony. Whipple published a string of articles in *Psychological Bulletin* (e.g., Whipple, 1911), as did many others (for details, see Loftus, 1979). Ceci and Bruck (1993) referred to the "dry middle years," a period that encompassed the 1930s thru the mid-1960s; they pointed to a resurgence of interest in child testimony that occurred in the late 1970s. Similarly, interest in eyewitness testimony was low to unremarkable in the decades or so before I entered this field. But at that time, I wasn't even particularly aware of any of this history.

## I THOUGHT I WAS STUDYING MEMORY

I went to graduate school at Stanford specifically because I wanted to study mathematical psychology, and Stanford was a top place in that field. Before long I realized that I was bored with mathematical psychology, and it wasn't until the later part of my graduate years that I developed an interest in semantic memory. Semantic memory concerns memory for words and concepts and general knowledge about the words, rather than memory about the episodes of our life. Inspired by a chance to work with professor Jonathan Freedman, I learned how to design and conduct experiments on how general knowledge is stored in the mind and how it is retrieved when we need it. We published a number of papers together, and for the first time I was truly excited about doing research (e.g., Freedman & Loftus, 1971). For the first few years post-PhD, I lived and breathed semantic memory. But I also had this nagging feeling that I wanted to do research that had more obvious social relevance.

What might that be? Since I'd built up some expertise and confidence in the area of memory, it seemed that it should be about memory. I also had a long-standing personal interest in legal cases. Then it hit me: What about studying the memory of witnesses to crimes and accidents and other legally relevant events? I got some funding from the U.S. Department of Transportation; they cared about accidents, which is why I started with accidents, but what I found extended well beyond accidents into memory for many different kinds of past experiences.

While the vast majority of other memory psychologists were using words or nonsense syllables, or sentences and simple photos, as experimental stimuli, I started showing people films of traffic accidents and studying their memory. In one early study I noticed that the questions I asked people could skew their answers. Asking, "How fast were the cars going when they smashed into each other?" led to higher estimates of speed than a more neutral question like, "How fast were the cars going when they hit each other?" The published paper describing this study has one of my favorite titles, "Reconstruction of Automobile Destruction;" I co-authored it with John Palmer, an undergraduate who would go on to become a fantastic researcher himself (Loftus & Palmer, 1974). These early studies on memory distortion caused by leading questions were followed by others (e.g., Loftus, 1975), and soon it became clear that leading questions are one way—among many others—by which witnesses' memories can be contaminated. I also found that memories can be contaminated when witnesses talk to one another or when they are exposed to media coverage that contains erroneous detail. Misinformation encountered after the fact can lead to problems with accurate memory, and the phenomenon became known as the "misinformation effect" (Loftus & Hoffman, 1989). During the 1978–1979 academic year I was fortunate to be free of routine academic responsibilities as I spent the year at the Center for Advanced Study in the Behavioral Sciences at Stanford. There I wrote my first book on eyewitness testimony (Loftus, 1979) and soaked myself in the work of Munsterberg, Whipple, and other early 20th-century pioneers in the field.

## A WALK IN THE WILD COURTROOM

A life-changing career move occurred in the mid-1970s when I wrote an article for *Psychology Today* magazine (Loftus, 1974). The article discussed some of the laboratory studies showing how leading questions contaminate memory, and I also wrote about a court case that I worked on with an experienced public defender in Seattle. The case involved a female defendant who was accused of killing her boyfriend, and her testimony and that of other witnesses had a bearing on whether the killing was or was not in self-defense. The woman was acquitted, and within days of the publication of my article, my phone was ringing off the hook. Some lawyers wanted me to analyze the memory issues in their cases. Other lawyers wanted me to speak at continuing legal education seminars about the psychology of memory and its implications for the legal system. I gave advice, I gave speeches, and I began to consult on legal cases and to appear in courtrooms as an expert witness on the psychological science of memory.

Over the next several decades, my professional life would be filled not only with laboratory and field research on memory but also with legal cases in which memory was critical. Sometimes a legal case gave me the idea for a new study to conduct. Sometimes new study results made their way into legal cases as scientific evidence.

## EYEWITNESS TESTIMONY—A REAL FIELD

By the early 1980s, I had a growing number of wonderful colleagues I could talk to about eyewitness testimony research. In England, Ray Bull and Brian Clifford were conducting influential studies, and they published a book on identification a year before mine (Clifford & Bull, 1978). In Canada, Dan Yarmey published a book on eyewitness testimony the same year that I did (Yarmey, 1979).

A few years later, one of the most influential researchers in the field, Gary Wells, would enter the scene. When we first met at a conference, he was already doing excellent research and had coined the distinction between estimator and system variables. He would focus much of his career on those system variables—things the system can change. In 1984, we published an edited volume together; he did the lion's share of the work, especially when it came to herding tardy contributors (Wells & Loftus, 1984). We ended our opening chapter this way: "The literature on the psychology of eyewitness testimony is neither perfect nor complete, and we have attempted here to help eyewitness researchers formulate better conceptual ideas as well as to encourage more and better empirical research on the subject" (Wells & Loftus, 1984, p. 11).

## EXPERT TESTIMONY BY PSYCHOLOGICAL SCIENTISTS

In the early 1970s, defense attorneys were trying hard to introduce expert testimony on eyewitness matters in their criminal cases. Brooklyn University psychology professor Robert Buckhout had been admitted a few times, including testimony he gave at the trial of social activist Angela Davis who had been implicated in a shooting that occurred in Marin County, California (for more details, see Doyle, 2005). However, often other attempts to introduce eyewitness testimony failed. Judges would typically exclude the testimony arguing that a psychologist could not tell the jury anything the jury didn't already know, or, put another way, the testimony was all a matter of common sense. Sometimes judges gave a different excuse—that the expert testimony invaded the province of the jury. Then, for me, something memorable happened on June 3, 1975. My testimony was admitted by Judge Janice Niemi in Seattle on a day I'll never forget. As I reminisced in a recent autobiography (Loftus, 2017, p. 7):

> My brother David called to tell me that our father had died that morning after a battle with melanoma. I had visited him only a couple of weeks before. I was still wiping away tears when the phone rang again. It was David Allen, a Seattle attorney, who asked me to come to the courthouse right away because it looked like the judge would admit my testimony. Could I really set aside my grief and do this? I somehow managed to collect myself and go to court. Judge Janice Niemi admitted my testimony into trial. Today, when prosecutors try to discredit me by asking how many times I have testified in court (translation: "you're a hired gun"), I often mention the exact date I first began testifying.

Prosecutors today sometimes stumble into a statement posing as a question, something like "I see you have no trouble remembering that date." After I inform them that it was the day my father died, they stop any further questioning.

Still, throughout the 1970s, judges continued frequently to exclude expert testimony about eyewitness questions. One famous case from the early 1970s was known as the San Quentin Six trial. A lawyer for one of the defendants tried to introduce my expert testimony that would have dealt with the effects of stress, the cross-racial identification problem, and other relevant factors. The judge did not permit the expert testimony, and we once again heard how this was all a matter of common sense. These experiences prompted my interest in finding out just what people in general and jurors in particular believe about memory. Is it all really common sense?

I wrote about an early pilot study (Loftus, 1979, p. 172) that revealed that many jury-eligible individuals appeared to hold beliefs that were contradicted by eyewitness science. I would subsequently collaborate on other publications revealing more about misconceptions that jurors have about eyewitness behavior (Deffenbacher & Loftus, 1982; Schmechel, O'Toole, Easterly, & Loftus, 2006). Many other researchers contributed to this literature; this would play a role in later convincing the courts that eyewitness science was not a matter of common sense.

Throughout the 1970s, though, judges continued to frequently exclude expert testimony. Convicted defendants who appealed to higher courts mostly got nowhere. The appellate and supreme courts of the state would routinely uphold convictions, deciding that the trial judges had broad discretion to exclude the expert testimony. Then something different happened with the decision of *Arizona v. Chapple* (1983). Dolan Chapple tried to introduce my testimony in his trial for murder and drug trafficking, but the judge refused on the grounds that it was all common knowledge. The Arizona Supreme Court thought otherwise and reversed the conviction, granting a new trial. A year later, the California Supreme Court followed Arizona, reversing Eddy Bobby McDonald's conviction for murder since the trial judge had excluded the expert psychologist (*People v. McDonald*, 1984). I wrote about these early "victories" for eyewitness science in an article based on my presidential address to the American Psychology–Law Society (Loftus, 1986) and also discussed them in a trade book called *Witness for the Defense* (Loftus & Ketcham, 1991). In the decades since

that time, there has been a string of reversals of convictions throughout the country for excluding expert testimony, with many higher courts
ruling that the science can and does tell the jurors something they don't
already know.

I predict that it will become even easier for defendants to introduce expert
testimony today, in part because of the publication of an important report
by the National Research Council (2014). The report described the work
of an ad hoc committee charged with assessing research in the social and
behavioral sciences on perception and memory, to identify gaps in the literature, and to suggest research questions to enhance our understanding of
witness performance and guide law enforcement and courtroom practice.
The report spoke favorably about expert testimony and explicitly noted the
trend toward greater acceptance of expert testimony regarding eyewitness
issues (National Research Council, 2014, p. 41), itemizing the advantages of
expert testimony over the "acceptable substitute" of jury instructions (p. 42).

## THE EVOLUTION OF RESEARCH
## ON EYEWITNESS TESTIMONY

Almost two decades after I had begun my research on eyewitness testimony and about 15 years after Judge Janice Niemi admitted my testimony
for the first time, I became involved in an unusual murder case. Eight-
year-old Susan Nason was murdered in the 1970s, and her murder was not
solved until two decades later when George Franklin, a former neighbor
of the Nason family, was charged. The only evidence against him was the
testimony of Franklin's daughter Eileen who claimed she had witnessed
the murder and repressed it. She also claimed to have repressed her memory for years of being sexually abused by him, and her testimony was sufficiently powerful to convict the father of the murder.

This case opened up a new line of scholarship for me. There was no
credible evidence of massive repression of the sort that Eileen claimed.
The work on memory distortion had mostly examined the details of events
that had actually occurred. Could you actually plant entire memories

into people's minds, and was there a way to study this? I spent consider-able time trying to think of a way to do this and eventually came up with the idea of planting a mildly traumatic event into the minds of research subjects—namely, that they were lost in a shopping mall, frightened, and rescued by an elderly person and reunited with the family (see Loftus, 1993; Loftus & Ketcham, 1994, chapter 7). We found a way to plant these memories and succeeded in about a quarter of our subjects (Loftus & Pickrell, 1995). Subsequently, many other researchers would adopt sim-ilar suggestive techniques and plant all kinds of memories of events that would have been traumatic had they actually happened, such as nearly drowning, or being hospitalized, or being attacked by a vicious animal.

Quite recently a research group developed a reliable coding system and coded the memory reports of 423 subjects who had participated in eight rich false memory studies (Scoboria et al., 2017). The results showed that 30% of the reports were classified as false memories and an additional 23% were classified as having accepted the event to some degree. So this one court case of George Franklin, with its puzzling fact pattern, spawned a whole series of studies. The research has enhanced our understanding of planting rich false memories of entire events that never occurred.

## THE MEMORY WARS

In the early days when I was developing the misinformation paradigm and testifying in criminal cases, I would encounter the occasional psychological expert who disagreed with the eyewitness conclusions and their applica-bility to legal cases. The discussions were typically polite. Occasionally an aggressive prosecutor would express displeasure with me in some ways that made me uncomfortable. But I was not prepared for the vitriol that would emerge when I began to publish my findings on rich false memories and would testify in court cases about them. After George Franklin's murder trial in the 1990s, thousands of other "repressed memory" cases emerged. Often they involved accusations of horrific sexual abuse. People were going into therapy with one sort of problem, like anxiety or depression, and coming out with a different problem, namely, horrific memories of sexual abuse allegedly perpetrated over years and purportedly banished into their unconscious minds until various procedures led to their emergence. People were suing their family members and destroying families in the process. I tried to speak out about these travesties, about the rather dubious nature of the whole concept of repression and the injustice of convicting people of crimes based on questionable memories. A great deal of anger came my way, primarily from the patients who were convinced of the veracity of their newly recovered memories, as well as some of the therapists who had helped them "recover" these memories. There were nasty letters and emails. There were death threats made to universities that had invited me to speak.

The worst episode of this type arose after I investigated a published case history that was being touted as the new proof of repressed memory. Jane Doe had accused her mother of sexual abuse when she was a child, in the midst of a nasty divorce and custody battle. The psychiatrist who had "blessed" the abuse story of the child also videotaped Jane Doe when she was much older, retrieving what seemed to be a lost memory. I investigated the case, now years after the mother had lost custody, and became convinced that she was probably innocent. After publishing some of my finding (still preserving Jane Doe's anonymity), the woman sued me and others for defamation, invasion of privacy, and other claims. The case went all the way through the California Supreme Court before it ended finally with Jane Doe declaring bankruptcy. People ask me, "Who won the case?" No one won, except perhaps the attorneys, who were the only ones compensated for their time. I wrote about this experience and tried to find some enduring lesson in this miserable legal process. Among other thoughts, I suggested that there is a profound need for our institutions to provide more protection for free speech (Loftus, 2003, 2008).

## SOME FINAL COMMENTS

In 2017 I gave a talk at the American Association for the Advancement of Science meeting that I titled "The Accidental Expert." I was part of a panel in which Shari Diamond and Rick Lempert presented the results of a new survey of scientists who had participated in the legal system. Many of their respondents had negative views about the legal system, but those who had actually participated had more favorable views. I was one of those participants. What started 40 years ago as an effort to learn more about actual witnesses in actual cases to augment my research on eyewitness testimony turned into a lifetime of walking the planet with a foot in two different camps: the psychological science camp and the legal camp. The court cases have stimulated my research ideas; the research findings then were distilled into expert testimony in the courtroom. That idea still appeals very much to me.

I've learned a lot from these experiences, even the unpleasant grueling cross-examinations. In my talk at the American Association for the Advancement of Science meeting I recounted one experience when I testified at a hearing for Scooter Libby who had been accused of outing a CIA agent (Valerie Plame). The special prosecutor scoured my publications and found places in the introduction where I had pointed out flaws and inconsistencies in previous research—a common practice for scientific authors who use the argument to set up the value of their new study. In the Libby hearing, I was citing the prior papers to bolster the argument that a memory expert would be useful in the case. The prosecutor shot back a question something like this: "Are you trying to fob flawed data on this court?" This caught me by surprise; he was using our scientific culture against me. Maybe it's best not to refer to previous scientific work as "flawed" if you still think it is valuable enough to use today.

The human stories that underlie these court cases have greatly enriched my teaching and my writings. Students are fascinated to hear more about some of the famous people I've met who have found themselves in legal hot water—Ted Bundy, Martha Stewart, Timothy McVeigh, and Oliver North, to name a few There are others whose cases I consulted on even if I never met them—Michael Jackson and Bill Cosby, for example. Yet the ones who meant the most to me were those little-known people whom I've been able to help at least a tiny bit, by presenting at their trials the science that is on their side.

Where is this field going? In terms of the basic science, I foresee a continuation of research on memory distortion, as we continue to investigate the extent to which our memories are malleable. The future might reveal even more powerful contaminating methods that may involve a combination of behavioral and pharmaceutical interventions. Hopefully, investigators will also learn something about ways in which people can protect themselves against these intrusions into memory. Many who work in this field have had a keen interest in applying the science toward solving real-world problems. Other scholars have devoted much time to documenting how law enforcement has made use of psychological science in collecting eyewitness evidence in actual cases (e.g., Wells, 2006). Some researchers have focused on how trial judges should handle eyewitness evidence when it is presented during actual cases, and the New Jersey case involving a defendant named Henderson stands out as a major development in this regard (*State v. Henderson*, 2011), for it created a whole legal standard for handling eyewitness evidence, and it was based on the extensive contributions of psychological science.

The legal arena is not the only place where malleable memories are important. Recent work showing that you can plant false memories and have a profound effect on people's behavior raises myriad ethical issues. When should we use this mind technology? And should we ban its use? We as psychological scientists can provide the data that can inform discussions of these issues. But it is up to a society, hopefully sufficiently informed and astute, to make these sorts of decisions.

## REFERENCES

Ceci, S., & Bruck, M. (1993). Suggestibility of the child witness: A historical review and synthesis. *Psychological Bulletin, 113*, 403–439.

Clifford, B. R., & Bull, R. (1978). *The psychology of person identification.* London: Routledge/Kegan Paul.

Deffenbacher, K. A., & Loftus, E. F. (1982). Do jurors share a common understanding concerning eyewitness behavior? *Law and Human Behavior, 6*, 15–30.

Doyle, J. M. (2005) *True witness.* New York: Palgrave MacMillan.

Freedman, J. L., & Loftus, E. F. (1971). Retrieval of words from long-term memory. *Journal of Verbal Learning and Verbal Behavior, 10,* 107–115.

Loftus, E. F. (1974). Reconstructing memory: The incredible eyewitness. *Psychology Today, 8,* 116–119.

Loftus, E. F. (1975). Leading questions and the eyewitness report. *Cognitive Psychology, 7,* 560–572.

Loftus, E. F. (1979). *Eyewitness testimony.* Cambridge, MA: Harvard University Press.

Loftus, E. F. (1986). Ten years in the life of an expert witness. *Law and Human Behavior, 10,* 241–263.

Loftus, E. F. (1993). The reality of repressed memories. *American Psychologist, 48,* 518–537.

Loftus, E. F. (2003). On science under legal assault. *Daedalus, 132*(4), 84–86.

Loftus, E. F. (2008). Perils of provocative scholarship. *Observer, 21*(5), 13–15.

Loftus, E. F. (2017). Eavesdropping on memory. *Annual Review of Psychology, 68,* 1–18.

Loftus, E. F., & Hoffman, H. G. (1989). Misinformation and memory: The creation of memory. *Journal of Experimental Psychology: General, 118,* 100–104.

Loftus, E. F., & Ketcham, K. (1991). *Witness for the defense: The accused, the eyewitness, and the expert who puts memory on trial.* New York: St. Martin's Press.

Loftus, E. F., & Ketcham, K. (1994). *The myth of repressed memory.* New York: St. Martin's Press.

Loftus, E. F., & Palmer, J. C. (1974). Reconstruction of automobile destruction: An example of the inter-action between language and memory. *Journal of Verbal Learning and Verbal Behavior, 13,* 585–589.

Loftus, E. F., & Pickrell, J. E. (1995). The formation of false memories. *Psychiatric Annals, 25,* 720–725.

Munsterberg, H. (1908). *On the witness stand.* New York: Doubleday/Page.

National Research Council. (2014). *Identifying the culprit: Assessing eyewitness identification.* Washington, DC: National Academies Press.

*People v. McDonald,* 37 Cal 3d 351 (1984).

Schmechel, R. S., O'Toole, T. P., Easterly, C., & Loftus, E. F. (2006). Beyond the Ken: Testing juror's understanding of eyewitness reliability evidence. *Jurimetrics Journal, 46,* 177–214.

Scoboria, A., Wade, K. A., Lindsay, D. S., Azad, T., Strange, D., Ost, J., & Hyman, I. (2017). A mega-analysis of memory reports from eight peer-reviewed false memory implantation studies. *Memory, 25,* 146–163.

*State v. Chapple,* 135 Ariz., 281, 660 p. 2d 1208 (1983).

*State v. Henderson,* 27 A. 3d 872 (N.J. 2011).

Thompson-Cannino, J., & Cotton, R. (2009). *Picking cotton.* New York: St. Martin's.

Wells, G. L. (2006). Eyewitness identification: Systemic reforms. *Wisconsin Law Review, 2006,* 615–643.

Wells, G. L., & Loftus, E. F. (1984). *Eyewitness testimony: Psychological perspectives.* Cambridge, UK: Cambridge University Press.

Whipple, G. M. (1911). The psychology of testimony. *Psychological Bulletin, 8,* 307–309.

Yarmey, A. D. (1979). *The psychology of eyewitness testimony.* New York: Free Press.

# 3

# Applying Social Psychology to Law and the Legal Process

MICHAEL J. SAKS

P sychology's application to law began early in the 20th century and then lay fallow for many years. When the 1970s arrived with a burst of interest in applying psychology to law, social psychology was near the forefront.

Some of the research centered on judges' decision-making. Ebbesen and Konecni (1975) found that judges made bail decisions in response to hypothetical scenarios in questionnaires by weighing factors as the law wishes them to, but in court the same judges responded to only one variable: the prosecutor's recommendation. Sentencing studies showed worrisome variability in how judges punished similar defendants for the same crimes (Eldridge & Partridge, 1974). Thibaut and Walker (1975) discovered the importance of procedural justice: The opportunity to assemble and present one's own evidence made the adversary process more satisfying and acceptable to litigants and observers alike, compared to inquisitorial procedures. Judicial instructions to juries were found to be no more helpful than no instruction at all (Doob & Kirschenbaum, 1973; Sue, Smith, & Caldwell, 1973), so Sales, Elwork, and Alfini (1977) used psycholinguistic principles to develop more effective instructions.

Juries quickly became a major focus of attention. Leading the way were Kalven and Zeisel (1966) and their colleagues (lawyers, sociologists, statisticians) in the Chicago Jury Project. Other work studied death qualification, the lack of representativeness of jury pools, correlates of prosecution versus defense inclinations, deciding insanity-defense cases, jury response to defendants' characteristics, and other topics (see Diamond, this volume). In the area of tort law, several researchers began to study how jurors attribute responsibility for injuries resulting from accidents—to the victim, to the tortfeasor, or at all (Chaikin & Darley, 1973; Shaver, 1970; Walster, 1966).

Social psychologists also played a role in the field's early fascination with problems of eyewitness identification. They were not the first to stage mock crimes and then question witnesses about what they thought they observed—Münsterberg (1908) and several of his colleagues beat them to that by many decades—but some showed bold creativity. For example, Robert Buckhout (1975) staged a mugging and purse-snatching and arranged to have it broadcast as part of the evening news on WNBC-TV in New York. Viewers were then shown a lineup and invited to choose the person they thought was the perpetrator. Researchers assessed their accuracy (one in five chose the actual mugger). Studies began to examine countless variables related to characteristics of the observer, the circumstances of the event, the conditions of retrieval, and so on (see Loftus, this volume).

I can offer no insight into why this variegated burst of psychological interest in law occurred at that particular historical moment. At the time, I was unaware that I was in the midst of something like a movement or a rebirth. Perhaps it was nothing more than the random occurrence of a number of unconnected individuals who became interested in a range of psychology–law topics close enough in time that they realized they were not alone. In finding others, they could draw a circle around themselves, put a name on it, and feel they shared an interest in law and psychology.

A field was being born, and I stumbled into it thanks to an inquisitive law student who was a complete stranger to me and to psychology.

## MY ARRIVAL INTO THIS WORLD

Early in the 1970s, having reached a certain point in my graduate student career at Ohio State University, the time had come for a meeting with my adviser to settle on a topic for my dissertation. I had a vague sense that I wanted to do "something relevant" with my education and my life. I was eager to deploy psychology's discovered phenomena, theories, and research methods in the service of helping to make the world better through psychology. But at that point in my life, I had not yet found the something. The something would turn out to be in the law, the legal system, and the legal process, but I did not yet know that.

I arrived at the office of my PhD adviser, Tom Ostrom, in the experimental social psychology program at Ohio State University with too many ideas. Before turning to my list of possibilities, however, Tom wanted to tell me of an encounter he'd had earlier that day with a student from the law school. The student, Charles Whetstone, was working on a law review note about several cases recently decided by the U.S. Supreme Court addressing the constitutionality of states eliminating the requirement of unanimous jury verdicts (*Apodaca v. Oregon*, 1972; *Johnson v. Louisiana*, 1972). In those cases, various defendants had been convicted of various charges by votes of 11–1, 10–2, and 9–3. In their opinions, a majority of justices put aside centuries of common law history and additional centuries of constitutional history to conclude that the process and product of decision-making under non-unanimous decision rules was sufficiently similar to decision-making under a unanimity requirement as not to violate rights of due process or equal protection. The portion of their reasoning that relied on social psychological assumptions was speculative. Two years earlier, the Court had followed the same logic to reach the conclusion that 6 jurors were the functional equivalent of 12 and, therefore, no less constitutional (*Williams v. Florida*, 1970).

Because Whetstone had been a biology major as an undergraduate, he recognized that the Court's test posed an essentially empirical question: Do juries behave differently when the requisite degree of consensus is changed? But to answer its empirical questions, the Court relied on guesswork about jury behavior. Whetstone suspected that some field of social or behavioral science might have conducted experiments on group decision processes that could illuminate whether the Court guessed correctly. So he went hunting for a behavioral scientist who might know and landed in my adviser's office.

Tom was not aware of such research, and we soon found that almost no relevant group decision research had been conducted. Tom asked if I would be interested in taking *that* on as my dissertation. Answer: Yes! Something that met all of my unarticulated requirements had fallen from the blue into my lap, and at that moment my career-long relationship with psychology and law began.

The completed dissertation was published as a small book (Saks, 1977). A year later, that book became one of a number of social science works cited in another opinion of the U.S. Supreme Court when the issue of jury size was again taken up (*Ballew v. Georgia*, 1978; see also, Zeisel, 1971; Zeisel & Diamond, 1974).

By the time I stepped into my first academic job, at Boston College, I was already hooked on commingling psychology with law, and I wasted no time in trying to teach an interdisciplinary course. During my first semester at Boston College, I approached its law school about offering a cross-listed seminar the following semester where law students and psychology graduate students could pair up, work together digging into published empirical research that could inform a legal or policy issue, and jointly write a paper about what they found. The law school directed me to their Curriculum Committee, which invited me to present my proposal at their next meeting.

There I was—a first-semester assistant professor of psychology telling the law school that whether they realized it or not, they needed psychology to enlighten their students. The committee was chaired by Associate Dean Charles "Buzzy" Baron. In addition to his law degree, Baron had a

PhD in philosophy. He already had interdisciplinary inclinations, thought law and legal education could benefit from infusions of knowledge from other fields, and knew enough about psychology to ask me what area of psychology I hailed from. Not only was my seminar approved, but Buzzy himself sat in on it. He and I became fast friends and still are.

Within a relatively short time, I somehow managed to touch nearly all of the bases that would keep me occupied the rest of my career. My explorations in the late 1970s were summed up mainly in two books: *Social Psychology in Court* (Saks & Hastie, 1978) and *The Use/Nonuse/Misuse of Applied Social Research in the Courts* (Saks & Baron, 1980). Here are their stories.

## SOCIAL PSYCHOLOGY'S POTENTIAL FOR LAW

News accounts of psychologists assisting lawyers in selecting jurors piqued my curiosity. This led me to do new analyses using my dissertation data, which contained demographic and attitudinal data as well as individuals' reactions to the video trial they viewed. Initially, I was disappointed to find only weak associations between jurors' characteristics and their verdicts. But after reviewing both basic and applied research on the relationship between decision makers' characteristics and their decisions, I realized that my "disappointing" findings were the real story. Situational factors and information presented typically overwhelmed the influence of individual differences (Diamond, 1990; Fulero & Penrod, 1990; Saks, 1976; Simon 1967; Visher, 1987). That meant that *evidence*, along with factual arguments and how they are presented, are the major drivers of trial outcomes.

Those early studies put me on my way to viewing the courtroom trial and its surround as an ideal place for applying social psychological knowledge and testing our theories. I decided to spread that notion by pulling together in one place what was known at the time about psychological phenomena that cast light on the trial process and to suggest psychology's potential to provide more. I asked Reid Hastie to join me in the effort. Our book, *Social Psychology in Court*, was published in 1978. We structured the book around the actors, influencers, and decision makers in the trial process.

The chapter "The Judge" reviewed studies of judicial decision-making, the characteristics of those appointed to the judiciary, the problems of judges instructing jurors on the law, and sentencing. Enough research existed to have two chapters on juries, covering research on jury composition, structure, and process and outcomes. The Outcome subsection described the (nonpsychology) field research of Kalven and Zeisel (1966), which famously found that judges and jurors hearing the same cases reached the same verdicts four-fifths of the time in both civil and criminal trials.

"The Lawyer" chapter provided an opportunity to connect already extensive areas of basic social psychology research to the tasks of the trial attorney. Lawyers face the challenge of persuading, and attitude formation and change were among the largest bodies of research in social psychology. Lawyers also try to manage social perception, and relevant work existed on impression management and even more on how observers form attributions about the person observed. Trial lawyers negotiate the settlement of most litigation, and a good bit of research existed on negotiation and conflict resolution.

"The Defendant" summarized research on two topics: the mental state of the criminal defendant, which included inferences about mens rea and the insanity defense, as well as the effects on jurors of the defendant's behavior, appearance (social and physical), prior criminal record, and explicit character evidence testimony. The "Evidence" chapter's most extensive discussion concerned eyewitness identification and was co-authored by Beth Loftus and Steve Penrod. More briefly, the chapter discussed principles of persuasion that pertained to witness credibility, techniques of lie detection, and research on the effects on jurors of sensational pretrial publicity.

The book's final chapter, "The Court as a Social System and as Part of a Social System," discussed, most importantly, the work of Thibaut and Walker (1975), which launched the subfield of procedural justice for psychology. The chapter also touched on roles of trial participants, discretion, social exchange, and courts within the larger society.

At that early point in my career, the exercise of summarizing the starting points of what was known and exploring their potential for the future expanded my own awareness of the range of issues to which law and psychology could contribute. Social psychology has continued to pursue many of the problems that Hastie and I explored in our book.

## COURTS' USE OF PSYCHOLOGICAL EVIDENCE

From 1978 to 1980, I took a leave from my academic job to work for the National Center for State Courts. Among other projects, I took on two that were also of a "pulling things together" kind. Although my research, and that of others, had been discussed and relied on in the lead opinion in *Ballew*, it was for a proposition that the research did not address. Though the research raised doubts about shrinking juries from 12 to 6, the opinion used it to prohibit reductions smaller than six, while *reaffirming* its decision in *Williams* authorizing juries of six. That aroused my interest in how courts used (or avoided using) social science research to inform their decisions.

I was all ears when an acquaintance, Clark Abt, founder of Abt Associates in Cambridge, Massachusetts, suggested that I organize the conference The Use/Nonuse/Misuse of Applied Social Research in the Courts. Sponsored by the Council for Applied Social Research, it was held in Washington, DC, in the fall of 1978. Nine panels addressed various topics (e.g., Misuses of Applied Social Research, What Judges and Lawyers Need to Know about Applied Social Science). The invited participants included an impressive array of scholars and practitioners—not only psychologists but also economists, statisticians, political scientists, sociologists, judges, and lawyers. The mix included legal consumers of social science research as well as producers. Perhaps not as a consequence of participating in our conference (though who can say for sure?), one of the younger participants (Robert Post) later became dean of Yale Law School and a still-young law professor (Stephen Breyer) later became a U.S. Supreme Court justice.

The presentations were professionally transcribed, and Buzzy Baron and I edited the transcript to produce the *Use/Nonuse/Misuse* book (Saks & Baron, 1980) through which the collective insights of the conferees could be widely shared. For me, this served as an eye-opening introduction to a wide assortment of perspectives, experiences, and possibilities for productive collaborations between social science and the law, as well as a warning of barriers that might forever slow the way.

Another project, growing in part from my interest in the power of evidence to drive trials, focused on expert witnesses of various kinds. I co-directed this review of law and practices related to use of expert witnesses, drawn from various literatures—some empirical, others on practices, legal analysis, commentaries, and recommendations—trying to identify the most persistent problems and promising solutions (Saks & Van Duizend, 1983). The project included an original empirical component: 10 intensive case studies of trials in which experts had played important (though not atypical) parts, selected from a spectrum of legal subject matter, around the United States. For each of those cases, we pored over relevant filings and portions of transcripts and traveled the country to interview the major participants in those trials: judge, lawyers, and expert witnesses.

That project exposed me for the first time to the possibility that much crime lab forensic science was a lot less scientific and more shaky than its image in popular culture had long suggested. One of the empirical studies we reviewed had sent various kinds of crime scene evidence (e.g., blood, bullets, hair, glass, handwriting) to 200 crime labs to perform standard testing (Peterson, Fabricant, & Field, 1978). When the researchers received the results, they assessed the accuracy of the reports. In a word, the performance of the labs was abysmal. Some areas of forensic science are derived from conventional science (e.g., applications of chemistry). For these, the main questions are whether the right tests are being employed, competently conducted, and properly interpreted. Other areas of forensic science have no conventional science from which to borrow (pattern comparison of tool marks, bullets, hair, handwriting, fingerprints, etc.). For these, the most fundamental questions of validity are in doubt.

After returning to Boston, a judge friend, Robert Hallisey, arranged a private tour for us of the state crime lab. Hallisey was not your average judge: Before attending Harvard Law School, he had majored in physics at Harvard College. Our crime lab visit reinforced my doubts about forensic science. For example, the firearms examiner explained to us that when he looked through his comparison microscope, he might initially be perplexed about whether the two bullets under examination had been fired from the same or different weapons. As he stared and pondered, he would eventually arrive at his conclusion, and, once he reached it, he was "100% sure" it was correct. He seemed utterly unaware that his subjective confidence was not the measure of validity.

Soon after that, two law professors, Michael Risinger and Mark Denbeaux, contacted me about working on what came to be called the "Case of the Mayflower Madame" (later a book and movie). The defendant, Sydney Biddle Barrows, descendant of a prominent family that had immigrated to America in the 17th century, was accused of operating an expensive call girl service in Manhattan. The major item of evidence linking her to the escort service was a handwritten log. The government's handwriting examiner claimed to be able to identify the writing in the log as hers. What did empirical research show about that asserted expertise? I dug through every possible journal (in English) that might contain a study on the question. The most important finding turned out to be that there were no findings. I unearthed exactly one attempt at an empirical study, from 1939, which found nothing of substance (Inbau, 1939). My report for the Mayflower Madam's legal team did not have to be lengthy. The law professors and I eventually wrote a more extensive article on the larger problem of a forensic science that had no science and no data undergirding it, as well as a legal process unable to recognize such deficiencies (Risinger, Denbeaux, & Saks, 1989).

## SOCIAL PSYCHOLOGY AND LAW IN RECENT YEARS

From the 1980s forward, social psychology's application to law grew broader and deeper, some of it perhaps encouraged by those early books and some of my own research. Right up to the present, the field is still working on many of the issues that interested those of us who were laying some of the groundwork. Let me describe some of that work in my final comments.

## Jury Research

Experiments designed to learn something basic about jury decision-making usually require a study of additional subject matter: that is, whatever the juries are asked to decide about. For example, my own jury research extended into factors affecting how jurors decide tort damages (Saks, Hollinger, Wissler, Evans, & Hart, 1997; Wissler, Hart, & Saks, 1999), how they react to the testimony of expert witnesses (especially forensic scientists; Koehler Schweitzer, Saks, & McQuiston, 2016), and whether juries are affected by neuroimages (Saks, Schweitzer, Kiehl, & Aharoni, 2014; Schweitzer et al., 2011), among other topics. Thus our jury research has taught us not only the effects of different instructions or innovative procedures, but also the body of knowledge about other legal issues has grown as well (Devine, 2012; also see Diamond, this volume).

## Eyewitness Identification

In the past decade, about twice as many articles on eyewitness research were published in *Law & Human Behavior* as were jury studies. My role in that body of work, if anything, was to try to steer some researchers toward other aspects of law and psychology (Saks, 1986). But I must concede that the intense interest in eyewitness research has led to deep empirical and theoretical understanding of how eyewitnesses can inadvertently lead police astray, how police sometimes lead eyewitnesses astray, and how we can reduce the rate of false-positive identifications with minimal loss of true positive identifications (Wells, 2016; also see Loftus, this volume).

## Procedural Justice

From the early work of Thibaut and Walker (1975), research on procedural justice has greatly expanded within the setting of formal adjudication as well as in numerous other directions: alternate forms of dispute resolution, negotiation, why people obey the law, police interactions with the public, cooperation in organizations, and others. If one word was to be chosen to capture the common thread to all of these, it would be whether the process accorded a person "voice." Still further expansion appears likely.

## Psychological Foundations of Evidence Law

Barbara Spellman, a psychologist and law professor, and I recently teamed up to see what cognitive and social psychology could now say about the underpinnings, logic, and likely effectiveness of the rules of evidence used in courts throughout the United States (Saks & Spellman, 2016). Evidence law provides the guidelines for filtering information that lawyers and witnesses seek to offer to jurors. The area is a cornucopia of ideas—contemplated and deployed for centuries by judges and lawyers—about relevance, bias, overvaluing, metacognition, being misled or misusing information, and more—all of which concern the risk of jurors drawing the wrong inferences from evidence. Common law judges and modern rules committees take on the role of amateur applied psychologists. They employ what they think they know about the ability and motivations of witnesses to perceive and retrieve information, about the effects of the litigation process on testimony and other evidence, and the capacity of jurors to comprehend and evaluate evidence. These are the same kinds of phenomena that cognitive and social psychologists systematically study. Though psychology has much to say on these questions, much, much more is needed.

## Forensic Science

In the nearly four decades since I first encountered their surprising weaknesses, a considerable amount of attention has been given to reevaluating, reconceptualizing, and rebuilding the forensic sciences. Two major forces facilitated this revolution. One was the advent of DNA typing. Analysis of the faulty evidence that leads to so many wrongful convictions has found forensic science errors second only to eyewitness errors as the source (Saks & Koehler, 2005). Moreover, DNA typing provided the first model of a scientifically defensible approach to forensic identification.

Second, in shifting the legal test of admissibility of expert evidence from consensus within a field to demonstrated validity, *Daubert v. Merrill Dow Pharmaceuticals* (1993) exposed many forensic sciences to attack for the lack of empirical testing of their claims. Immediately after *Daubert* was decided, David Faigman conceived the idea of a continually updated book (which has grown to a five-volume treatise) that would follow the impact of *Daubert* going forward on the law's treatment of a wide range of areas of expert evidence (Faigman et al., 2016).[1]

Forensic identification involves much that is psychological: issues of perception, judgment, decision-making, cognition regarding quantitative phenomena, and the communication of conclusions to lawyers, judges, and jurors (Thompson & Cole, 2006; also see McQuiston & Saks, 2008). One of the most social psychological of problems is that of context effects (or observer effects). Examiners of ambiguous patterns whose conclusions are reached subjectively make no attempt to blind themselves to other information about a case (Risinger, Saks, Rosenthal, & Thompson, 2002). The most dramatic demonstration of this effect was a study by Dror, Charlton, and Péron (2006), showing that only one of five fingerprint experts gave the same conclusion when reexamining pairs of prints that they had given opinions about several years earlier. The most fundamental shortcoming is that the beliefs and techniques of those fields developed without serious (or any) empirical testing of their assumptions and without testing the reliability or validity of the techniques (e.g., Faigman et al., 2016; National Research Council, 2009; President's Council of Advisors on Science and Technology, 2016; Risinger et al., 1989; Saks & Koehler, 2005, 2008; Saks et al., 2016).

---

1. The original line-up of editors in 1997 consisted of David Faigman, David Kaye, Michael Saks, and Joe Sanders. Two of us have rolled off, and others joined. The current line-up is Faigman, Sanders, Edward Cheng, Erin Murphy, Jennifer Mnookin, and Chris Slobogin.

Much research and reform remain to be accomplished, but the corner has been turned. Under a mandate from Congress, the National Research Council formed a committee to review and evaluate the forensic sciences, relying in part on studies and analyses by social and cognitive psychologists. The committee's unanimous report (National Research Council, 2009, p. 53) concluded: "The bottom line is simple: In a number of forensic science disciplines, forensic science professionals have yet to establish either the validity of their approach or the accuracy of their conclusions, and the courts have been utterly ineffective in addressing this problem."

## The Tort System

Periodic "tort liability crises" burst onto the front pages, along with rash explanations and proposals for solutions. Past controversy over what the real facts were, what effects the law was or wasn't having, the benefits and harms of proposed reforms—as well as fundamental psychological processes involved in attributing cause, responsibility, liability, and assessing harm and compensation—have attracted the interest of researchers from a variety of fields. In recent decades, a critical mass of psychologists (in the dozens) have become interested in tort law (accidental harm and its compensation) and related phenomena and theory. For a book-length review of the psychology of tort litigation, see Robbennolt and Hans (2016).[2]

The enormous gap between what has been learned from the empirical work of psychologists and many others, and the legal policies that are adopted, is another fascinating and disturbing aspect of the problem. For example, the research findings about medical malpractice have consistently been that serious medical errors are so frequent as to be the third leading cause of preventable death in the United States, while legal claims for compensation are filed in a small fraction of those cases (James, 2013; Makary

2. An earlier law review article by a psychologist, integrating the relevant empirical research to create a picture of the behavior of the tort litigation system *as a system*, has become the most-cited tort law article of the past generation (Saks, 1992).

& Daniels, 2016; Saks, 1994; Vidmar, 1995; Votruba & Saks, 2013; Weiler et al., 1993). Yet law reforms have been concentrated on reducing the ability of victims to obtain compensation (Paik, Black, & Hyman, 2013).

Given the declining ability of the litigation system to create incentives for safety in the healthcare arena, some of us are suggesting that research and policy attention turn to new and different steps that can be taken by the law to increase patient safety and reduce iatrogenic harm, harnessing both economics and behavioral economics (Saks & Landsman, in press).

## CONCLUSION

So much of my own travels across the terrain of law and psychology, and consequently the work I have undertaken, has been the product of chance encounters or the quests of others (especially our legal colleagues) that I sometimes wonder whether I would have done anything interesting without them. Were I to give advice on the basis of my own career's experience, it would be to welcome those accidental collisions of people, ideas, and experience. They might be the best things that could ever happen to us.

## REFERENCES

*Apodaca v. Oregon*, 406 U.S. 404 (1972).
*Ballew v. Georgia*, 435 U.S. 223 (1978).
Buckhout, R. (1975). Note. Social Action and the Law Newsletter, 2, 7.
Chaikin, A. L., & Darley, J. M. (1973). Victim or perpetrator? Defensive attribution of responsibility and the need for order and justice. *Journal of Personality and Social Psychology, 25*, 268–275.
*Daubert v. Merrell Dow Pharms., Inc.*, 509 U.S. 579 (1993).
Devine, D. (2012). *Jury decision making: The state of the science*. New York: NYU Press.
Diamond, S. S. (1990). Scientific jury selection: What social scientists know and don't know. *Judicature, 73*, 178–183.
Doob, A. N., & Kirschenbaum, H. M. (1973). Bias in police lineups—Partial remembering. *Journal of Police Science and Administration, 1*, 287–293.
Dror, I. E., Charlton, D., & Péron, A. E. (2006). Contextual information renders experts vulnerable to making erroneous identifications. *Forensic Science International, 156*, 74–78.

Ebbesen, E. B., & Konecni, V. J. (1975). Decision-making and information integration in the courts: The setting of bail. *Journal of Personality and Social Psychology, 32*, 805–821.

Eldridge, W. B., & Partridge, A. (1974). *The Second Circuit sentencing study: A report to the judges of the Second Circuit.* Washington, DC: Federal Judicial Center.

Faigman, D. L., Cheng, E. K., Mnookin, J. L., Murphy, E. E., Sanders, J., & Slobogin, C. (2016). *Modern scientific evidence: The law and science of expert testimony.* St. Paul, MN: West.

Fulero, S. M., & Penrod, S. D. (1990). The myths and realities of attorney jury selection folklore and scientific jury selection: What works. *Ohio Northern University Law Review, 17*, 229–253.

Inbau, F. (1939). Lay witness identification of handwriting (an experiment). *Illinois Law Review, 34*, 433–443.

James, J. T. A. (2013). A new, evidence-based estimate of patient harms associated with hospital care. *Journal of Patient Safety, 9*, 122–128.

*Johnson v. Louisiana*, 406 U.S. 356 (1972).

Kalven, H., & Zeisel, H. (1966). *The American jury.* Chicago: University of Chicago Press.

Koehler, J. J., Schweitzer, N. J., Saks, M. J., & McQuiston, D. E. (2016). Science, technology, or the expert witness: What influences jurors' judgments about forensic science testimony? *Psychology, Public Policy and the Law, 22*, 401–413.

Makary, M. A., & Daniels, M. (2016). Medical error—the third leading cause of death in the US. *British Medical Journal, 353*, 1–5.

McQuiston, D., & Saks, M. J. (2008). Communicating opinion evidence in the forensic identification sciences: Accuracy and impact. *Hastings Law Journal, 59*, 1159–1189.

Münsterberg, H. (1908). *On the witness stand: Essays on psychology and crime.* New York: Doubleday.

National Research Council of the National Academies, Committee on Identifying the Needs of the Forensic Science Community. (2009). *Strengthening forensic science in the United States: A path forward.* Washington, DC: National Academies Press.

Paik, M., Black, B., & Hyman, D. (2013). The receding tide of medical malpractice litigation: Part 1. National trends. *Journal of Empirical Legal Studies, 10*, 612–638.

Peterson, J., Fabricant, E. L., & Field, K. S. (1978). *Crime laboratory proficiency testing research program.* Washington, DC: GPO.

President's Council of Advisors on Science and Technology. (2016). *Forensic science in criminal courts: Ensuring scientific validity of feature-comparison methods.* Washington, DC: Executive Office of the President.

Risinger, D. M., Denbeaux, M. P., & Saks, M. J. (1989). Exorcism of ignorance as a proxy for rational knowledge: The case of handwriting identification "expertise." *University of Pennsylvania Law Review, 137*, 731–792.

Risinger, D. M., Saks, M. J., Rosenthal, R., & Thompson, W. (2002). The *Daubert/Kumho* implications of observer effects in forensic science: Hidden problems of expectation and suggestion. *California Law Review, 90*, 1–56.

Robbennolt, J., & Hans, V. (2016). *The psychology of tort law.* New York: NYU Press.

Saks, M. J. (1976). The limits of scientific jury selection: Ethical and empirical. *Jurimetrics Journal, 17*, 3–22.

Saks, M. J. (1977). *Jury verdicts: The role of group size and social decision rule.* Lexington, MA: D.C. Heath.

Saks, M. J. (1986). The law does not live by eyewitness testimony alone (editorial). *Law & Human Behavior, 10,* 279.

Saks, M. J. (1992). Do we really know anything about the behavior of the tort litigation system—And why not? *University of Pennsylvania Law Review, 140,* 1147–1292.

Saks, M. J. (1994). Medical malpractice: Facing real problems and finding real solutions. *William & Mary Law Review, 35,* 693–726.

Saks, M. J., Albright, T., Bohan, T. L., Bierer, B. E., Bowers, C. M., Bush, M. A. . . . Zumwalt, R. E. (2016). Forensic bitemark identification: Weak foundations, exaggerated claims. *Journal of Law & the Biosciences, 3,* 538–575.

Saks, M. J., & Baron, C. H. (Eds.). (1980). *The use/nonuse/misuse of applied social research in the courts.* Cambridge, MA: Abt.

Saks, M. J., & Hastie, R. (1978). *Social psychology in court.* New York: Van Nostrand.

Saks, M. J., & Koehler, J. J. (2005). The coming paradigm shift in forensic identification science. *Science, 309,* 892–895.

Saks, M. J., & Koehler, J. J. (2008). The individualization fallacy in forensic science. *Vanderbilt Law Review, 61,* 199–219.

Saks, M. J., & Landsman, S. (in press). *Closing death's door: Patient safety and the law.* New York: Oxford University Press.

Saks, M. J., & Spellman, B. A. (2016). *The psychological foundations of evidence law.* New York: NYU Press.

Saks, M. J., Schweitzer, N. J., Kiehl, K., & Aharoni, E. (2014). The impact of neuroimages in the sentencing phase of capital trials. *Journal of Empirical Legal Studies, 11,* 105–131.

Saks, M. J., & Van Duizend, R. (1983). *The uses of scientific evidence in litigation.* Williamsburg, VA: National Center for State Courts.

Sales, B. D., Elwork, A., & Alfini, J. J. (1977). Improving comprehension for jury instructions. In B. D. Sales (Ed.), *Perspective in law and psychology: Vol 1. The criminal justice system.* New York: Plenum.

Schweitzer, N. J., Saks, M. J., Murphy, E. R., Roskies, A. L., Sinnott-Armstrong, W., & Gaudet, L. M. (2011). Neuroimages as evidence in a mens rea defense: No impact. *Psychology, Public Policy, and Law, 17,* 357–393.

Shaver, K. G. (1970). Defensive attribution: Effects of severity and relevance on the responsibility assigned for an accident. *Journal of Personality and Social Psychology, 14,* 101–113.

Simon, R. J. (1967). *The jury and the defense of insanity.* Boston: Little, Brown.

Sue, S., Smith, R. E., & Caldwell, C. (1973). Effects of inadmissible evidence on the decisions of simulated jurors: A moral dilemma. *Journal of Applied Social Psychology, 3,* 345–353.

Thibaut, J., & Walker, L. (1975). *Procedural justice: A psychological analysis.* Hillsdale, N.J.: Erlbaum.

Thompson, W., & Cole, S. (2006). Psychological aspects of forensic identification evidence. In M. Constanza, D. Krauss, & K. Pezdek (Eds.), *Expert psychological testimony for the courts* (pp. 9–31). Mahwah, NJ: Erlbaum.

Vidmar, N. (1995). *Medical malpractice and the American jury: Confronting the myths about jury incompetence, deep pockets, and outrageous damage awards.* Ann Arbor: University of Michigan Press.

Visher, C. A. (1987). Juror decision making: The importance of evidence. *Law and Human Behavior, 11,* 1–17.

Votruba, A., & Saks, M. (2013). Medical adverse events and malpractice litigation in Arizona: By-the-numbers. *Arizona State Law Journal, 45,* 1537–1561.

Walster, E. (1966). Assignment of responsibility for an accident. *Journal of Personality and Social Psychology, 3,* 73–80.

Weiler, P., Hiatt, H., Newhouse, J. P., Johnson, W. G., Brennan, T., & Leape, L. (1993). *A measure of malpractice: Medical injury, malpractice litigation, and patient compensation.* Cambridge, MA: Harvard University Press.

Wells, G. L. (2016). Eyewitness identification. In D. Faigman, E. K. Cheng, J. L. Mnookin, E. E. Murphy, J. Sanders, & C. Slobogin. (Eds.), *Modern scientific evidence: The law and science of expert testimony* (pp. 451–479). St. Paul, MN: West.

*Williams v. Florida,* 399 U.S. 78 (1970).

Wissler, R. L., Hart, A. J., & Saks, M. J. (1999). Decision-making about general damages: A comparison of jurors, judges, and lawyers, *Michigan Law Review, 98,* 751–826.

Zeisel, H. (1971). ". . . and then there were none": The diminution of the federal jury. *University of Chicago Law Review, 38,* 710–724.

Zeisel, H., & Diamond, S. S. (1974). Convincing empirical evidence on the six-member jury. *University of Chicago Law Review, 41,* 281–295.

# 4

# Jury Research

**SHARI SEIDMAN DIAMOND**

I was hardly the first to become fascinated with jury behavior. The American jury has long attracted scholarly and popular interest. In 1929, the jury was under attack, a situation that should sound familiar (Diamond & Ryken, 2013). Prominent evidence scholar John Henry Wigmore wrote a spirited defense, concluding, "Jury trial, properly reformed, is on the whole superior to judge trial" (Wigmore, 1929, p. 166), but he had no systematic empirical evidence to support most of his claims.

## MY INTRODUCTION TO PSYCHOLOGY AND JURIES

It was the law professor and sociologist/lawyer team of Harry Kalven Jr. and Hans Zeisel who carried out the first extensive empirical investigation of the American jury. In 1966, they published *The American Jury*, which inventively used a survey of judges to compare the agreement/

disagreement between judges and juries (Kalven & Zeisel, 1966). The judges reported on the characteristics of 3,576 criminal trials, including the jury's verdict, and how the judge would have decided the case. The authors found that in 78% of the cases, the judge agreed with the jury's verdict. The jury acquitted when the judge would have convicted in 19% of the cases but convicted when the judge would have acquitted in only 3% of cases. Disagreement was reduced when the judge viewed the evidence as clear as opposed to close but was unaffected when the judge viewed the evidence as difficult versus easy to understand. These results led Kalven and Zeisel to conclude that juries are competent decision makers, at least if the judge is the benchmark.

Critics complained of sample limitations and expressed skepticism about the "reason analysis" that depended on judges to evaluate what jurors were likely to think (Goldstein, 1967; also see Hans & Vidmar, 1991). Nonetheless, the research was recognized as path-breaking, inspiring generations of jury researchers. Moreover, most of the basic findings have endured (e.g., Eisenberg et al., 2005).

Psychologists came later to the jury table,[1] and that timing was perfect for me. I was in college when *The American Jury* (Kalven & Zeisel, 1966) was published. It was not until graduate school that I discovered it, met Hans Zeisel, and developed my lifelong interest in the jury and in psychology and law. When I was in college at the University of Michigan in the late 1960s, questions of authority, altruism, conformity, and justice dominated discussion. The civil rights movement put issues of inequality front and center. The Vietnam War pitted government and adult authority ("Don't trust anyone over 30") against youth. I began college as a math major intending to become an actuary(!), but outside events changed my path, diverting me to worry about conformity and obedience (Milgram, 1963), how important decisions are made, and how people in authority can exert irresponsible and disproportionate influence. I ended

1. Although many other scholars have contributed to the empirical literature on the jury, my focus in this essay is on the psychologists who made the jury a dominant topic in psychology and law.

up majoring in psychology and sociology and headed for graduate school at Northwestern in social psychology.

My first encounters with law were in graduate school where I helped to train interviewers to gather information on the exorbitant purchase prices paid by black homebuyers in the Contract Buyers League case then being tried as a federal class action in Chicago. Hans Zeisel, co-author of *The American Jury*, was the statistical expert in the case, and I observed him in court explaining how sampling procedures could enable us to describe the pattern of discrimination in housing prices by collecting data on only a portion of the homebuyers. My interest grew in how law and the legal system control and influence—and, of course, are influenced by—human behavior. I also came to believe that empirical research could have a crucial impact on policy, which fit with the thrust of Northwestern's social psychology program. The program chair, Donald Campbell, offered the vision of an experimenting society (Campbell, 1969) and pushed, with my advisor Tom Cook, for methodologically rigorous field research initiatives (Campbell & Stanley, 1963; Cook & Campbell, 1979). I also learned how hard it was to conduct such research.

My next encounter with Hans Zeisel was near the end of graduate school when I was looking for a teaching or post-doc position in Chicago because my husband was an Illinois municipal lawyer. I contacted Zeisel because of a letter he had written to the editor of the *Chicago Tribune*. In the letter he warned that the U.S. Supreme Court was going down a dangerous path with jury size. Zeisel reported that the Court had authorized juries composed of as few as six people. It was in 1970, in the case of *Williams v. Florida*. I went to see him, telling him, which he of course already knew, that this seemed to me to be a very bad idea if the goal of the jury was thorough deliberation and decision-making. We talked at great length. It turned out that he was initiating a project on jury selection in the federal courts. So he hired me as a post-doc to run the project, and I began spending time in court with jurors and jury trials. Our field study of jury selection compared the real jury with two shadow juries, one composed of those excused on peremptory challenge during jury selection and one chosen at random from the jury pool. The comparison raised questions about the ability of attorneys to deselect unfriendly jurors, at least under the limited voir dire conditions in federal court (Diamond & Zeisel, 1974; Zeisel & Diamond, 1978).

I confess that I began studying the jury with some skepticism. Why should we expect amateurs to be able to competently handle legal conflicts? I shared my doubts with Zeisel, who was an unabashed jury fan. Zeisel was a fascinating man of enormous complexity: a dedicated opponent of guns and the death penalty, an ardent fan of Shakespeare, and a statistical expert. He arrived in the United States from Austria in 1938 at age 32, three months after Germany annexed Austria, escaping the threat of the Nazis. His appreciation for democracy may partially explain his devotion to the jury, but he was also hard-nosed when it came to empirical evidence, including evidence on the jury. Working with him was extraordinary. Although he had the courtly demeanor of a typical Austrian gentleman, when you got involved in an academic or intellectual discussion with him, everything changed. He had no patience with claims you couldn't support with evidence, and he expected you to treat his claims with equal critical evaluation; there was no expectation of deference to seniority. But it wasn't Zeisel's persuasiveness that led me to see the jury as a remarkably, inexplicably functional institution. That conversion came later and, as Hans would have appreciated, from the data. Yet Hans left his mark in other ways on my jury research: on my interests in jury size, jury selection, interactions between the jury and the law, and death penalty decisions.

In a moment, I will return to my research on some of these topics in the 1970s and 1980s. First, it may be helpful to acknowledge the importance of jury research as a major topic within Psychology and Law across the years. Few other areas in the field have been studied so thoroughly.

## FIFTY YEARS OF JURY RESEARCH

While I was getting acquainted with the jury, psychologists across the country were making the same discovery. Since the 1970s, the jury has been a dominant topic of research in psychology and the law, particularly among social psychologists, later joined by psychologists interested in social cognition. It is easy to see why: Social psychologists study how social perception, influence, and interaction affect individual and group behavior, a fair description of the activities of jurors and juries. As an important nonexpert actor in the legal system, charged with reaching decisions about contested events and states of mind, the jury is an obvious legal group for psychologists to study.[2]

In the first three years of *Law and Human Behavior* (1977–1979), a quarter of its articles focused on the jury. Many of the new studies used a jury (actually, predominantly, juror) simulation paradigm, joining the dominant methodological tool of social psychology with this new research topic. Content analyses reveal the dramatic growth of jury research: Weiten and Diamond (1979) reported that jury simulations had grown from 7 studies between 1964 and 1966 to 62 studies between 1973 and 1975. Roesch (1990) reported that jury research along with eyewitness testimony and expert witnesses accounted for a substantial portion of the articles published in *Law and Human Behavior* since the journal's inception. In the early years, books on the jury focused on individual jury simulations: studies of group size and decision rules (Saks, 1977; Hastie, Penrod, & Pennington, 1983). Based on Small's (1993) analysis, jury decision-making accounted for 44 of the 105 experimental articles that appeared in *Law and Human Behavior* between June 1986 and December 1991. Devine (2012) reported (based on Greene et al., 2002) that about 825 studies of juror or jury decision-making were published between 1997 and 1999, and he estimated that, by 2011, 1,500 studies had been published in total.

By 2000, books using expanded jury methods and new topics accompanied the growing numbers of articles: the observational and interview study of medical malpractice by Vidmar (1995) and the multiple methods study of business trials by Hans (2000). Researchers were addressing some complaints about the early literature (e.g., the civil jury was

2. Political scientists interested in professional decision-making show a similar fascination with courts, particularly with the U.S. Supreme Court.

receiving increased attention; see Greene & Bornstein, 2003). Other areas remained underaddressed, notably the relative dearth of jury, as opposed to juror, studies. The empirical literature on the jury has continued to grow, and authors of many of the most recent volumes on jury research have attempted to take stock of the jury in light of that literature. In 2017 alone, two books on the jury were published: *The Jury under Fire* (Bornstein & Greene, 2017) and *The Psychology of Juries* (Kovera, 2017).

This volume focuses only on the earliest work of the 1970s and 1980s and on the authors' contributions in those days when their own research was contributing to the early foundation of the field. So, in what follows, I focus on just a few of the jury topics that attracted my attention in the early days, played important roles in my scholarly career, and contributed to developments in the field of Psychology and Law. To do this, I set aside research I later conducted on other important jury topics, such as expert testimony, race, jury selection, and perceptions of the jury, as well as research on important jury topics that others have studied and I have not, such as pretrial publicity and punitive damages.

## STUDIES OF JURY SIZE

*Williams v. Florida* (1970) acted as something of a call to arms for the growing group of social psychologists interested in Psychology and Law. The Court said it was basing its decision on functional, rather than historical or legal, claims about jury size to determine that six-person juries would pass constitutional scrutiny. The Court concluded that juries of 6 and 12 would not differ in representativeness or quality of decision-making. Yet the Court cited no statistical or behavioral evidence that supported these claims. The case stimulated empirical research on jury size that the Court cited three years after *Williams* when it approved six-member juries in federal civil cases. The methodological weaknesses in the new studies that the Court referred to as "convincing empirical evidence" made it clear that science was not a strong suit for judges, even Supreme Court justices. Zeisel and I wrote an article (Zeisel & Diamond, 1974) critiquing the Court's opinion and the "empirical" evidence on which the Court had said it relied. I reanalyzed the one experimental study the Court had cited to show why it could not have detected differences (Diamond, 1974). New empirical work by Michael Saks (1977) and others made it clear that the Court's conclusions were wrong: 6 and 12 members juries do behave differently.

A few years later, the State of Georgia tested whether the jury could be reduced even further. The question in *Ballew v. Georgia* (1978) was whether criminal juries of five were constitutional. The lead opinion, by Justice Blackmun, was at its heart a literature review of the empirical research on group size effects, including Saks's (1977) work, that had been completed since *Williams*, as well as the critiques and reanalyses of the flawed studies cited with approval in *Colgrove v. Battin* (1973) (Diamond, 1974; Zeisel & Diamond, 1974). It reached a strange conclusion. Blackmun concluded that the research comparing 6-person groups to 12-person groups showed that a reduction from six to five raised grave concerns about the ability of a jury to serve its necessary constitutional functions.

Though it took the justices four different opinions to provide some justification for their votes, by 9–0 every justice chose to stop the slippery slide of juries toward ever smaller numbers, and they reset the constitutional minimum at six, affirming *Williams*. Blackmun (joined by Stevens) concluded that serious problems arose only when the reduction went from 6 to 5 and did not suggest a return to 12.

Michael Saks[3] found what may be an explanation in Justice Blackmun's papers at the Library of Congress. In one memo about the *Ballew* case, a law clerk reported to Justice Blackmun about the empirical research he found and of the findings of that research and concluded by suggesting that *Williams* was decided in error and ought to be reversed. Blackmun responded that *Williams* is "on the books"—implying that it cannot (easily) be changed. But Justice Blackmun also noted that he saw where this game was heading. If the Court approved five-person juries, he believed, next it would be confronted by states authorizing four, then three, two, or one (Smith & Saks, 2008). So, one way or another, the destruction of

---

3. Thanks to Michael Saks for this analysis.

the American jury had to be halted there and then. And it was. But why include all of that research, which pointed far more clearly to the need to return juries to 12 than it did to a need to keep juries from shrinking to 5?

Saks guesses, and I concur, that Justice Blackmun saw the need to return the constitutional minimum to 12, or closer to 12, but realized that his colleagues would not agree to do so only a few years after they had approved the historic reduction to 6. The most that Blackmun could do, and remain the author of the opinion announcing the Court's judgment, was to plant the research where future justices and lawyers could most easily find it—like seeds to sprout another time when conditions are more favorable. He was doing the best he could to help some future Court to restore the American jury to twelve.

It appears that Justice Blackmun's approach did have some impact. The New Hampshire legislature asked their Supreme Court for an advisory opinion on whether the court would hold reduction in jury size to be constitutional. The Court responded that, in view of Justice Blackmun's opinion in *Ballew* (not the holding but the discussion of empirical studies), a reduction in jury size below 12 would violate the jury trial guarantee of the New Hampshire Constitution (Opinion of the Justices, 1981). Some of the seeds sprouted.

In an amicus brief, a number of legal scholars and psychologists urged the U.S. Supreme Court to revisit the issue and restore the 12-person jury.[4] But the crop, apparently, was not yet ready for harvest (*Gonzalez v. Florida*, 2008). Important lesson: psychologists interested in court influence have to take a long view.

## RESEARCH ON JURIES AND JUDGES

While I was in federal court working on that first jury selection project, I learned that the Northern District of Illinois was operating a judicial

4. Steven G. Calabresi, Shari S. Diamond, Phoebe C. Ellsworth, Samuel R. Gross, Valerie Hans, Saul Kassin, Stephan Landsman, Richard O. Lempert, Steven D. Penrod, Mary R Rose, Michael J. Saks, and Neil Vidmar.

sentencing council designed to reduce sentence disparity. Judges on the council received presentence reports on defendants who were to be sentenced, wrote down their independent sentence preferences, and then discussed the cases. The sentencing judge retained the final decision-making power. Intrigued by the problem of unwarranted variability in sentencing, a topic I would later revisit in studies of jury death penalty sentencing, I initiated research on sentencing councils that showed that differences in judgments among judges are common (Diamond, 1981; Diamond & Zeisel, 1975). We also found that sentencing council input had only a modest effect on that variation. I found the same variability in other groups (Diamond, 1983). Judges, like jurors, are human. The genius of the jury, of course, is that its verdict is based on what Wigmore (1929, p. 171) called "reconciliation of varied temperaments and minds," the pooling of variation in the group. Although a majority position may disproportionately influence outcomes, the group must approach consensus (or at least a supermajority in a few jurisdictions). The decisions of trial judges, in contrast, even of those who sit on sentencing councils, are decisions of one person and thus subject to individual variation.

Early jury research was dominated by investigations of ways in which laypersons are susceptible to extralegal influence (e.g., for the attractiveness of the defendant, see Efran, 1974; for an admonition to ignore inadmissible evidence, see Wolf & Montgomery, 1977). These are interesting questions, but as Wigmore (1929) pointed out, and Lempert (1993) later reminded us, the evaluation of jury performance makes sense only in the context of a comparison with the alternative: the judge. Modern research has partially corrected the record (e.g., Landsman & Rakos, 1994; Wistrich, Guthrie, & Rachlinski, 2005), but only partially.

## SIMULATION RESEARCH ON THE JURY

Psychologists' use of mock jury (or juror) studies as a preferred methodology to study the jury has given rise to concerns from both courts and inside the academy about the ability to generalize to the behavior of real juries. In 1979, I edited a special issue of *Law and Human Behavior* in which I asked: "Does the microscope lens distort?" I pointed out, "Astronauts walked on the moon because planning research was able to study in the laboratory much of what would be encountered in space" (Diamond, 1979, p. 1), but I recognized that social research on legal issues might present special problems of inference. I suggested that the key was to identify factors that would modify the ability to extrapolate and the ability to persuade others (courts) that extrapolation was justified. Wayne Weiten and I described six methodological characteristics that might threaten the validity of conclusions from simulation research: inadequate sampling, inadequate trial simulations, lack of jury deliberation, inappropriate dependent variables, lack of corroborative field data, and the nature of decisions based on role playing (Weiten and Diamond, 1979). In the years that followed, researchers conducted more elaborate simulations and tested the impact of variations in the ecological validity of simulations on results (e.g., see later contributions: Bornstein, 1999; Diamond, 1997).

Courts have been an inconsistent audience for jury simulations, a source of frustration for those of us who would like to have our research lead to improvements in the legal system. For example, Phoebe Ellsworth and her colleagues provided an extensive body of jury simulation evidence in *Lockhart v. McCree* (1986), demonstrating that lack of opposition to the death penalty was associated with a greater willingness to convict, so that "death-qualifying" the jury seated to decide whether to convict a defendant was likely to increase that defendant's likelihood of conviction. Justice Rehnquist, writing for the majority on the U.S. Supreme Court, dismissed the empirical evidence, expressing doubt that such studies could predict the behavior of real juries.

## JURORS AND THE LAW

The second issue of *Law and Human Behavior* included an innovative experiment (Alfini, Sales, & Elwork, 1977) showing that jury instructions on the law could be rewritten to improve comprehensibility. This seminal piece addressed a common criticism of jury decision-making and showed how it might be addressed, but there seemed to be little appetite in the legal system to take on the task. Later studies replicated evidence that jurors struggled with legal instructions, which were often, and continued to be, written in incomprehensible, poorly organized, opaque language. Researchers studied particular pockets of comprehension problems: for example, "beyond a reasonable doubt" (Horowitz & Kirpatrick, 1996; Severance & Loftus, 1982; Stoffelmayr & Diamond, 2000) and death penalty instructions (Ellsworth, 1989).

In 1992, when Hans Zeisel's health was failing and just before he died, we worked together again on a case involving death penalty jury instructions. James Free had been convicted of rape and murder and was sentenced to death. As often happens, the instructions in his case had been opaque in crucial ways, and Hans conducted research with the MacArthur Justice Center to support an appeal of the death sentence, based on the failure to provide the jury with understandable instructions about the rules involving death sentences. I testified about Zeisel's survey and some other research on jury instructions. A thoughtful federal judge, Marvin Aspen, overturned the death sentence and ordered a new sentencing hearing. With psycholinguist Judith Levi, I conducted further experimental research showing that the instructions could be made more comprehensible (Diamond & Levi, 1996), but it was too late. On appeal, the Seventh Circuit reinstated the death sentence. One of my most surreal experiences as a jury scholar was testifying at the defendant's clemency hearing about jury instructions—a procedurally peculiar and ultimately unsuccessful effort. Procedural fairness in sentencing was no longer a concern at this point. The panel was mildly polite, but what I had to say was of little interest to them. The focus had shifted. When a nun testified on behalf of Mr. Free, the only question she got was whether she was in favor of or opposed to the death penalty. Mr. Free was eventually executed in 1995.

## STUDYING THE ACTIVE JURY

Ever since psychologists began studying the jury, scholars have complained that jury research is under-theorized. Although there have been a few exceptions—for example, Jim Davis's social decision scheme (Davis, 1973) and Pennington and Hastie's (1991) story model—that charge is probably still warranted today. But there is no doubt that our general understanding of jurors and jury decision-making has expanded over time as empirical researchers have studied jury behavior, particularly as we have observed jury behavior in the more elaborate simulations and in field experiments where jurors are able to actively engage with the trial stimulus and each other. My early interactions with the shadow jurors and the posttrial interviews I conducted with the real jurors in my first jury study (Zeisel & Diamond, 1978) taught me to expect that active engagement. In later research, Jay Casper and I showed that treating jurors like adults, providing them, where possible, with explanations for legal rules, can reduce the likelihood that information will be used inappropriately (Diamond & Casper, 1992).

## CHANGES OVER TIME AND A LOOK AT THE FUTURE

In considering those early days of psychology and law, I am mostly elated but in some ways dissatisfied with what the years have produced for juries and jury research. On the positive side, early researchers identified important features of the jury that were not well understood or even previously considered by the legal system and corrected mistaken beliefs about how the jury actually works. My personal experience in the 1970s with the developing field generated for me a growing fascination with legal decision-making by both juries and judges. That interest led me in 1981 to conduct a study of English lay and professional magistrates as another way to understand lay performance in the courtroom (Diamond, 1990). It also led me to law school in 1982, where I originally intended to spend a year "boning up" on law and ended up graduating three years later. The jury accompanied me throughout, and today I teach a course on juries and jury behavior at Northwestern University Law School that I like to think is a healthy mix of psychological research and legal doctrine. My own empirical research on the jury has continued as the field of research on psychology and jury behavior has dramatically expanded, building on those early foundations.

The pioneering Chicago Jury Project by Kalven and Zeisel, which I described earlier, included an aborted effort to study actual jury deliberations. The authors of *The American Jury* referred to it as the "purple heart" of the project when the fact that they had taped five civil jury deliberations became public and resulted in "public censure by the Attorney General of the United States, a special hearing before the Sub-Committee on Internal Security of the Senate Judiciary Committee, [and] the enactment of statutes in some thirty-odd jurisdictions prohibiting jury-taping" (Kalven & Zeisel, 1966, p. vii).

Times have changed, at least in some jurisdictions. While some courts have continued to be suspicious of empirical jury studies, others have embraced the opportunity to learn from that research. Some courts, too, have come to recognize that the jury is not the potted plant reflected in the legal system's early template and as a result have been open to ideas about how to optimize trial procedures to improve juror and litigant experiences. In one such effort, Arizona permitted us to videotape actual jury deliberations as part of a randomized experiment on one of its reforms (Diamond, Vidmar, Rose, Ellis, & Murphy, 2003). As a result of this opportunity, we have uncovered much that is consistent with prior laboratory research, but we have also found some surprises.

The topic of improving jury instructions now receives some of the attention it deserves. Most recently, California rewrote its entire pattern of jury instructions in "plain English" with the help of psycholinguist Peter Tiersma. Psychologists have worked with the courts to implement procedural changes that can help with comprehension, like providing individual written copies of the instructions. The Arizona Jury Project showed that jurors in real civil jury deliberations made regular and productive use of the instructions each received at the end of the trial, but also identified omissions and structural defects that are obstacles to optimal jury comprehension and use of legal instructions (Diamond, Murphy, & Rose, 2012). So there is still more to do.

An unexpected benefit of jury research has been its international spread. For example, some provinces in Argentina have relied on the jury research we've conducted in the United States to inform their choices in designing their new jury trial procedures.

On the negative side, while jury research in the United States has attracted an active and creative new generation of researchers studying previously underexplored topics like emotion (e.g., Salerno & Peter-Hagene, 2015), the jury as an institution is no longer a standard method of case resolution, with plea bargaining and settlement now dominant. The shadow of the jury (what would a jury do if the case went to trial?) is still a crucial influence, but researchers have yet to study the contours of that impact. Similarly, the greater costs of jury versus juror research and the greater ease, lower cost, and speed of conducting juror research online have discouraged needed research on deliberations.

I mentioned earlier that I began my acquaintance with the jury as a skeptic. One of the joys of scholarship is to test a pet theory and find support for it. Just as important are those occasions when the evidence forces you to reject a pet theory. And so it was with me. My studies of the jury persuaded me that this remarkable institution is in fact an impressive and remarkably competent decision maker. I came to view the jury as early scientists viewed the hummingbird. It shouldn't be able to fly, but it does—and in fact it can fly backward. Now how does it do that? The challenge with the jury is the same. And that continues to be a challenging question for all of us who study juries. At the same time, we should never forget that the jury is a human institution, so it sometimes makes mistakes. A second task for jury researchers, therefore, at least for those interested in policy, is how to identify and test the effects of potential system features (Wells, 1978) that can be implemented to optimize jury performance.

## REFERENCES

*Ballew v. Georgia*, 435 U.S. 223 (1978).

Bornstein, B. H. (1999). The ecological validity of jury simulations: Is the jury still out? *Law and Human Behavior, 23*, 75–91.

Bornstein, B. H., & Greene, E. (2017). *The jury under fire: Myth, controversy, and reform.* New York: Oxford University Press.

Campbell, D. T. (1969). Reforms as experiments. *American Psychologist, 24,* 409–429.

Campbell, D. T., & Stanley, J. C. (1963). *Experimental and quasi-experimental designs for research.* Boston: Houghton Mifflin.

*Colgrove v. Battin,* 413 U.S. 149 (1973).

Cook, T. D., & Campbell, D. T. (1979). *Quasi-experimentation: Design and analysis issues for field settings.* Chicago: Rand McNally.

Davis, J. H. (1973). Group decision and social interaction: A theory of social decision schemes. *Psychology Review, 80,* 97–125.

Devine, D. J. (2012). *Jury decision making: The state of the science.* New York: New York University Press.

Diamond, S. S. (1974). A jury experiment reanalyzed. *University of Michigan Journal of Law Reform, 7,* 520–532.

Diamond, S. S. (1979). Simulation: Does the microscope lens distort? *Law and Human Behavior, 3,* 1–4.

Diamond, S. S. (1981). Exploring patterns in sentence disparity. In B. Sales (Ed.), *Perspectives in law and psychology: The trial process.* (pp. 387–411). New York: Plenum.

Diamond, S. S. (1983). Order in the court: Consistency in criminal court decisions. In C. T. Scheirer & B. L. Hammonds, (Eds.), *The master lecture series:* Vol. 2. *Psychology and the law* (pp. 123–146). Washington, DC: American Psychological Association.

Diamond, S. S. (1990). Revising images of public punitiveness: Sentencing by lay and professional English magistrates. *Law & Social Inquiry, 15,* 191–221.

Diamond, S. S. (1997). Illuminations and shadows from jury simulations. *Law and Human Behavior, 21,* 561–571.

Diamond, S. S., & Casper, J. D. (1992). Blindfolding the jury to verdict consequences: Damages, experts, and the civil jury. *Law & Society Review, 26,* 513–563.

Diamond, S. S., & Levi, J. N. (1996). Improving decisions on death by revising and testing jury instructions. *Judicature, 79,* 224–232.

Diamond, S.S., Murphy, B., & Rose, M.R. (2012). The "Kettleful of Law" in real jury deliberations: Successes, failures and next steps. *Northwestern University Law Review, 106,* 1537–1608.

Diamond, S. S., & Ryken, A. (2013). The modern American jury: A hundred year journey. *Judicature, 96,* 315–322.

Diamond, S. S., Vidmar, N., Rose, M., Ellis, L., & Murphy, B. (2003). Juror discussions during civil trials: Studying an Arizona innovation, *University of Arizona Law Review, 45,* 1–81.

Diamond, S. S., & Zeisel, H. (1974). A courtroom experiment on juror selection and decision-making. *Personality and Social Psychology Bulletin, 1,* 276–277.

Diamond, S. S., & Zeisel, H. (1975). Sentencing councils: A study of sentence disparity and its reduction. *University of Chicago Law Review, 43,* 109–149.

Efran, M. G. (1974). The effect of physical appearance on the judgment of guilt, interpersonal attraction and severity of recommended punishment in a simulated jury task. *Journal of Research in Personality, 8,* 45–54.

Eisenberg, T., Hannaford-Agor, P. L., Hans, V. P., Waters, N. L., Munsterman, G. T., Schwab, S. J., & Wells, M. T. (2005). Judge–jury agreement in criminal cases: A partial replication of Kalven and Zeisel's "The American Jury." *Journal of Empirical Legal Studies, 2,* 171–207.

Ellsworth, P. C. (1989). Are twelve heads better than one? *Law and Contemporary Problems, 52,* 205–224.

Elwork, A., Sales, B. D., & Alfini, J. T. (1977). Juridic decisions: In ignorance of the law or in light of it? *Law and Human Behavior, 1,* 163–189.

Goldstein, A. S. (1967). Book review. *Law & Society Review, 1,* 148–152.

*Gonzalez v. Florida,* 555 U.S. 1056 (2008) [denial of certiorari].

Greene, E., & Bornstein, B. H. (2003). *Determining damages: The psychology of jury awards.* Washington, DC: American Psychological Association.

Greene, E., Chopra, S., Kovera, M., Penrod, S., Rose, V. G., Schuller, R., & Studebaker, C. (2002). Jurors and juries: A review of the field. In J. Ogloff (Ed.), *Taking psychology and law into the twenty-first century* (pp. 225–284). New York: Kluwer/Plenum.

Hans, V. P. (2000). *Business on trial: The civil jury and corporate responsibility.* New Haven, CT: Yale University Press.

Hans, V. P., & Vidmar, N. (1991). *The American Jury* at twenty-five years. *Law & Social Inquiry, 16,* 323–351.

Hastie, R., Penrod, S. D., & Pennington, N. (1983). *Inside the jury.* Cambridge, MA: Harvard University Press.

Horowitz, I. A., & Kirpatrick, C. (1996). A concept in search of a definition: The effects of reasonable doubt instructions on certainty of guilt standards and jury verdicts. *Law and Human Behavior, 20,* 655–670.

Kalven, H., Jr., & Zeisel, H. (1966). *The American jury.* Boston, MA: Little, Brown.

Kovera, M. B. (Ed.). (2017). *The psychology of juries.* Washington, DC: American Psychological Association.

Landsman, S., & Rakos, R. F. (1994). A preliminary inquiry into the effects of potentially biasing information on judges and jurors in civil litigation. *Behavioral Sciences and the Law, 12,* 113–126.

Lempert, R. O. (1993). Civil juries and complex cases: Taking stock after twelve years. In Robert E. Litan (Ed.), *Verdict: Assessing the civil jury system* (pp. 181–247). Washington DC: Brookings Institute.

*Lockhart v. McCree,* 476 U.S. 162 (1986).

Milgram, S. (1963). Behavioral study of obedience. *Journal of Abnormal and Social Psychology, 67,* 371–378.

*Opinion of the Justices* [of the Supreme Court of New Hampshire], 121 N.H. 480 (1981).

Pennington, N., & Hastie, R., (1991). A cognitive theory of juror decision making: The story model. *Cardozo Law Review, 13,* 519–557.

Roesch, R. (1990). From the editor. *Law and Human Behavior, 14,* 1–3.

Saks, M. J. (1977). *Jury verdicts: The role of group size and social decision rule.* Lexington, MA: Heath.

Salerno, J. M., & Peter-Hagene, L. C. (2015). One angry women: Anger expression increases influence for men, but decreases influence for women, during deliberation. *Law and Human Behavior, 39,* 581–592.

Severance, L. J. & Loftus, E. L. (1982). Improving the ability of jurors to comprehend and apply criminal jury instructions. *Law & Society Review, 17,* 153–198.

Small, M. A. (1993). Legal psychology and therapeutic jurisprudence. *St. Louis University Law Journal, 37*, 675–700.

Smith, A., & Saks, M. J. (2008). The case for overturning *Williams v. Florida* and the six-person jury: History, law, and empirical evidence. *Florida Law Review, 60*, 441–470.

Stoffelmayr, E., & Diamond, S. S. (2000). The conflict between precision and flexibility in explaining "beyond a reasonable doubt." *Psychology, Public Policy and Law, 6*, 769–787.

Vidmar, N. (1995). *Medical malpractice and the American jury: Confronting the myth about jury incompetence, deep pockets, and outrageous damage awards.* Ann Arbor: University of Michigan Press.

Weiten, W., & Diamond, S. S. (1979). A critical review of the jury simulation paradigm: The case of defendant characteristics. *Law and Human Behavior, 3*, 71–93.

Wells, G. L. (1978). Applied eyewitness-testimony research: System variables and estimator variables. *Journal of Personality and Social Psychology, 36*, 1546–1557.

Wigmore, J. H. (1929). A program for the trial of jury trial. *Judicature, 12*, 166–171.

*Williams v. Florida*, 399 U.S. 78 (1970).

Wistrich, A. J., Guthrie, C., & Rachlinski, J. L. (2005). Can judges ignore inadmissible information? The difficulty of deliberately disregarding. *University of Pennsylvania Law Review, 53*, 1251–1345.

Wolf, S., & Montgomery, D. A. (1977). Effects of inadmissible evidence and level of judicial admonishment to disregard on the judgments of mock jurors. *Journal of Applied Social Psychology, 7*, 205–219.

Zeisel, H., & Diamond, S. S. (1974). "Convincing empirical evidence" on the six member jury. *University of Chicago Law Review, 41*, 281–295.

Zeisel, H., & Diamond, S. S. (1978). The effect of peremptory challenges on jury and verdict. *Stanford Law Review, 30*, 491–531.

# 5

# Mental Health Law and the Seeds of Therapeutic Jurisprudence

DAVID B. WEXLER

I am the only author in this project who is not a psychologist. Yes, my name sounds like that of a psychologist (David Wechsler of intelligence test fame). And, if you look up even my properly spelled name in Amazon.com, you'll find a California psychologist named David B. Wexler who is more prolific than I! We are often confused by others and regularly receive invitations to speak and write intended for the other. A university press that had asked me to do an essay on therapeutic jurisprudence (TJ) for an encyclopedia even published it under the "other" David B. Wexler, thanks to an overeager editorial assistant doing a last-minute Google check of credentials who identified me as a psychologist from San Diego, California.

As much as I love psychology, and though many of my best friends are psychologists, I lack even a single unit of psychology in my training. I attended a college where Intro to Psych was an eight-unit "rat lab" course, and I was accordingly denied permission, not having taken that prerequisite, to enroll in Abnormal Psychology or Social Psychology. I did manage to major in sociology, and it served me well as a background for law school, as an attorney in the Criminal Division of the U.S. Department of Justice, and as a legal academic.

My passion and life's work—apart from fully enjoying my domestic/ family life, as well as my professorial, social, and cultural life in San Juan, Puerto Rico, and in travels beyond—is in Therapeutic Jurisprudence. As I will explain, TJ's official "birth" can be traced to a presentation given in October 1987 in an National Institute of Mental Health (NIMH) work- shop on law and mental health coordinated by Saleem Shah and Bruce Sales. But the purpose of this book is to look especially at the 1970s when American Psychology–Law Society was getting started, and at that time I was creating some of the field's early works on mental health law. This retrospective assignment has given me an opportunity to consider, more closely than I have before, how the seeds of TJ were evident in my earliest mental health law projects.

My objective, then, is to fine tune the early history of TJ to show where it came from. Some of that history is provided in an essay presented long ago at the University of Virginia (Wexler, 1999) at a conference organized by John Monahan as a 25-year retrospective on mental health law.[1] But before going back to the 1970s, let me provide a brief "pod" of TJ into which I will, in the next section, place the TJ seeds.

TJ is an approach that regards the law itself as a potential therapeutic (or antitherapeutic) agent. It looks at the law in action, not simply at the law in books, and it views the law as consisting of rules of law, legal procedures, and the roles of legal actors (judges, lawyers, mental health, and other professionals working in a legal context). TJ is interested in examining the therapeutic and antitherapeutic consequences of the law and in proposing ways that the law may be made or administered in a more therapeutic (or

---

1. See also a recent academic biographical essay written about me and TJ by the distin- guished legal scholar and legal historian University of Ottawa Professor Constance Backhouse (Backhouse, 2016). I would also like to take this opportunity to thank my research assistant, Rocío Alonso, for her diligent aid in the preparation of this chapter.

less antitherapeutic) way but without privileging therapeutic results over due process or other constitutional and related values.

## THE 1970S: MENTAL HEALTH LAW

I left my position as an attorney at the Criminal Division of the U.S. Department of Justice in 1967 to begin teaching at the University of Arizona College of Law. Given my interest and experience, my courses were Criminal Law and Criminal Procedure. I was not the only mental health law scholar to make my way into academia in those early years. Two others who made extraordinary contributions to our field across the following decades were Bruce Winick and Michael Perlin. Bruce, about whom I will say much more later, had been a lawyer for the New York City Department of Mental Health before he took his life-long position at the University of Miami in the 1970s. During the 1970s, Michael Perlin was serving in legal advocacy positions in the Department of the Public Advocate in Trenton, New Jersey, before joining New York Law School in 1984. Michael's contributions began in the late 1970s and later had a significant impact on the growth of mental health law, including his well-known multivolume work *Mental Disability Law: Civil and Criminal* (Perlin, 1989, 1998) and his book on *The Jurisprudence of the Insanity Defense* (Perlin, 1994), which won the Guttmacher Award from the American Psychiatric Association in 1995.

When I began teaching in the late 1960s, the criminal procedure "revolution" was in full swing, with cases like *Miranda* taking center stage. My earliest publications had to do with witness immunity, criminal discovery, and prisoners' rights. But the criminal procedure revolution was spilling over into other, related areas: Juveniles are also being deprived of freedom, the argument went, and even though those proceedings are technically *civil*, that label is merely a technicality, and many of the criminal safeguards, such as the right to a hearing and assigned counsel, should apply to them as well (*In re Gault*, 1967).

And then, what about mental patients, often confined against their will for extended periods, again without a hearing and counsel. Shouldn't something like the criminal-type rights apply to them as well?

So, a few years into my teaching career—in the 1970–1971 academic year—Dean Charles Ares, who has just now celebrated his ninetieth birthday, invited me to teach a seminar in law and psychiatry, an offer I jumped at. Note that the course was law and *psychiatry*, not law and *psychology*, which I don't think existed in law schools in those days. Nor was the course then called Mental Health Law, which similarly didn't then exist. There was no published casebook, only a large mimeographed volume (officially published several years later) by Rutgers Professor Alexander Brooks, called *Law, Psychiatry, and the Mental Health System*.

Interestingly, 10 years later, when I published my first book—Volume 4 in Bruce Sales's *Perspectives in Law and Psychology*—the book was entitled *Mental Health Law: Major Issues* (Wexler, 1981). Apparently, by then, the term *mental health law* had taken root. The book consists of revised essays all originally published between 1971 and 1979—the exact period of interest to the present project. Of the 11 chapters, 4 have been of enduring interest to me. Not surprisingly, those four are the ones that contain the seeds of TJ, and it is thus to those four that I will now turn.

## The Administration of Psychiatric Justice

"The Administration of Psychiatric Justice" (Wexler & Scoville, 1971), a law review article, was a major book-length (269 pages) project that I undertook in connection with my Law and Psychiatry seminar and a group of law review students. Among those students was Dan Shuman, who later became a leading contributor to mental health law. The project was unique in law school education in terms of its group project method. Moreover, it was unique in engaging not only in careful doctrinal analysis but also in bringing the area to life through extensive field work: observing many commitment hearings, examining court files, visiting the Arizona State Hospital and various county hospitals, and conducting interviews with physicians, lawyers, and judges in every Arizona county. Substantively, the study covered material now regarded as standard in mental health law courses—the civil commitment process, criminal commitment of those found incompetent or acquitted by reason of insanity, the role of counsel in all such proceedings, and the rights of patients, including the right to treatment.

The project enabled us to learn a tremendous amount about the law and its application (and misapplication) in the course of a year-long study. And we were gratified that it led to widespread legislative reform and was awarded the very first Manfred Guttmacher Award of the American Psychiatric Association.

Lessons for the eventual development of TJ? This project was a seed for the later development of TJ. The project used a standard approach except for its important field work component. But the field work made an important impression regarding the need for understanding the law in action, an approach that has become crucial to TJ and to what we now call *therapeutic application of the law*, as discussed later in this chapter.

More to the point of the TJ framework of the law as a therapeutic agent, we encountered an important example of an antitherapeutic rule of law, something that especially stood out in an area of the law explicitly designed to help persons with mental disability. A young man willing to go to the hospital as a voluntary patient had no means of transportation, leading the court to issue an involuntary commitment order, thereby requiring the sheriff's department to provide the transport. This measure, of course, added to the stigma of the hospitalization and likely to the enhanced security measures that follow involuntary commitment, such as the inability freely to exercise "ground privileges." In any case, this example of a statute that provided publicly funded transportation only for involuntary patients—thus discouraging voluntary admission in certain cases—is an antitherapeutic rule of law and a TJ seed of the study that has remained vivid to me from the moment I encountered it, as have a number of others.[2]

---

2. In another example, a patient found incompetent to stand trial and therefore confined under criminal commitment laws to the maximum security ward, was later reclassified as a mere

## Token and Taboo (Wexler, 1973)

"Token and Taboo" (Wexler, 1973), a *California Law Review* article—on law, behavior modification, and token economies operative in mental hospitals—is the best-known of my works, at least among behavioral psychologists of that time. Mostly, it was a straight-forward legal/constitutional analysis of the challenges posed by token economies, where important items—food, beds, privacy—were, under the token system, only available contingent on appropriate patient behavior. Yet, at the same time, cases like *Wyatt v. Stickney* (1969) were mandating minimum constitutional standards for hospital life, and those constitutional rights meant that the items should be given as a matter of right, not merely as reinforcers for good conduct.

What was unique about the piece was the extensive use of the literature of behavioral psychology and the description of the actual operation of token systems in the hospitals. An interdisciplinary approach became a later staple of much TJ writing, as did the notion that therapeutic goals should not take precedence over basic rights but must try to accommodate those rights. Finally, an approach was suggested to capture the positive value of reinforcers without violating the basic constitutional rights of the patients. If reinforcers could be found by observing patient preferences (the Premack principle; Premack, 1959), or even by the less-pure method of merely asking patients for their preferences, individual idiosyncratic reinforcers could be established. And given that they were in fact idiosyncratic, they would, by definition, not threaten the basic, general rights of the hospitalized population. Thus, the piece involved a thorough examination and use of the pertinent psychological literature, and it paved the way for the TJ approach in seeking both to affirm patient rights and, at

civilly committed patient and thus moved to a less secure ward. The reclassification, however, was not done for clinical concerns. Instead, it somehow came at the request of the county Board of Supervisors, as criminal commitments were a charge to the county, but the civilly committed were a charge to the state. Other antitherapeutic laws and policies discovered during the field work of the project relate to prison-to-hospital transfers, but, since they were also discussed as part of another publication, they will be mentioned in the following Criminal Commitment Contingency Structures section.

the same time, to navigate creatively to use behavioral psychological principles to achieve therapeutic results.

## Criminal Commitment Contingency Structures

In 1974 or 1975, Saleem Shah invited me to prepare a monograph for NIMH entitled *Criminal Commitments and Dangerous Mental Patients* (Wexler, 1976). The monograph's approximate 100 pages contained much standard doctrinal mental health law analysis. But certain parts captured my attention more than others. These parts were accordingly plucked out and put together under the name "Criminal Commitment Contingency Structures," an essay presented in the mid-1970s at a University of Nebraska conference (sponsored by Bruce Sales), then printed in Volume 1 of Bruce Sales's (1977) *Perspectives in Law and Psychology: The Criminal Justice System* (see Wexler, 1977) and again in two of my books—*Mental Health Law: Major Issues* (Wexler, 1981) and *Therapeutic Jurisprudence: The Law as a Therapeutic Agent* (Wexler, 1990).

From the title of that article, the reader can see we are getting closer to what might now be considered an almost full-blown TJ analysis. It is surely an implicit TJ paper. Its focus was basically the incentive structures in various rules and procedures and how those incentives could help or hinder therapeutic gains. In this paper, four incentive structures were examined:

- *Indeterminate confinement*—Where it is proposed that release is best gained by meeting objective conditions (e.g., obtaining a high school equivalency diploma) rather than by subjective criteria (e.g., demonstrating socially constructive attitudes) or, even worse, by practices where the confined population is never informed of the release criteria.
- *Defendants found incompetent to stand trial (IST)*—Although developments increasingly allow for outpatient treatment of ISTs, some expressed a concern that such an incentive structure

could encourage unwanted behavior: "By *remaining* clinically
IST while at large in the community, a patient may indefinitely
postpone 'pending' criminal proceedings without sacrificing
liberty" (Wexler, 1981, p. 122, emphasis in original).

- *Prison-to-hospital transferees*—Here, the piece concentrated on
disincentives for a prisoner with mental health issues to seek
transfer—even voluntary transfer—to a mental hospital. These
include a transferred prisoner possibly losing good time credits
while in a mental hospital, parole board policies disfavoring
conditional release of prisoner-patients, and policies in some
jurisdictions requiring maximum security confinement of all
transferred prisoners—including those who in prison were able
to serve as outside trustees.

- *Defendants found not guilty by reason of insanity (NGRI)*—To me,
the most interesting of these incentive contingencies relates to the
NGRI release structure. When a patient is merely civilly committed
to an institution, release usually lies unilaterally in the hospital's
hands. Nothing more is required. But for the NGRI population,
there is often an extra protective layer required for release: court
approval of the hospital's release recommendation.

At first glance, this release procedure may seem to disadvantage the
NGRI population, and some courts and legislatures have moved to equal-
ize the release procedures for the two patient groups. But interviews of
hospital officials and an examination of the diffusion of responsibility
literature led me to pose the question (obviously ultimately an empirical
one) whether the extra requirement of court approval might, in the aggre-
gate, inure to the benefit of NGRI release at a time the hospital believes
release is clinically warranted. Hospital officials are fearful of releasing
NGRI patients completely on their own. The officials are fearful that the
person being released might commit a violent act on release, and the hospital would then be the target of litigation or legislative budget cuts or, at
least, of seriously adverse publicity. The patients may thus be held longer
than the hospital actual believes necessary. On the other hand, if the

hospital recommends release to the court, the court is likely, in most cases, to approve the hospital recommendation:

The sharing of responsibility may thus lessen improper inhibitions. The hospital knows the court will scrutinize the hospital recommendation, and the court will know the hospital's decision is based on an evaluative judgment of professionals who have had a considerable amount of time to observe the patients proposed for release. It seems a win–win situation. Thus, the shared release procedure may lead to the timely release of those clinically regarded as ready for release—something that ironically might not occur if the professionals alone were in charge.

In the language of TJ seeds, we see in these examples, and dramatically in the example of the NGRI release structure, the therapeutic design of a procedure, and also how necessary it is to examine not only the written law but also the law's likely impact in practice. Interestingly, especially in retrospect, I closed the chapter by noting, "It seems that lawyers, behavioral psychologists, and others have reached the stage where they may begin cooperating to formulate a 'behavioral jurisprudence'" (Wexler, 1981, p. 130). Perhaps. But such a jurisprudence would seemingly be restricted to the therapeutic design of the law—to proposing and evaluating rules and procedures for their incentive structure. In fact, though, we were well on our way to completing the ingredients of the broader and more robust TJ framework. What we are missing, at this stage, is the crucial component of roles or behaviors of legal actors (judges, lawyers, mental health professionals, and others working in a legal context). The component of roles—practices and techniques—is essential to a full picture of TJ. The next section will provide that component.

## The Tarasoff Case and Its Victimological Virtues

In 1979, just under the wire to be included in work published during the 1970s, I wrote a paper (Wexler, 1979) giving a different twist to the important and controversial *Tarasoff* case (1976), a California case that held that a therapist owes a duty of reasonable care to third parties who may be endangered by the therapist's patient. The case was widely attacked by mental health professionals who were worried that the trusted therapist–patient relationship might be impaired by this additional obligation to nonpatient third parties.

I, too, was initially wary of *Tarasoff* and its potential impact on effective therapy. But then I received a telephone call from a worried therapist whose patient believed his wife was having affairs and told the therapist there would be "big trouble unless she cuts it out." The therapist did not know if this was a case of true infidelity or, instead, of "morbid jealousy" but was worried about liability if he failed to warn the wife. *Tarasoff* wasn't binding in our jurisdiction, but, needless to say, he did not want to be the defendant in a future Arizona case that might accept the *Tarasoff* rule. Nor, of course, did he want—ethically or legally—to violate his patient's confidence. I asked him how he thought his patient would react if he were told, "Mr. P, if you're so agitated about this, what would you think of my calling your wife, telling her of your agitation, and finding out what she has to say for herself?" He thought the patient would consent—and I thought such a strategy would finesse the legal dilemma: Neither the patient nor the spouse would then have a claim against the therapist.

Then, when I reviewed the victimological literature and the literature on marital jealousy, I realized that the involvement of the spouse seemed not only legally advisable but also therapeutically warranted—we needed more of an interpersonal rather than an intrapsychic approach. Yet, without the pressure generated by *Tarasoff,* such spousal involvement would likely not occur. My pro-*Tarasoff* thesis then began to take shape.

But *Tarasoff* would be of potential therapeutic benefit only if mental health professionals skillfully discharged the *Tarasoff* duty in an appropriate manner. It would not be therapeutic, for example, if the therapist simply called the police and mentioned the patient's statement. Nor would it be therapeutic if the therapist merely took the unilateral step of calling the spouse. *Tarasoff,* in other words, is not self-executing. If it is to work out, it calls for a proper and sensitive therapeutic application of the law. The *Tarasoff* article provides a suggested step-by-step sensitive way in which a therapist can navigate to achieve a therapeutic application of the rule.

(Today this component is essential and is evident especially in the recommended roles for judges and their court conversations; Wexler, 2016).

So there we have it: the 1970s coming to a close with all the pieces of the TJ jigsaw puzzle—some implicit articles, most clearly, "Criminal Commitment Contingency Structures" (Wexler, 1977; also see Wexler 1981, 1990) and the just-mentioned article on the *Tarasoff* case (Wexler, 1979). The pieces were, albeit mixed with other mental health law pieces, published in *Mental Health Law: Major Issues* (Wexler, 1981), but the jigsaw still was not assembled to form a perspective of the law as a therapeutic agent. For some reason, there would be a delay. Let's try to figure out why.

## TJ'S LONG GESTATION PERIOD

I've looked back at my list of publications following the 1979 *Tarasoff* article (Wexler, 1979) and am surprised to see a developmental delay. True, there is one paper immediately following the *Tarasoff* article—a 1980 piece, which, by its title, is clearly an implicit TJ work—a *Yale Law Journal* review essay entitled "Doctor–Patient Dialogue: A Second Opinion on Talk Therapy through Law" (Wexler, 1980). "Talk therapy through law" sounds *so* TJ. In 1980, its birth seemed imminent.

But, curiously, my subsequent publications are instead general mental health law topics: civil commitment, seclusion and restraint, and a sprinkling relating to insanity defense issues. Insanity defense issues? Hmm. *Aha*! In retrospect, I remember that the surprising 1982 *Hinckley* NGRI verdict caused shock waves through the mental health law community and, for many, including myself, interrupted the preexisting trajectory of scholarship.

Finally, then, more than a few years later—in 1986—I again wrote an implicit TJ piece that struck me at the time as being remarkably similar, at least in approach, to my 1979 *Tarasoff* article: This article was called "Grave Disability and Family Therapy: The Therapeutic Potential of Civil Libertarian Commitment Codes" (Wexler, 1986). The thesis and particulars are not important for our purposes. Instead, what seems relevant is that I was again in a "TJ kind of mood."

About then I received an invitation to participate in the October 1987 NIMH law and mental health workshop, and since I had done quite a bit of writing in the general area of law and therapeutic practice—*Tarasoff*, token economies, an analysis of the *Kaimowitz* psychosurgery case (Wexler, 1981)—I was asked by the workshop organizers to focus on the area of law and therapy.

It was then, preparing my written work during the summer of 1987, that it struck me that my enduring interest was not in law *and* therapy in general, but rather in law *as* therapy, and that was the TJ lightbulb— therapy *through* law, just as "talk therapy through law" was the title of the review essay I had written in 1980 right before the *Hinckley* "disruption."

The TJ puzzle pieces then came clearly and quickly together in a paper first named "Juridical Psychotherapy," a title that didn't survive the feedback at the October meeting (feedback that included Bruce Sales's persistent difficulty pronouncing "juridical"). The title was accordingly promptly changed to the first-runner up of "Therapeutic Jurisprudence"—a term that has always had its own set of problems but which, helped by its acronym "TJ," has now firmly taken hold.

Because of publishing delays and other snafus, the paper was actually not officially published for several years, when it appeared as the first chapter in my edited book, *Therapeutic Jurisprudence: The Law as a Therapeutic Agent* (Wexler, 1990). That book contained my essay explaining and naming TJ, followed by chapters (by myself and others) that were implicitly TJ (such as the *Tarasoff* piece and, once again, "Criminal Commitment Contingency Structures"). Actually, for newcomers to TJ, I think the best introductory route at the present time would be later-written essays that were revisions of talks, such as "Therapeutic Jurisprudence: An Overview" (Wexler, 2000; see also Wexler, 2010).

Curiously, therefore, because of the substantial publishing delay, the first articles to use the TJ name were in 1989—two pieces coauthored by me and Robert Schopp, now a long-time member of the University of

Nebraska law faculty (and involved in Nebraska's law and psychology program; Schopp & Wexler, 1989; Wexler & Schopp, 1989). Schopp came to the University of Arizona law school after a 10-year career as a PhD clinical psychologist. At Arizona, he entered a law/philosophy JD/PhD concurrent degree program. He served as an off-the-charts brilliant research assistant and then launched a remarkable academic career combining his many interests, which include TJ and much more.

## BRUCE WINICK

Because of the structure and requirements of this chapter, I have not yet mentioned the enormous contribution to TJ of my late friend, colleague, and collaborator, Bruce Winick. In the most wonderful of coincidences, Bruce and I first met in 1975, when I was on a semester sabbatical at the University of Miami and was given an office adjoining a brand-new law professor named Bruce Winick. As noted earlier, Bruce had been a lawyer for the New York City Department of Mental Health and, believe it or not, was assigned to teach mental health law! We became fast friends and mental health law colleagues who were able to finish each other's sentences. We were constant stimulants for each other's work. We did not write together until 1991, but from then until Bruce's untimely death several years ago, we were the principal co-developers of TJ, known as "the Ws." We wrote *Essays in Therapeutic Jurisprudence* (Wexler & Winick, 1991)—the first book to deal completely and explicitly with TJ, all chapters by me (including a reprint of my 1990 essay conceptualizing TJ), by him, by Schopp and me, and a conclusion by Bruce and me. In 1996, we attracted a number of other writers and edited a mammoth (1,000 page) book, *Law in a Therapeutic Key* (Wexler & Winick, 1996): the main contribution of that work was converting TJ from a new approach to mental health law to a mental health/well-being approach to law in general. In 2000, together with Dennis Stolle as first editor, we produced *Practicing Therapeutic Jurisprudence* (Stolle, Wexler, & Winick, 2000), extending TJ to an office counseling approach that drew also on insights from preventive law, and in 2003, Bruce and

I followed with *Judging in a Therapeutic Key* (Winick & Wexler, 2003), my personal favorite.

We each, of course, continued to write (books and articles) separately as well, and Bruce's body of work in TJ is enormous and inspirational. His work remains incredibly influential, constantly cited in today's scholarship.

## TODAY AND TOMORROW

Today, TJ is a flourishing international and interdisciplinary movement. The *International Journal of Therapeutic Jurisprudence* has been launched, a product of the Arizona Summit Law School in Phoenix, and the non-profit International Society of Therapeutic Jurisprudence is, at this writing, soon to be launched. TJ work has been published in 14 languages, and there is an Iberoamerican TJ Association active in Spain, Portugal, and Latin America. There is a "TJ in the Mainstream Blog," edited by Pauline Spencer. a magistrate of Victoria, Australia, working with an international advisory group from 18 countries. The blog is an easy-to-join and user-friendly resource, available at http://www.mainstreamtj.wordpress.com

The TJ in the Mainstream project—which seeks to use TJ even beyond the familiar problem-solving court (e.g., drug treatment court) area where it is best known—has been facilitated by a methodology that looks at the legal structure (rules and procedures) as "bottles" and the legal roles (practices and techniques of lawyers, judges, mental health and correctional professionals, etc.) as "liquid" or "wine" (Wexler, 2014). Conceptually, TJ remains true to its original conceptualization but now emphasizes the important interrelationship of the components: It is now clear that for true, meaningful, and sustainable law reform to take place, we need to concentrate on the therapeutic application of the law (the liquid or wine) as well as the therapeutic design of the law (the bottles; Wexler, 2015). We urge a seamless process entailing both dimensions. The wine and the bottles should be examined and thought of together.

The mainstreaming effort began principally in the criminal law domain (Wexler, 2014), but the methodology has already expanded, internationally, to juvenile law, child protection law, and public housing law. And a current international mainstreaming proposal urges the use of the TJ perspective to add an explicit well-being component to the achievement of court excellence, employing as an important tool the *International Framework for Court Excellence* (see Richardson, Spencer, & Wexler, 2016). It is an exciting time for TJ.

## REFERENCES

Backhouse, C. (2016). An introduction to David Wexler, the person behind therapeutic jurisprudence. *International Journal of Therapeutic Jurisprudence, 1*, 1–21.

*In Re Gault*, 387 U.S. 1 (1967).

Perlin, M. (1989). *Mental disability law: Civil and criminal.* Charlottesville, VA: Michie.

Perlin, M. (1994). *The jurisprudence of the insanity defense.* Durham, NC: Carolina Academic Press.

Perlin, M. (1998–2002). Mental disability law: Civil and criminal (2nd ed.). 5 vols. Charlottesville, VA: Lexis Law.

Premack, D. (1959). Toward empirical behavior laws: 1. Positive reinforcement. *Psychological Review, 66*, 219–233.

Richardson, E., Spencer, P., & Wexler, D. (2016) The international framework for court excellence and therapeutic jurisprudence: Creating excellent courts and enhancing wellbeing. *Journal of Judicial Administration, 25*, 148–166.

Sales, B. (1977). *Perspectives in law and psychology: The criminal justice system.* New York: Plenum.

Schopp, R., & Wexler, D. (1989). Shooting yourself in the foot with due care: Psychotherapists and crystalized standards of tort liability. *Journal of Psychiatry and Law, 17*, 163–203.

Stolle, D. P., Wexler, D., & Winick, B. J. (2000). *Practicing therapeutic jurisprudence: Law as helping profession.* Durham, NC: Carolina Academic Press, 2000.

*Tarasoff v. Regents of University of California*, 17 Cal. 3d 425 (1976).

Wexler, D., & Scoville, S. (1971). The administration of psychiatric justice: Theory and practice in Arizona. *Arizona Law Review, 13*, 1–259.

Wexler, D. (1973) Token and taboo: Behavior modification, token economies, and the law. *California Law Review, 61*, 8–109.

Wexler, D. (1976). *Criminal commitments and dangerous mental patients.* Washington, DC: National Institute of Mental Health.

Wexler, D. (1977). Criminal commitment contingency structures. In B. D. Sales (Ed.), *Perspectives in law and psychology: The criminal justice system.* (Vol. 1, pp. 121–138). New York: Plenum.

Wexler, D. (1979). Patients, therapists and third parties: The victimological virtues of *Tarasoff. International Journal of Law and Psychiatry, 2*, 1–28.

Wexler, D. (1980). Doctor–patient dialogue: A second opinion on talk therapy through law. *Yale Law Journal, 90,* 458–472.

Wexler, D. (1981). *Mental health law: Major issues.* New York: Plenum.

Wexler, D. (1986). Grave disability and family therapy: The therapeutic potential of civil libertarian commitment codes. *Journal of Law and Psychiatry, 9,* 39–56.

Wexler, D. (1990). *Law as a therapeutic agent.* Durham, NC: Carolina Academic Press.

Wexler, D. (1999). The development of therapeutic jurisprudence: From theory to practice. *Revista Juridica UPR, 68,* 691–705.

Wexler, D. (2000) Therapeutic jurisprudence: An overview. *Thomas M. Cooley Law Review, 17,* 125–134.

Wexler, D. (2010). Therapeutic jurisprudence and its application to criminal justice research and development. *Irish Probation Journal, 7,* 94–107.

Wexler, D. (2014). New wine in new bottles: The need to sketch a therapeutic jurisprudence "code" of proposed criminal processes and practices. *Arizona Summit Law Review, 7,* 463–479.

Wexler, D. (2015). *Moving forward on mainstreaming therapeutic jurisprudence: An ongoing process to facilitate the therapeutic design and application of the law.* Arizona Legal Studies Discussion Paper no. 15–10, University of Arizona.

Wexler, D. (2016). *Guiding court conversation along pathways conducive to rehabilitation: Integrating procedural justice and therapeutic jurisprudence.* Arizona Legal Studies Discussion Paper no. 15–33, University of Arizona.

Wexler, D., & Winick, B. (1991) *Essays in therapeutic jurisprudence.* Durham, NC: Carolina Academic Press.

Wexler, D., & Winick, B. (1996). *Law in a therapeutic key.* Durham, NC: Carolina Academic Press.

Wexler, D., & Schopp, R. (1989). How and when to correct for juror hindsight bias in mental health malpractice litigation: Some preliminary observations. *Behavioral Sciences and the Law, 7,* 485–504.

Winick, B., & Wexler, D. (2003). *Judging in a therapeutic key: Therapeutic jurisprudence and the courts.* Durham, NC: Carolina Academic Press.

*Wyatt v. Stickney,* 344 F. Supp 373 (1969).

# Mental Disability, Criminal Responsibility, and Civil Commitment

STEPHEN J. MORSE

The early, formative years of American Psychology–Law Society (AP–LS) were generative for legally relevant psychological and psychiatric science and transformative politically. This chapter begins with an autobiographical sketch that explains my early interest in law and psychology and in issues of criminal responsibility and civil commitment in particular. It then turns to the history of the legal landscape in these contexts in the formative years, followed by a section that diagnoses the problems that beset these fields. Then I describe my attempts to remedy some of the problems. The conclusion assesses where we are now.

## A PORTRAIT OF THE LAWYER-PSYCHOLOGIST AS A YOUNG MAN

I entered Harvard Law School in 1966. The mid-1960s were heady for those of us eager to use the law as a tool for social reform, especially the expansion of civil liberties. The Civil Rights Act was two years old and it did not require a crystal ball to understand that the thinking undergirding this historic legislation would apply to other groups that had been treated shabbily by the law, including women and people with mental disabilities. I loved law school's intellectual challenges and learned three essential things. First, I was mostly interested in crime, people with mental disorders, and kids, interests I dubbed the "human law package." Second, the law was a blunt instrument that generally responded only after people's problems had surfaced and then typically reacted counterproductively. Third, I concluded that the law lacked the internal resources to accomplish just reforms and needed input from the social sciences to achieve this goal.

A particularly formative experience was a year-long sequence called Prediction and Prevention of Harmful Behavior co-taught by Alan Dershowitz and Alan Stone, who became mentors. I became interested in the issues of responsibility, involuntary civil commitment, and preventive detention generally. This course also led me to believe that psychology could contribute to making the law more just and effective. I therefore applied to graduate school.

I chose the program in personality and developmental studies in Harvard's Department of Psychology and Social Relations. It was a rigorous empirical and experimental program that appealed to my methodological individualism and that would turn me into a scientist. I also pursued clinical training, first at the Massachusetts General Hospital and then at McLean. I was fortunate to have Robert (Bob) Rosenthal as my thesis advisor. Bob is a consummate scientist and gentleman. Working with him shaped the way I understood studies and data.

During my graduate training, I had two other influential experiences. The first was exposure to the type of unscientific and narrow-minded thinking that too often dominated American psychiatry at the time and that became a focus of my work. For example, clinicians then were quite certain that they could accurately predict human behavior despite the already substantial literature, pioneered by Paul Meehl's epochal monograph, *Clinical v. Statistical Prediction* (Meehl, 1954), that clinical prediction was poor. Second, I discovered that I was more interested in investigating normative rather than empirical issues and wanted to use my scientific and clinical training to inform normative legal analysis and reform proposals. Equally important, I realized that neither psychology nor psychiatry had the good, legally relevant data base that would be necessary to support reform efforts.

In 1974, I was offered a position at the University of Southern California, then and now one of the most intellectual and interdisciplinary law schools in the nation. My job talk was on the seminal case of *Lessard v. Schmidt*, the 1973 decision by the federal district court in Wisconsin holding that the Wisconsin civil commitment statute violated substantive and procedural due process. This talk prefigured work I would do for the rest of my career. I was on my way to LaLa Land to teach criminal law and mental health law. I threw away my overcoats and did not look back.

Not long after arriving in Los Angeles, I started receiving calls to consult on civil and criminal cases that involved mental health issues. The calls mostly resulted from things I had written or talks that I had given to professional groups. I had not planned to become a forensic psychologist, and there were few real training programs then, but I had a good deal of clinical experience and thought that I understood the relation between the law and mental health sufficiently to be of use. Thus, I became a practicing forensic psychologist by default.

## THE LEGAL LANDSCAPE IN THE FORMATIVE YEARS OF AP–LS

In criminal responsibility law, the U.S. Supreme Court had taken two modest early steps in substantive doctrine. In *Robinson v. California* (1962), the Court held that it violated the Eighth and Fourteenth Amendments to blame and punish a person for being an addict. It was unclear what the basis of the holding was, however. In *Powell v. Texas* (1968), the Court was asked to hold that a "compulsion" excuse was constitutionally required. The Court ruled that no such constitutional defense was required and clarified that *Robinson* only prohibited punishment of a status.

Most of the substantive doctrinal action in the state legislatures and courts and lower federal courts was concerned with the insanity defense and so-called diminished capacity, a doctrine most clearly promulgated by the influential California Supreme Court. The *Durham* (1954) "experiment" in legal insanity ended when the federal Court of Appeals for the District of Columbia overruled it in *United States v. Brawner* (1972) and adopted the Model Penal Code test (§4.01,1962). The Model Penal Code's insanity provision appeared to be the wave of the future as the majority of legislatures and courts addressing the issue of insanity defense reform adopted it.[1]

The court-created diminished capacity doctrine was in disarray because courts failed to distinguish two different variants of using mental abnormality evidence. In one, the defendant was claiming that he lacked the mens rea required by the definition of the offense. In the other, even if the mens rea was present, the defendant was arguably less responsible. This confusion led many courts to reject the former because they incorrectly believed that the defendant was claiming the latter, which was a type of mitigation defense claim the courts thought was the province of the legislatures.

The confusion was potentiated by the California Supreme Court. Its doctrine applied only in murder cases and it created the "defense" by judicial reinterpretation of the mens rea elements of murder so that they resembled mini-insanity defenses. With respect, the California court was torturing traditional meanings of murder. The California legislature took action in 1980 after the homophobic ex-police officer and city supervisor, Dan White, assassinated Mayor George Moscone and Supervisor Harvey Milk. Although the homicides were clearly intentional and premeditated and would otherwise have resulted in a capital murder conviction, White was convicted only of voluntary manslaughter based on the court's diminished capacity doctrine. The legislature abolished the court's doctrine, but

1. There was no uniform federal insanity defense until Congress passed the Insanity Defense Reform Act in 1984 in the wake of John W. Hinckley's acquittal by reason of insanity for attempting to assassinate President Reagan.

permitted defendants to introduce mental abnormality evidence to negate mens rea in a limited number of cases.

In the early days of AP–LS, the civil rights revolution extended to people with mental disabilities. New York's Mental Hygiene Law and California's Lanterman–Petris–Short Act were new attempts to inject due process into the civil commitment process. During the 1970s and early 1980s, federal and state courts were holding civil commitment laws unconstitutional. The U.S. Supreme Court decided *O'Connor v. Donaldson* (1975; requiring dangerous to self or others for civil commitment if the person could live safely in the community) and *Addington v. Texas* (1978; requiring that the criteria for commitment had to be proven by clear and convincing evidence). In *Youngberg v. Romeo* (1983), the Court did not hold that there was a right to treatment, but held that a severely intellectually disabled institutionalized patient was entitled to safety and freedom from restraint and to the habilitation necessary to preserve those rights. The question was whether the judicial and legislative changes in that era would also change actual practice.

## ANNALS OF ERRANCY IN THE FORMATIVE YEARS

At the time, psychiatry ruled the roost in the forensic world. Psychologists were just starting to become licensed and the whole field of forensic work was dominated by medical thinking and power. There were pioneering psychologists who were primarily forensic practitioners, but they were few and had limited influence. Mental health law was a set of unsystemized rules that treated mentally disordered people differently in many civil and criminal law contexts.

Bad thinking was both attitudinal and conceptual, and it was fueled by bad data. The attitudinal part was the arrogance among many mental health professionals about how much they knew about human behavior and what was in people's best interests. The belief that they were accurate predictors of human behavior, a practice crucial to both postinsanity-acquittal commitments and involuntary civil commitment, is a good example. There simply was no adequate data base, and clinicians still trusted their judgment despite Meehl (1954). Most of the legally relevant research was then in psychiatric journals, but psychiatry was in the lamentable grip of the *Diagnostic and Statistical Manual of Mental Disorders* (2nd edition; American Psychological Association, 1968) until 1980, which had utterly poor reliability and no validity, and the journals were full of scientifically poor-quality research (White, 1979; for an egregious example, see Lagos, Perlmutter, & Saexinger, 1977). Mental health research has gotten much better and some was excellent even then, but during the formative years, the general quality of research was poor by methodologically rigorous standards. Not understanding the limits of their knowledge promoted paternalism among mental health professionals. They thought they knew best because they thought they knew more than they did and because they conflated empirical and normative claims. They did not realize that maximizing health and safety at the expense of autonomy and liberty is a normative choice, and they systematically underestimated the capacity of people with mental disorders to make rational decisions concerning their own welfare.

There were two major conceptual failures in thinking about criminal responsibility in the formative years: misunderstanding determinism and free will and the erroneous belief that a cause of behavior, especially an abnormal cause, was per se an excusing or mitigating condition (which I later termed the *fundamental psycholegal error;* Morse, 1994). Together and separately, they led to "Creeping Krupke-ism (from the marvelous *West Side Story* number, "Gee, Officer Krupke").[2] Many mental health professionals and lawyers, including judges and legal academics, had an unsophisticated view of the meanings of determinism, free will, responsibility, and the relation among them. They failed to recognize, as philosophers had known for centuries, that determinism is a working hypothesis that cannot be confirmed or disconfirmed by

---

2. "Gee, Officer Krupke, you're really a square; this boy don't need a judge, he needs an analyst's care! It's just his neurosis that oughta be curbed. He's psychologic'ly disturbed!" (Bernstein & Sondheim, 1996).

science and that, even if determinism is true, there is a regnant philosophical position—compatibilism—that holds that ordinary people have
sufficient freedom to be held responsible. Some even made the error of
claiming that determinism could be partial or apply selectively to different groups. They were using determinism to support a normative agenda
it could not possibly support. If determinism is true and inconsistent
with responsibility, then no one is responsible. This could not possibly
explain our responsibility practices, which hold most people responsible
and excuse some.

The related error of thinking that causation per se mitigates or excuses
suffers from the same defects as the determinism argument. If this is a
causally closed universe and there is universal causation, as most scientists
think, then *all* behavior is caused and causation excuses everyone. Every
time a "new syndrome" was tentatively identified and linked to antisocial behavior, proponents of the causal theory of excuse would claim that
the offender was not responsible. But one cannot pick and choose favored
causes under this theory because causation excuses everyone. This theory
was founded on a basic conceptual error, and it was then used again to
support a normative agenda that it could not support.

There is a genuine metaphysical debate about whether determinism
is inconsistent with responsibility, but this debate has no legal purchase
within our doctrines and practices. Free will is not a legal criterion and
is not even foundational for responsibility. Nonetheless, people writing
about criminal responsibility and applying its doctrines in the formative
years consistently misused determinism and causation to support positions that were adopted on other, normative grounds. They had no idea
that they were special pleading. They argued for expansion of excusing
conditions because an offender had been deprived, had bad parents, had
underlying conflicts, lived in a bad neighborhood, had the wrong genes,
had a broken brain, and so on ad infinitum. These variables may be causally related to antisocial behavior, but they are not per se excusing. They
may cause a genuine excusing condition, such as lack of rational capacity, but then it is this deficit and not causation per se that is doing the
excusing work.

The bad practice stemmed from the belief that mental health professionals knew more than they did, the attempt to impose a particular politic position, and the failure to understand the legal doctrines of responsibility that psychology and psychiatry were supposedly helping to elucidate. Researchers and practitioners infused legal concepts with meanings that facilitated their moral agenda but that did not exist in law. In this, they were aided and abetted by like-minded lawyers or by unwitting judges. Transcripts of expert testimony and appellate decisions during the formative years provide striking evidence of this phenomenon.

For example, in one case I handled, the defense experts testified that the mentally disordered murder defendant lacked the capacity to form the intent to kill when he killed the victims to obey God's will. What could the experts have possibly meant? The defendant clearly formed the intent to kill. His psychotic perceptions and ideation were precisely the reason he did form the intent to kill. Of course, he had the capacity to form the intent as law defines it, which is simply to do something on purpose. Either the experts were cynically trying to get the defendant off by any means, or they erroneously believed that lack of rational understanding negates intent. Irrationally motivated intentions are still intentions. In summary, criminal responsibility and civil commitment doctrine and practice during the 1970s and 1980s were subject to many serious problems.

## A PORTRAIT OF THE LAWYER-PSYCHOLOGIST AS A (SOMEWHAT) OLDER MAN

My own contributions at that time were responses to the mess as I saw it. My first major mental health law article (Morse, 1978) tried to systematize the various civil and criminal laws that treated people with mental disorder differently. I claimed that all mental health laws had the same structure and underlying theoretical foundation. They all asked two questions: Is the person mentally disordered? and Is the person responsible in the context in question? And some asked a third question: What will the person do in the future?

I pointed out that the foundation for all these laws was the responsibility question because, in a liberal political and legal order, people should not be subject to special treatment that typically denied both liberty and autonomy unless the basis for liberty and autonomy, being responsible, was severely compromised. The article next addressed the role of experts, claiming that thick description of behavior was the best evidence rather than tests of any kind and that experts had less expertise than they were credited with. I suggested numerous reforms, including the exclusion of diagnoses and ultimate legal opinions because the former were legally irrelevant and confusing and the latter were not matters of psychological expertise. I also recommended recording all forensic evaluations to permit assessment of the underlying data of the expert's opinion and to expose potential confirmation bias. The final part examined many specific mental health laws through the lens of the preceding analyses. In retrospect, I believe this was the least successful part, because my strongly liberal position concerning the capacities and rights of people with mental disorder led me to some incorrect and unjust views that I later (but not much later) recanted, such as proposing the abolition of the defense of legal insanity. This article engendered fruitful debates.

In two articles (Morse, 1979, 1984) I tried to clarify the diminished capacity doctrine, demonstrating that it dealt with two distinct issues: the mens rea variant (whether mental disorder negated mens rea) and the partial responsibility variant (whether it diminished culpability even if it did not negate mens rea). I argued that relevant mental abnormality evidence should be introduced without restriction to negate mens rea and that adopting a partial responsibility variant was the province of the legislature because this variant was a form of partial affirmative defense. This work was influential in state and federal cases, especially in federal cases asked to interpret the mens rea provisions of the Insanity Defense Reform Act of 1984. I was also critical of California's expansion of the diminished capacity concept previously described and debunked the notion that Dan White received a lesser conviction for his homicides as a result of the "Twinkies" defense. I showed that his ingestion of junk food was simply used by White's defense experts to bolster his then-standard diminished capacity claim in California. I will say more about that shortly.

In two more articles—fun interchanges with Norman Poythress (Morse, 1982c) and Richard Bonnie and Christopher Slobogin (Morse, 1982a)—I tried to defend my views on the role of expertise. In the first, I attempted to show how a forensic expert could realistically behave as I had suggested, and in the second I produced an extended critique of psychodynamic psychology as the basis for expert testimony.

Finally, I wrote a detailed critique of the practice of involuntary civil commitment on largely consequential grounds (Morse, 1982b). By then, I had softened my stance on the capacities of people with severe mental disorder and believed some could properly be treated differently *in theory*. Nevertheless, I concluded that involuntary civil commitment created injustice and scarcely helped needy sufferers and that factually there were not enough mental health professionals in the United States to treat all of the severely disordered who might voluntarily accept treatment offered with respect. I recommended complete abolition.

In those early years, my concerns about mental health law involved me directly in two noteworthy public policy interventions. After the Dan White conviction for manslaughter rather than murder, California had had enough of the California Supreme Court's diminished capacity doctrine. There were hearings before the Joint Committee on Revision of the Penal Code. I was one of many experts to testify. After hearing my testimony, the chair, Senator David Roberti (D., West Hollywood), enlisted me to draft with one of his aides, Ned Cohen, an innovative legislative approach. It proposed that the partial responsibility variant effectively adopted by the California Supreme Court should be abolished but that mental abnormality could be introduced to negate any mens rea. To avoid spurious testimony about capacity, the bill also prohibited experts from testifying about a defendant's capacity to form mens rea. Experts were limited to testifying about whether the defendant *in fact* formed the mens rea. I was the lead witness for the bill, which became law. In a sad coda, the law-and-order people thought it had gone too far by permitting negation of all mens rea, which virtually never happens as a practical matter. As a result, the year after the bill became law there was emergency legislation to restrict testimony to negation of the mens rea only for so-called specific intent crimes and to prohibit such testimony for general intent crimes. This was unnecessary for public safety, and it propagated a confusing distinction.

The second event occurred in the wake of the unpopular Hinckley verdict, when many jurisdictions and Congress considered abolishing the insanity defense. By then, I had publicly recanted my 1978 argument that the defense should be abolished and was a strong proponent of it. The American Psychological Association asked me to be its witness before the House Subcommittee on Criminal Justice, chaired by John Conyers (D., Michigan). I argued for retaining the cognitive form of the defense and demonstrated that the major justice ground for abolishing the defense— that poverty was a much stronger cause of crime than mental disorder, and we don't excuse the poor—rested on the confusion that causation is per se an excusing condition. I opposed including a control test because it was insufficiently conceptualized and could not be operationalized, a position also adopted by both the American Psychiatric Association and the American Bar Association. I claimed in addition that diagnoses and ultimate opinion testimony should be banned.

Rep. Conyers put all three recommendations in the next mark-up of the bill and invited me to testify again. In the interim, the psychiatrists had howled about the exclusion of diagnoses. Just before my second appearance, Rep. Conyers told me privately that he agreed with me about diagnoses, but that there were 35,000 psychiatrists and only one of me, so the psychiatrists won. Congress passed the Insanity Defense Reform Act in 1984, which retains a limited cognitive insanity defense, shifts the burden of persuasion on legal insanity to the defendant, and prohibits expert testimony on the ultimate legal conclusions about mens rea and legally insanity. In the House Committee report, Rep. Conyers was gracious enough to specially thank me for my assistance to the Committee.

## A PORTRAIT OF THE LAWYER-PSYCHOLOGIST
## AS A (MUCH) OLDER MAN

Research on law and psychology has become a broader field than in the formative years. Work on mental health law and forensic psychological topics is now joined by the investigation and application of scientific psychology to a broad range of criminal and civil justice topics. This is the mark of a mature discipline.

The law of legal insanity is not much different from the middle 1980s. Few jurisdictions have readopted a control test despite claims that justice demands one. It appears that shifting the burden of persuasion is more outcome determinative than narrowing the insanity defense test (e.g., Steadman et al., 1993). The Supreme Court has never decided whether the insanity defense is constitutionally required, and it still does not exist in four states that abolished it. The U.S. Supreme Court was squarely presented with the issue in a 2013 case (*Delling v. Idaho*), but declined to grant certiorari. I was the primary author of an amicus brief in *Delling* (with Richard Bonnie), signed by 50 other law professors of every political persuasion, arguing that the petition should be granted and that the Court should hold that some insanity defense was required, a brief cited in Justice Breyer's dissent from the denial of certiorari (see Morse & Bonnie, 2013, which expanded the brief into a scholarly article).

Specialty courts for mentally disordered and addicted defendants that divert and treat nonviolent offenders have become common. They have dedicated proponents, but the research indicating their value is as sparse as they are popular. And they have many critics who object to their lack of due process and paternalism.

In 2006, the Supreme Court held in *Clark v. Arizona* that Arizona's narrowest possible insanity defense did not violate the Constitution but also held that a state could exclude all evidence of mental abnormality to negate mens rea except direct behavioral observation evidence. The former was not surprising, because the Court gives jurisdictions great leeway in setting their substantive doctrines. But Judge Morris Hoffman and I believed the latter procedural due process holding was simply wrong (Morse & Hoffman, 2007). The majority of states still permit defendants to use mental abnormality evidence to negate mens rea but only in limited circumstances.

In most jurisdictions, experts still testify about ultimate legal issues, although the prohibition in federal criminal cases seems to have caused no mischief. Diagnoses are permitted everywhere and are indeed required in cases involving the potential application of the death penalty to defendants with intellectual disability (*Atkins v. Virginia*, 2002). Recording evaluations anecdotally appears to be increasingly common. The quality of expert testimony seems much improved, largely because of specialized professional training and credentialing.

Civil commitment continues everywhere, but at least long-term hospitalization is rare. Despite the development of good actuarial risk prediction tools and the superiority of structured professional judgment, too often weak clinical prediction continues to be used. The newer, so-called sexual predator civil commitments that can be imposed after a sexual offender has completed his prison term for the same behavior have been adopted in a substantial minority of states and were approved by the U.S. Supreme Court (*Kansas v. Hendricks*, 1997; *Kansas v. Crane*, 2002). In my opinion, these commitments are abusive of civil liberties and rest on an incoherent definition of mental abnormality (Morse, 2002). They are simply imposing punishment by other means, and the conditions of confinement are dreadful (*Karsjens v. Jesson*, 2015).

Many people think that the new neuroscience fueled by noninvasive functional imaging will transform criminal law, mental health law, and law more generally. With respect, proponents of the extensive relevance of neuroscience suffer from Brain Overclaim Syndrome BOS), a disorder I have provisionally identified (Morse, 2006; Morse, 2013; also recommending Cognitive Jurotherapy (CJ) as the safe, effective, and inexpensive treatment of choice). Imaging is insufficiently sensitive to diagnose even major mental disorder, and it is a fantasy to believe that it can identify whether someone is delusional, hallucinating, knows right from wrong, or can control himself. For now and for the foreseeable future, the level of analysis most useful for addressing questions in criminal and mental health law is psychological. Forensic psychology is indispensable.

## A PERSONAL NOTE

It has been my great good fortune to be part of the AP–LS since its inception and to work with many of the wonderful people who are contributing to this volume. I was honored to be elected president of the Society twice, once when it was free-standing and again after it was incorporated into the American Psychological Association. I am very grateful to the organization and the field. Although the MacArthur Foundation Research Network on Mental Health and Law, brilliantly led by John Monahan, was created just after the formative years, it made and is still making immense contributions to the issues discussed in this chapter. I was fortunate to be a member.

## REFERENCES

*Addington v. Texas,* 441 U.S. 418 (1978).

American Psychiatric Association. (1968). *Diagnostic and statistical manual of mental disorders* (2nd ed.). Washington, DC: American Psychiatric Association.

*Atkins v. Virginia,* 536 U.S. 301 (2002).

Bernstein, L. (composer), & Sondheim, S. (lyrics). (1996). Gee, Officer Krupke (score). On *The Songs of West Side Story* [CD]. New York: RCA Victor.

*Clark v. Arizona,* 548 U.S. 735 (2006).

*Durham v. United States,* 214 F.2d 862 (D.C. Cir. 1954).

Insanity Defense Reform Act of 1984 (IDRA) 18 U.S.C. § 17 (2012).

*Kansas v. Hendricks,* 521 U.S. 346 (1997).

*Kansas v. Crane,* 534 U.S. 407 (2002).

*Karsjen v. Jesson,* 109 F.Supp.3d 1139 (D. Minn., 2015).

Lagos, J. M., Perlmutter, K., & Saexinger, H. (1977). Fear of the mentally: Ill. Empirical support for the common man's response. *American Journal of Psychiatry, 134,* 1134–1137.

*Lessard v. Schmidt,* 349 F.Supp.1078 (D.Wisc, 1973).

Meehl, P. (1954). *Clinical versus statistical prediction: A theoretical analysis and a review of the evidence.* Minneapolis: University of Minnesota Press.

Morse, S. J. (1978). Crazy behavior, morals and science: An analysis of mental health law. *Southern California Law Review, 51,* 527–654.

Morse, S. J. (1979). Diminished capacity: A moral and legal conundrum. *International Journal of Law and Psychiatry, 2,* 271–298.

Morse, S. J. (1982a). Failed explanations and criminal responsibility: Experts and the unconscious. *Virginia Law Review, 68,* 973–1084.

Morse, S.J. (1982b). A preference for liberty: The case against involuntary commitment of the mentally disordered. *California Law Review, 70,* 54–106.

Morse, S. J. (1982c). Reforming expert testimony: An open response from the tower (and the trenches). *Law and Human Behavior, 6,* 45–47.

Morse, S. J. (1984). Undiminished confusion in diminished capacity. *Journal of Criminal Law and Criminology, 75,* 1–55.

Morse, S. J. (1994). Culpability and control. *University of Pennsylvania Law Review, 142,* 1587–1600.

Morse, S. J. (2002). Uncontrollable urges and irrational people. *Virginia Law Review, 88,* 1025–1078.

Morse, S. J. (2006). Brain overclaim syndrome: A diagnostic note. *Ohio State Journal of Criminal Law, 3,* 397–412.

Morse, S. J. (2013). Brain overclaim redux. *Law & Inequality, XXXI,* 509–534.

Morse, S. J. & Bonnie, R. J. (2013). Abolition of the insanity defense violates due process. *Journal of the American Academy of Psychiatry and Law, 41,* 488–495.

Morse, S. J. & Hoffman, M. B. (2007). The uneasy entente between insanity and mens rea: Beyond *Clark v. Arizona. Journal of Criminal Law & Criminology, 97,* 1071–1149.

*O'Connor v. Donaldson,* 422 U.S. 563 (1975).

*Powell v. Texas,* 392 U.S. 514 (1968).

*Robinson v. California,* 370 U.S. 660 (1962).

Steadman, H. J., McGreevy, M. A., Morrisey, J. P., Callahan, L. A., Robbins, P. C., & Cirincione, C. (1993). *Before and after Hinckley: Evaluating insanity defense reform.* New York: Guilford.

*United States v. Brawner,* 471 F.2d 969 (D.C. Cir. 1972).

White, S. J. (1979). Statistical errors in papers in the British Journal of Psychiatry. *British Journal of Psychiatry, 135,* 336–342.

*Youngberg v. Romeo,* 457 U.S. 307 (1983).

# Framing, Institutionalizing, and Nurturing Research in Psychology and Law

BRUCE D. SALES

Starting law school in the fall of 1969, I experienced a eureka moment during the second week of law classes. I was so excited I called my girlfriend who was living in another state, now my wife of 46 years, to tell her that I saw an intellectual future that was exciting and that combined my work in psychology and psycholinguistics with law. I need to back up, however, to provide some context.

As an undergraduate psychology major at the University of Rochester, my mentor Ralph Haber opened his lab to me, helped to secure a National Science Undergraduate Research Fellowship for me, mentored me in carving out my own psychological science studies, and taught me how to write as a scientist-scholar. His mentoring and our collaboration resulted in my co-authoring 11 peer reviewed articles with him during my undergraduate and graduate training in psycholinguistics (Cole, Haber, & Sales, 1968, 1973; Cole, Sales, & Haber, 1969, 1974; Sales, Cole, & Haber, 1969a, 1969b, 1974; Sales, & Haber, 1968; Sales, Haber, & Cole, 1968; Standing, Haber, Cataldo, & Sales, 1969; Standing, Sales, & Haber, 1968).

Although my graduate studies went extremely well, including an unsolicited offer to stay on as an assistant professor, I doubted whether I would be able to sustain my enthusiasm for psycholinguistics. I needed time to reflect, and I chose to pursue another degree, selecting law because the thought of learning a new language and reasoning process was fascinating. Once there, something else excited me even more. My law professors regularly made assumptions about how people act and how their actions are best controlled or facilitated, yet they were not talking about psychology. I knew then that there should be a field of psychology and law.

## FINDING A SUITABLE POSITION

In my third year of law school, my concern became finding a position that would allow me to pursue my psychology and law interests, while allowing me to frame, institutionalize, and nurture the field. My commitment was unshakeable. By the end of the first semester of my third year, I had three unsolicited and easily declined offers to join major law firms in Chicago and New York City.

The Department of Psychology at the University of Nebraska–Lincoln (UNL) emerged as the best academic possibility. Some prestigious psychology departments were interested in my teaching psycholinguistics and would allow me to do some of my research in psychology and law topics. However, they made it clear that they wanted a commitment from me to stay in psycholinguistics. A very good law school invited me to be a traditional assistant professor of law while a business school sought me to teach the legal environment of business.

UNL was different. Although I was being hired on a psycholinguistic line in the psychology department, the department chair told me that if I brought in grants, he would allow me to become solely invested in psychology and law research, teaching, and training. He also arranged for me to meet Harvey Perlman, a law professor, who was excited about the possibility of my developing this new field at UNL.

## FRAMING THE FIELD

To achieve my goals for developing psychology and law, I needed a framework that would identify the major ways that the two disciplines relate to each other. Four pathways and their interactions were apparent to me before I went to UNL. They were formally presented in the first Master Lectures in Psychology and Law, with the editors of the ensuing published book selecting my paper to be the lead chapter (Sales, 1983). During those early years, it was important to me to focus my scholarship in a way that would make the pathways and their connections clear.

### First Pathway—Psychological Science on Law and Law-Related Topics

Psychological science could provide a scientific lens through which to view law and law-related matters. Such work would involve applying existing psychological theories to improve the administration of the law and achieve legal goals of justice, fairness, and efficiency, as well as lead to programmatic empirical testing of these theories in the legal context. The alternative approach was for psychologists to use empirical methods to gather information about law and law-related activities and then let the emerging data inform theory to explain legal phenomena and make future predictions. This latter approach had been promoted by sociologist Arthur Stinchcombe (1968) but was also reflected in some psychologists' works in the 1970s (e.g., see Ebbesen & Konečni, 1981; Konečni & Ebbesen, 1981; Konečni, Mulcahy, & Ebbesen, 1980).

The importance of this pathway was clear to me early in law school. A classmate, James Alfini, who also worked for the American Judicature Society, and I talked about how we might merge his organization's interests in juries and the justice system with my training in psychology and psycholinguistics. I was certain that a sizeable proportion of jurors had no idea about the meaning of what judges read to them during the jury instruction process, and I thought it would be a great first project. If jurors miscomprehended the law, it would increase their likelihood of relying on whim, sympathy, bias, and prejudice.

Based on our agreed upon mutual interest in the topic and with one of my first graduate students at UNL, Amiram Elwork, we wrote a grant application initially funded by National Institute of Mental Health (NIMH), with subsequent grant awards from the National Science Foundation and the National Institute of Justice. We sought to explore failures in comprehension of jury instructions, their causes, and methods of rewriting instructions to improve comprehension. Our empirical research showed that juror comprehension stagnated between 50% and 60% with some instructions being so poorly conceived and/or written that approximately one-third of the people tested would acquit a guilty defendant because of miscomprehension (Elwork, Sales, & Alfini, 1977, 1982; Sales, Elwork, & Alfini, 1977). Our research used two rewrites of instructions: rewrite #1 followed by comprehension testing, and rewrite #2 correcting additional problems followed by more comprehension testing. We were able to improve juror understanding to 80%. We were confident that with additional funding we could have achieved 90% accuracy for most instructions. However, because I needed to spend more time on larger psychology and law goals, we never sought additional funding.

One subsequent National Science Foundation–funded project was studying empirically the work of state trial court judges. This grant allowed colleagues and me to spend time with judges in urban and rural settings around the country, observe their professional behaviors, and interview and survey them about their work. This topic had not been systematically investigated before, and it involved working in multidisciplinary teams of political scientists, psychologists, and lawyers. Our findings were published as a book entitled *American Trial Judges* (Ryan, Ashman, Sales, & Shane-Dubow, 1980), which was chosen as a selection by the Lawyers Literary Club.

Another psychology and law topic that struck me as worth pursuing scientifically was jury selection. In my first year at UNL, I taught a graduate seminar in nonverbal communication that identified easily observed nonverbal paralinguistic and kinesic behaviors that could be used to understand prospective jurors' responses to questions posed by the judge and attorneys. To collect data to explore these predictions, I needed access to numerous trials and the type of funding that my other two projects received. I could not find a federal agency that would fund such applied work. The agencies' rationale was that if lawyers wanted to make more money through better jury selection techniques, let them fund it. To finish this story we need to go to the second pathway.

## Second Pathway—Psychologists Aiding in the Law

Psychological scientists and practitioners could provide knowledge in legal settings to achieve legal and societal goals. Such services include trial consultation services, evaluating a litigant for an attorney or the court, providing expert testimony, providing treatment services to alleged or adjudicated offenders, and advising government committees or agencies. Ideally, such services would be based on existing scientific literature. Where such literature does not exist, the services should be used to stimulate new research in the first pathway to ensure that there is scientific evidence for these law-related practices, if not immediately, then in the long term. Conversely, research in the first pathway can and should lead to further opportunities for psychology's input into the law.

Returning to jury selection, I was not the first psychologist to find this topic interesting. Social psychologist Richard Christie from Columbia University was using his knowledge of Machiavellian and authoritarian personality traits to assess potential jurors during the voir dire. In 1971 Christie worked with Jay Shulman, a sociologist, on the famous Harrisburg Seven political trial. Shulman, who later joined Columbia University, pioneered the use of community surveys and regression analyses to determine the characteristics of juror pool members that related most strongly to being pro-prosecution, pro-plaintiff, or pro-defense in criminal and civil trials (Berman & Sales, 1977).

I met Shulman in 1974 while both of us were testifying in one of the Wounded Knee Trials in South Dakota. I told him about my interests, and he was sufficiently intrigued that he invited me to work with him on a major antitrust case during that year. Comparing my predictions in that trial using in-court observations to his using the community survey approach, Shulman concluded that we agreed about 90% of the time. Based on this information, he asked me to join his organization, the National Jury Project. I declined, and he then asked that I train his National Jury Project staff in the technique. Once again I declined; I was not interested in consulting at the cost of my research scholarship and larger psychology and law agenda. However, David Suggs, one of my graduate students who worked with me in several trials, and I co-authored an article describing the nonverbal in-court observational approach (Suggs & Sales, 1979). I also co-authored other articles discussing the field of jury selection (Herbsleb, Sales, & Berman, 1979; Suggs & Sales, 1978). For a critical look at Shulman's and more recent approaches to jury selection, see Lieberman and Sales's (2007) book *Scientific Jury Selection*.

Interacting with judges, juries, and trials in the judicial branch of government was fascinating, but I also wanted to focus on topics that would require me to gain familiarity with the legislative and executive branches. If psychology was going to promote better law, we needed to understand all facets of law and how its different components interact. Mental health law seemed like an obvious initial focus for me. Statutes (part of the legislative branch's work) defined many parts of mental health law (see the following discussion of the third pathway), but it was the executive branch that oversaw the public agencies that provided services under the law. I decided to tackle an important constitutional topic of the time in mental health law—the involuntary civil commitment of mentally ill persons. In 1974, I believed that Nebraska's law violated emerging constitutional interpretations of minimal standards for commitment, which led me to contact the chair of the relevant legislative committee. It was made clear to me that the committee had no time to deal with the matter. Still, if I could write the draft law and receive the support of the Nebraska Psychiatric Association, the Nebraska Bar Association, and the Nebraska Psychological Association, the legislative committee would create a hearing for the draft bill. I contacted those associations and created a working group with members from each of the associations, and our draft bill was subsequently passed by the Nebraska legislature (Sales, Hirsch, Hornstein, Gunderson, & Hoffman, 1976).

I had now acquired some experience and expertise in the workings of the three branches of government and the interactions between them. I believed that this information could lead to a blueprint for significant new psychology and law empirical research (for a more detailed discussion, see Sales & Krauss, 2015). It also led to empirical research on one aspect of understanding commitment law—the role of attitudes in shaping law and its administration (Kahle & Sales, 1978, 1980; Kahle, Sales, & Nagel, 1978). The NIMH invited me to present in an invitation-only workshop on law and attitudes (Sales & Kahle, 1980).

In 1975, I had an opportunity to expand my contribution to state legislation relating to the rights of mentally and developmentally disabled persons. I participated with the American Bar Association in submitting a grant to the U.S. Department of Health, Education, and Welfare, which was funded as a "Grant of National Significance." Some of the funding allowed me, as project director, to invite a dozen or so national organizations to send a representative to join our advisory board. Our goal was to draft model state legislation using the best information from psychology, law, and other disciplines that had expertise relevant to the needs of mentally and developmentally disabled persons. The project, started in 1977, culminated in a 3,000-typed-page book (Sales, Powell, Van Duizend & Associates, 1982) that influenced state and federal legislative discussions for several decades. One empirical project (first pathway) exposed a troubling reality that was not previously documented: parental opposition to deinstitutionalization of their mentally or developmentally disabled children (Frohboese & Sales, 1980).

## Third Pathway—Law Affecting Psychology

Law regulates or otherwise controls or facilitates the science and practice of psychology. Additional laws focus on the subjects, clients, and patients of those practices/services and what obligations, if any, psychologists have to them. For example, in respect to mental health law, I was curious what other laws needed to be understood by attorneys, judges, and psychologists. With support from the Nebraska Bar Association, I put together a volume on mental disability law in the state (Sales, 1977c). Michael Miller and I created the book series Law and Mental Health Professionals, for the American Psychological Association, with the first volume being published in 1986, although I had started work on it in earnest in the middle of the 1970s (Miller & Sales, 1986). Expanding the focus somewhat more broadly than mental health issues, Thomas Grisso and I guest-edited the special issue on Law and Professional Psychology for the journal *Professional Psychology: Research and Practice* (Grisso & Sales, 1978; Sales & Grisso, 1978).

The third pathway logically relates to the first two pathways. We have to update our knowledge of the relevant laws and their proposed or enacted revisions (this pathway), so that we can scientifically study their intended and unintended consequences for psychologists, clients, patients, families, and friends, and the public (first pathway). Empirical findings can lead to more informed laws and to better systems, structures, and procedures for implementing such laws. For example, see Swoboda, Elwork, Sales, and Levine (1978) about mental health professionals' knowledge of and compliance with privileged communication and child abuse reporting laws and Sales and Kahle (1980) with regard to the relationship between law and attitudes. The third pathway can also interact with the second pathway because some expert consulting psychological scientists and practitioners directly consider what laws to have, how they should be structured, and the consequences of different alternatives.

Fourth Pathway—Using Legal Insights to Improve Psychology
and Create Integrated Psycholegal Interventions

If psychological science and practice can be used to improve law, isn't it possible that some legal practices might provide insights into how to more effectively structure psychological science and practice, and psychology and law interactions? Levine (1974) wrote about law providing a model for psychology to evaluate its theories, and Wexler (1981) described the law interacting more effectively with psychology to achieve better outcomes (see Wexler, this volume). My expectation in this pathway was that through experimentation in structural and procedural design alternatives suggested by the law, we could go beyond disciplinary interactions between psychology and law to interdisciplinary collaborations. David Hargrove and I called them *psycholegal interventions*. For example, some courts were already specializing in limited areas of adjudication (e.g., mental health law) where cases involved multidisciplinary interaction. However, we assumed that specifying structural and procedural alternatives (e.g., different ways judges might interact with psychologists) and the scientific testing of them (first pathway) could achieve psycholegal (collaborative) interventions. Unfortunately, as noted in the next section, my other efforts in institutionalizing and nurturing prohibited my going further than raising the possibility.

## INSTITUTIONALIZING AND NURTURING THE FIELD

Framing and personally testing the value of the frame were necessary but not sufficient to help institutionalize and nurture the entire field. I sought to create a model for training in psychology and law, to develop publication outlets for psychology and law research and scholarship, and to convince the psychological and legal professions that they should seek the consistent input of the other.

### Training in Psychology and Law

A first step for me in nurturing the field was to develop integrated training. In 1973, I planned a training program and wrote a draft NIMH grant application before I started teaching that year. Harvey Perlman had arranged for me to meet with Norval Morris, a professor at the University of Chicago Law School and an international expert on criminal law and justice, to talk about my ideas. At the time, he also was chairing NIMH's Antisocial and Violent Behavior Branch's review panel, so his opinions were critical to me. At the end of our two-hour face-to-face conversation, he asked me to send him a copy of my draft grant application. Shortly after he received it, he asked me to send it to Saleem Shah who led the branch. Once again I received a quick response. Shah asked for minor revisions, so I was able to submit the grant in time for full committee review, which resulted in funding for five years beginning the summer of 1974.

The training grant allowed for students to pursue either the PhD–JD or a PhD in psychology and law (including forensic clinical psychology). A few years later, I was awarded a postdoctoral training grant, which allowed for the funding of PhDs and lawyers who wanted to expand their research/scholarly expertise in psychology and law. Creating what NIMH labeled a model training program in psychology and law in turn stimulated the creation of other such programs in the field. For example, by 1979, the University of Maryland combined with Johns Hopkins University in Baltimore, while Hahnemann Medical College combined with Villanova University, to offer training in psychology and law.

## Developing Publication Outlets for the Field

There was a critical need for another class of institutionalizing and nurturing activities, namely, developing a journal and a book series to promote psychology and law research and scholarship. When I spoke to the leadership of the American Psychological Association (APA) about starting a journal, I was told that the field of psychology and law did not exist so APA could not be the publisher. After discussions with other publishers, I signed a contract to publish *Law and Human Behavior* in 1975 with the first issue coming out in 1977. I served as the journal editor for the first nine volumes (1977–1985) and, before my editorship ended, transferred the journal to the American Psychology–Law Society (AP–LS).

Some decades later I proposed the creation of the APA journal *Psychology, Public Policy, and Law,* I served on the two APA task forces to consider the proposal and, once approved, was selected to serve as the journal's first editor (Volumes 1–6).

I also believed in the importance of developing a book series in psychology and law because it could present broader perspectives on the field. In 1974–1975, I already had been working on a collection of readings in psychology and law (Sales, 1977a) but quickly realized that I needed one publisher who would commit long term to such a publishing venture. The result was a contract for the series Perspectives in Law and Psychology, which included both edited and authored works. The first volume focused on criminal justice and contained papers presented at a NIMH supported conference on the topic at UNL (Sales, 1977b). After eight volumes were published and a ninth was under contract, I turned over this series to AP–LS, which continued overseeing its publication under the series editorship of Tom Grisso.

## Convincing the Psychological and Legal Communities of the Importance of Psychology and Law

My third approach to institutionalizing and nurturing psychology and law was to participate as often as possible in governance activities and to give addresses before meetings of national organizations. It did not take long before those organizations sought me out. During that first decade, I was often being asked to do work for the APA, the American Bar Association, federal grant agencies, other public and private organizations, law firms, and the judiciary.

Prior to my first year at UNL, I learned from June Louin Tapp about the brief history of the AP–LS, which was founded in 1969. Fairly quickly, I was nominated and elected to the AP–LS board of directors (1974–1978) and agreed to run the AP–LS newsletter. Tapp did not hide the fact that the organization was started with a practice focus, and she strongly supported my building its research base. The goal was not to minimize psychologists' practices in law-related matters but rather to have it tied to a strong research foundation, similar to the goal for psychological science being applied to law. I immediately put out a call for persons interested in psychology and law to attend a meeting at APA's annual meeting to discuss their research in the area. Eighteen people showed up, counting myself and one of my graduate students. I then was elected president of AP–LS for the 1976–1977 term. After the society moved to become both free standing and a division of APA, I was elected to its board of directors (1981–1991) and again served as its president (1985–1986).

Some APA staff became fascinated with the announcement that NIMH was funding a psychology and law training program at UNL. When our first conference on the topic of psychology and law's links to criminal justice was held in 1975, an APA staff person attended. Not long after, I was contacted by other APA staff, nominated to serve on two APA committees, and subsequently elected by their overseeing boards. I served on the Board of Scientific Affairs Committee on Tests and Assessment (1976–1978; chair, 1978), which was relevant to first and second pathways, and on the Board of Professional Affairs Committee on State Legislation (1976–1978, chair, 1978), which was relevant to the second and third pathways. Around the same time, I was appointed to APA's Task Force on Legal Action (1976–1977). Psychologist Patrick DeLeon, who worked for U.S. Senator Daniel Inouye, wanted APA to become more directly involved in psychologists providing expertise to legal decision makers (second pathway). Subsequently, in 1979, DeLeon chaired the newly formed Committee on Legal Issues, which was the progeny of the task force's work. I was appointed as a member of that group from 1979 to 1991 (chair, 1991). Also in 1979, I was appointed to serve on APA's Board of Professional Affairs (1979–1981). By the end of the 1970s, APA leadership had moved from not believing psychology and law existed to wanting our input regularly.

Other groups relevant to psychology and law also sought out my input. For example, the American Association of State Psychology Boards, the umbrella group that represented psychologists serving on state licensure boards, had me serve on its Committee on Legal Issues (1976–1978). I also served on the Advisory Board to the British Psychological Society's

International Conference on Psychology and Law (1981–1982), and became a Fellow of APA in 1981 and of the Association for Psychological Science in 1986. I received a similar response from law-related groups, serving on the American Bar Association's Committee on Psychiatry and Criminal Law (1975–1977), Commission on the Mentally Disabled (1976–1983), Pretrial Release Committee (1976–1977), Committee on Behavioral Sciences and Law (chair, 1976–1985), and the Task Force on the Roles of Mental Health Professionals in the Criminal Process (1981–1984).

Finally, similar responses occurred with the attorney and judicial communities. For example, one nationally prominent law firm asked me to spend the summer teaching its lawyers about the possibilities for psychological science to inform law. Their expressed hope was that I would join the firm permanently if they and I worked well together during the summer stint. I declined. From the judiciary, in 1974 I received a call from Frank M. Johnson, a nationally prominent federal judge in Alabama. In 1971 Johnson had held that mentally ill patients "have a constitutional right to receive such individual treatment as will give each of them a reasonable opportunity to be cured or to improve his or her mental condition" (*Wyatt v. Stickney*, 1971). The next year, he held that "the mentally retarded patients have a constitutional right to such individual habilitation as will give each of them a realistic opportunity to lead a more useful and meaningful life and to return to society" (*Wyatt v. Stickney*, 1972). He also ordered the Alabama officials "to implement a detailed set of standards designed to ensure the provision of minimally adequate treatment and habilitation at the institutions" (*Wyatt v. Aderholt*, 1974). Alabama officials did not comply, including Alabama's Governor George C. Wallace, which is why Judge Johnson called me. He asked that I become the receiver responsible for ensuring the state's compliance with his rulings. My responsibilities would be substantial, including overseeing whether improvements were appropriately made and selling Alabama public lands and property if the state did not provide appropriate funds to carry out the needed improvements. Although I had the greatest respect for the judge and the importance of his constitutional rulings, I had to decline to continue my pursuits in psychology and law.

## GOING FORWARD

It is satisfying to see how far psychology and law has come since those early days. Still, so much of the written law, legal systems, and law-related behaviors have gone unstudied that there is work enough to keep ourselves and future generations of psychology and law researchers and scholars fully occupied. This is important work. As a country of laws, we should use our expertise to help identify weaknesses in law, legal systems, and law-related behaviors of legal and nonlegal actors, and the ways in which these weaknesses can be overcome (Sales, 1983; Sales & Krauss, 2015). We are not the only field engaged in this process, but we bring unique perspectives that need to be represented to improve the functioning of both the law and our society.

## REFERENCES

Berman, J., & Sales, B. D. (1977). A critical evaluation of the systematic approach to jury selection. *Criminal Justice and Behavior, 4,* 219–240.

Cole, R. A., Haber, R. N., & Sales, B. D. (1968). Mechanisms of aural encoding. I: Distinctive features for consonants. *Perception and Psychophysics, 3,* 281–284.

Cole, R. A., Haber, R. N., & Sales, B. D. (1973). Mechanisms of aural encoding. VI: Consonants and vowels are remembered as subsets of distinctive features. *Perception and Psychophysics, 13,* 87–92.

Cole, R. A., Sales, B. D., & Haber, R. N. (1969). Mechanisms of aural encoding. II: The role of distinctive features in articulation and rehearsal. *Perception and Psychophysics, 6,* 343–348.

Cole, R. A., Sales, B. D., & Haber, R. N. (1974). Mechanisms of aural encoding. VII: Decay of consonants and vowels in a Peterson and Peterson short-term memory task. *Memory and Cognition, 2,* 211–214.

Ebbesen, E. B., & Konečni, V. J. (1981). The process of sentencing adult felons: A causal analysis of judicial decisions. In B. D. Sales (Ed.), *Perspectives in law and psychology: Vol. 2. The trial process* (pp. 413–458). New York: Plenum.

Elwork, A., Sales, B. D., & Alfini, J. (1977). Juridic decisions: In ignorance of the law or in light of it? *Law and Human Behavior, 1,* 163–190.

Elwork, A., Sales, B. D., & Alfini, J. (1982). *Making jury instructions understandable.* Charlottesville, VA: Michie.

Frohboese, R. F., & Sales, B. D. (1980). Parental opposition to deinstitutionalization: A challenge in need of attention and resolution. *Law and Human Behavior, 4,* 1–88.

Grisso, T., & Sales, B. D. (Eds.). (1978). *Special Issue: Law and applied psychology. Professional Psychology, 9*(3).

Herbsleb, J., Sales, B. D., & Berman, J. (1979). When psychologists aid in the voir dire: Legal and ethical consequences. In L. E. Abt & I. Stuart (Eds.), *The social psychology of discretionary law* (pp. 197–218). New York: Van Nostrand Reinhold.

Kahle, L. R., & Sales, B. D. (1978). The attitudes of clinical psychologists toward involuntary civil commitment law. *Professional Psychology: Research and Practice, 9,* 428–439.

Kahle, L. R., & Sales, B. D. (1980). Due process of law and the attitudes of professionals toward involuntary civil commitment. In P. Lipsitt & B. D. Sales (Eds.), *New directions in psycholegal research* (pp. 265–292). New York: Van Nostrand Reinhold.

Kahle, L. R., Sales, B. D., & Nagel, S. (1978). On unicorns blocking commitment law reform. *Journal of Psychiatry and Law, 6,* 85–105.

Konečni, V. J., & Ebbesen, E. B. (1981). A critique of theory and method in social-psychological approaches to legal issues. In B. D. Sales (Ed.), *Perspectives in law and psychology:* Vol. 2. *The trial process* (pp. 481–498). New York: Plenum.

Konečni, V. J., Mulcahy, E. M., & Ebbesen, E. B. (1980). Prison or mental hospital: Factors affecting the processing of persons suspected of being "mentally disordered sex offenders." In P. D. Lipsitt & B. D. Sales (Eds.), *New directions in psycholegal research* (pp. 87–112). New York: Van Nostrand Reinhold.

Levine, M. (1974). Scientific method and the adversary model: Some preliminary thoughts. *American Psychologist, 29,* 661–677.

Lieberman, J. D., & Sales, B. D. (2007). *Scientific jury selection.* Washington, DC: American Psychological Association.

Miller, M. O., & Sales, B. D. (1986). *Law and mental health professionals: Arizona.* Washington, DC: American Psychological Association.

Ryan, J. P., Ashman, A., Sales, B. D., & Shane-Dubow, S. (1980). *American trial judges: Their work styles and performance.* New York: Free Press.

Sales, B. D. (Ed.). (1977a). *Psychology in the legal process.* New York: Spectrum.

Sales, B. D. (Ed.). (1977b). *The criminal justice system.* New York: Plenum.

Sales, B. D. (Ed.). (1977c). *Mental disability law in Nebraska.* Lincoln: Nebraska State Bar Association.

Sales, B. D. (1983). The legal regulation of psychology: Professional and scientific interactions. In C. J. Scheirer & B. L. Hammonds (Eds.), *The master lecture series:* Vol. 2. *Psychology and the law* (pp. 5–36). Washington, DC: American Psychological Association.

Sales, B. D., Cole, R. A., & Haber, R. N. (1969a). Mechanisms of aural encoding. V: Environmental effects of consonants on vowel encoding. *Perception and Psychophysics, 6,* 361–365.

Sales, B. D., Cole, R. A., & Haber, R. N. (1969b). Mechanisms of aural encoding. IV: Hear-see, say-write interactions for vowels. *Perception and Psychophysics, 6,* 385–390.

Sales, B. D., Cole, R. A., & Haber, R. N. (1974). Mechanisms of aural encoding. VIII: Phonetic interference and context-sensitive coding in short-term memory. *Memory and Cognition, 2,* 596–600.

Sales, B. D., Elwork, A., & Alfini, J. (1977). Improving comprehension for jury instructions. In B. D. Sales (Ed.), *The criminal justice system* (pp. 23–90). New York: Plenum.

Sales, B. D., & Grisso, T. (1978). Law and professional psychology: An introduction. *Professional Psychology: Research and Practice, 9*, 363–366.

Sales, B. D., & Haber, R. N. (1968). A different look at perceptual defense for taboo words. *Perception and Psychophysics, 3*, 156–160.

Sales, B. D., Haber, R. N., & Cole, R. A. (1968). Mechanisms of aural encoding. III: Distinctive features for vowels. *Perception and Psychophysics, 4*, 321–327.

Sales, B. D., Hirsch, R., Hornstein, B., Gunderson, S., & Hoffman, R. (1976). An act for the commitment of mentally ill dangerous people. Passed by the Nebraska Legislature (Legislative Bill 806) and signed into law by the Governor. Laws 1976, LB 806. Currently referred to as the Nebraska Mental Health Commitment Act, Nebraska Revised Statute 71-901 – 71-963 (2017).

Sales, B. D., & Kahle, L. R. (1980). Law and attitudes toward the mentally ill. *International Journal of Law and Psychiatry, 3*, 391–403.

Sales, B. D., & Krauss, D. A. (2015). *The psychology of law: Human behavior, legal institutions, and law*. Washington, DC: American Psychological Association.

Sales, B. D., Powell, D. M., Van Duizend, R., & Associates (1982). *Disabled persons and the law*. New York: Plenum.

Standing, L. G., Haber, R. N., Cataldo, M. F., & Sales, B. D. (1969). Two types of short term visual storage. *Perception and Psychophysics, 5*, 193–196.

Standing, L. G., Sales, B. D., & Haber, R. N. (1968). Repetition versus luminance as a determinant of recognition. *Canadian Journal of Psychology, 22*, 442–448.

Stinchcombe, A. L. (1968). *Constructing social theories*. Chicago: University of Chicago Press.

Suggs, D., & Sales, B. D. (1978). The art and science of conducting the voir dire. *Professional Psychology: Research and Practice, 9*, 367–388.

Suggs, D., & Sales, B. D. (1979). Using communication cues to evaluate prospective jurors during the voir dire. *Arizona Law Review, 20*, 629–642.

Swoboda, J., Elwork, A., Sales, B. D., & Levine, D. (1978). Knowledge of and compliance with privileged communication and child abuse reporting laws. *Professional Psychology: Research and Practice, 9*, 448–457.

Wexler, D. B. (1981). *Mental health law: Major issues*. New York: Plenum.

*Wyatt v. Aderholt*, 503 F.2d 1305 (1974).

*Wyatt v. Stickney*, 325 F.Supp. 781, 784 (MD Ala.1971).

*Wyatt v. Stickney*, 344 F.Supp. 387, 390 (MD Ala.1972).

# Assessment, Interventions, and Practice in Legal Contexts

# Forensic Mental Health Services and Competence to Stand Trial

RONALD ROESCH

My career as an academic in forensic psychology did not begin on the path of most academics. A sequence of events in my adolescence and early twenties shaped much of the research in my career on issues like competency to stand trial and jail mental health. When I was 17, I dropped out of high school and lived on my own. Those of you who know the risk assessment literature will recognize that as risk factor #1. In 1967, when I was 19, a friend and I broke into a golf course shop and stole golf clubs. Because they were worth thousands of dollars, we were charged with burglary and grand theft, both felonies. I spent a couple of weeks in jail before getting out on bail. I eventually pleaded guilty to one of the charges, but during the many months between arrest and sentencing (thankfully the justice system then, as now, moved slowly!), I got a job, obtained a GED, and also enrolled in courses at a community college. Judge William Gooding, to whom I am forever grateful, commented favorably on this and sentenced me to two years of probation with the added condition that if I successfully completed probation he would have my record expunged. Here was an example of diversion before diversion was common, including expungement of my record when I completed probation.

My friend did not fare as well because he had a prior record and got a prison sentence. For those who are counting, you can check off risk factor #2—hanging around with delinquent or criminal friends. Despite these risk factors, I do not think I would have been assessed as a high-risk offender if the risk instruments we have today were available then. I did not have a prior delinquency history and was not a violent offender. Indeed, as it turns out, I now know that I would be classified by Terrie Moffitt as an adolescent-limited rather than a life-course-persistent offender (Moffitt & Caspi, 2001).

Judge Gooding's diversion decision set me on a career path in psychology and law in which I have tried to create similar opportunities for others, by helping to start a formal pretrial diversion program, ensuring that mentally ill people in our jails and prisons are afforded treatment rather than punishment, and seeking to improve forensic mental health evaluation services, especially related to competency to stand trial.

## ARIZONA STATE HOSPITAL AND THE DEINSTITUTIONALIZATION MOVEMENT

I decided to major in psychology due in large part to a positive experience I had in my first psychology course taught by Dr. Roger Strachan. After two years at a community college I transferred to Arizona State University (ASU). At the same time, my probation officer alerted me to an opening for a full-time job at the Arizona State Hospital (ASH). ASH opened as the Insane Asylum of Arizona during the late-19th-century era when mental hospitals were being created throughout the country, led by reformers such as Dorothea Dix, as a humane alternative to housing persons with mental illness in jails. Regrettably, the hospitals created a class of chronic mental patients who would spend decades in the hospital.

The position required two years of college with the expectation that those hired would continue with their education while working full time. It was one of a new class of positions for mental health workers who would eventually replace the psychiatric aides who had long been the frontline workers. The hospital planned to discharge current patients into the community and reduce the length of hospitalization of new patients. This was during the early days of the deinstitutionalization movement, fueled by a growing knowledge of the negative effects of psychiatric hospitalization (e.g., Ken Kesey's *One Flew Over the Cuckoo's Nest*, 1962; David Rosenhan's *On Being Sane in Insane Places*, 1973), as well as new psychopharmacological ways to stabilize patients, thus freeing them from confinement to allow for their care through community mental health services. Large numbers of chronic patients were being discharged while at the same time reducing admission rates or, if admitted, reducing length of stay.

As 1 of 10 mental health workers, each assigned to 10 patients in an adult treatment unit, my job was to work with families and community mental health centers to get my patients back into the community. In reality, many patients no longer had any family or ties to the community, so that the main options often were to discharge them to halfway houses or other community lodges. I approached the job with a sense of excitement, that I would be helping people return to community life.

While this turned out to be a positive experience for some patients, there were many others who did not want to leave the hospital. One patient approved for discharge to a halfway house had been at ASH for decades and had worked on the hospital grounds for many years on a garbage truck. When he was on the ward, he rarely talked to anyone, preferring to keep to himself in the evening, often sitting on the floor against a wall. One day a nurse informed me that the man had not come to the nursing station for his medications. I approached him and asked him to do so. He said nothing, got up, grabbed the lid of a cigarette canister and attempted to hit me over the head with it. I managed to restrain him, and the nurse gave him his medication by injection. This patient never talked about why he attacked me. I checked his record, and he had no history of aggression, but I learned that he was scheduled to be discharged to a half-way house the following week.

I am convinced that the man acted out because he did not want to leave the hospital. He may have been experiencing what our field was just beginning to realize: that deinstitutionalization was simply sending patients into communities that were ill-prepared and underfunded to provide quality mental health and other services to the large number of discharged patients (Roesch & Golding, 1985). Many patients languished in hastily created halfway houses run by individuals with little or no training. Indeed, it is likely that for many their quality of life was not as good as it was in the hospital. During the deinstitutionalization era, sociologists later affirmed a pattern of patient resistance to discharge from hospitals on which they had come to rely as a way of life (Braginsky, Braginsky, & Ring, 1982).

After working at ASH for two years, I was asked to be an instructor in the education department at ASU that provided preservice and in-service training for mental health workers like myself. I am grateful to Dr. Ron Holler, the director of that department, who selected me and provided mentorship as I finished my bachelor's degree at ASU. During that time I was elected president of the newly formed Arizona Society of Mental Health Technology, a professional group representing mental health workers, and I was the founding editor of a professional journal, the *Journal of Mental Health Technology*. I must have enjoyed the experience as I later became editor of two psychology and law journals—*Law and Human Behavior* and *Psychology, Public Policy, & Law*. Unfortunately, that first journal only survived for a few years, but I found the experience helpful when my Simon Fraser University colleague Stephen Hart and I later started the *International Journal of Forensic Mental Health*, which is now in its sixteenth year.

## GRADUATE SCHOOL AND JAIL/DIVERSION REFORM

At ASH I had an opportunity to organize a conference for mental health workers, allowing funding to invite speakers from out of state. I had read an article by a professor at the University of Illinois (UI), Julian Rappaport, who wrote about his research on paraprofessionals working in mental hospitals. I invited him to come to this conference in Arizona and that began a life-long friendship. I had nearly finished my bachelor's degree, and he invited me to consider applying to UI in the clinical and community graduate psychology program. I was admitted in the fall of 1972 and in my first semester took a clinical research methods course from Stephen Golding. This began a relationship that led to later collaboration on the competency research that became a career focus for both of us. Edward Seidman, a community psychologist who had just joined the UI faculty, was my dissertation supervisor, and he and Julian eventually became my lifelong friends.

There were no psychology and law graduate programs in the United States when I started graduate school (the University of Nebraska would start the first one in 1974), but I had a clear interest in that direction. I took courses in political science, sociology, and the law school to broaden my training in legal and policy issues, and I looked for projects that reflected my interest in applying psychology to the legal system.

Before I got involved in my dissertation research, I initiated two projects that grew directly out of my arrest and jail experience: bail release and diversion. I recalled that five years ago, when I had been released on bail, many of the inmates I met in jail had been there for lengthy periods because they were not able to raise the bail funds. And Judge Gooding had used his own "diversion logic" to keep me out of prison and give me a chance in the community.

I got interested in alternatives to a cash bail system through a pilot study, by two UI senior graduate students that was done at the Champaign County jail, to identify alternatives to the cash bail system (Nietzel & Dade, 1973). They created a measure of the strength of a defendant's ties to the community. A cut-off score to make a recommendation to the court for release on recognizance, which meant a cash bail was not needed for release, resulted in an increase in release on recognizance.

At that time I was doing a practicum with a local African-American community agency called the Kenneth Kuumba Shackleford Community Institute, named after a youth who was shot and killed in a police encounter.

The Nietzel and Dade (1973) study led the community group and me to approach the Champaign County court to ask if they wanted to restart the bail project. The court agreed, and we relied on undergraduate volunteers and members of the community group to interview the defendants, rate them on another bail eligibility measure that had been developed by the Vera Institute, and then make recommendations to the court when bail was being set. Many individuals were subsequently released without having to post a cash bail.

My development of a pretrial diversion project, still as a graduate student, was during a time when there were few formal diversion programs and none in Champaign County. They arose primarily in the 1970s and 1980s, and the first formal diversion program in Arizona did not begin until 1978. Judge Gooding had provided me a first-hand appreciation of the benefits of diversion, and I wanted to create a more formal program. Coincidently, the Champaign County prosecutor was also interested in diversion, and I was among a group of 20 citizens he invited to develop guidelines for the program. I served as vice-chair of the Citizen's Committee that was formed. We wrote a proposal for federal funds and obtained support that provided staffing and services for three years.

I had hoped to evaluate the effectiveness of diversion and to use that as my dissertation research, having reviewed the field and found that many diversion programs had been created but few had been evaluated. But that was not to be. The randomly assigned control group that I recommended (eligible for diversion but processed as usual through the legal system) was rejected by the project's evaluation subcommittee on the grounds that it would be unethical to deny these valuable services. My counterargument that we did not know whether the program was beneficial, and that a design of the type the subcommittee recommended was needed to determine whether it was effective, was to no avail. After spending nearly a year on this project, I was left with no prospects for a dissertation. But all was not lost. I wrote about my diversion experience[1] and, in retrospect, losing

---

1. I wrote about this experience in an article and subsequent comments in an exchange with the director of the Champaign County diversion program (Gottheil, 1979; Roesch, 1978, 1979).

the diversion topic may have been fortuitous. It required me to look for another dissertation idea, which was the competency research I began as a graduate student and continued to do throughout my career.

## FORENSIC MENTAL HEALTH SYSTEMS AND COMPETENCY TO STAND TRIAL

One of my jobs during graduate school was with the National Clearinghouse for Criminal Justice Planning and Architecture. This was a UI program federally funded and mandated to review proposals from state and local prisons and jails that had requested federal funds for expanding existing facilities or building new ones. While most requests were from prisons or jails, an unusual request came in from a forensic unit located within a state hospital. I was asked to consult with them, and this project eventually formed the basis of my dissertation. The forensic unit conducted evaluations of criminal defendants referred for questions of competency to stand trial or the insanity defense and also housed those found incompetent or not guilty by reason of insanity.

To put this in historical context, in the 1970s virtually all forensic evaluations took place in hospitals, and there were no standards for evaluating competence. As we would learn in our research, most evaluators equated incompetency with a diagnosis of psychosis. A psychiatrist, A. Louis McGarry, had just completed the first major study of competency evaluations and published the first competency assessment tool, the Competency Assessment Instrument (McGarry & Curran, 1973), but it was not widely used.

Digging into this project, my graduate training in community psychology led me to think about the potential for community-based alternatives to traditional models of forensic assessment and treatment. That sort of thinking had also influenced our discovery that bail reform would reduce the need to build new jails (Roesch, 1976). The National Clearinghouse for Criminal Justice Planning and Architecture hired Steve Golding as a consultant to work on this project. We devised a series of studies that examined the forensic evaluation procedures currently being used, as well as the feasibility of a brief competence screening method as an alternative to automatically sending defendants to inpatient settings for evaluation. We found two things of importance.

First, defendants found incompetent were typically diagnosed with a psychosis or intellectual impairment, while competent defendants rarely had either diagnosis. This reflected a prevailing view of evaluators at the time that psychosis/mental retardation meant incompetency. Steve and I challenged that association, arguing that individuals with a diagnosis of psychosis or mental retardation could be competent to stand trial. We suggested that paramount consideration be given to how the defendant's behavior and symptoms affect the demands of her legal case. As we described it in our book (Roesch & Golding, 1980), severe psychopathology was only a threshold issue; incompetency rested on whether that condition resulted in actual deficits in competency-related abilities, given the specific circumstances of this defendant. This came to be known as a functional definition of competency. Others were arriving at this view roughly at the same time (McGarry & Curran, 1973), and at least by the late 1980s, this was becoming the best-practices perspective (e.g., Grisso, 1986). Later research showed that this view took hold to the extent that forensic evaluators rarely made this conceptual "diagnostic" error by the 1980s and 1990s (Heilbrun & Collins, 1995; Nicholson & Norwood, 2000).

Another key finding of our examination of the hospital evaluation process was that the majority of the defendants were found to be competent. The evaluations took an average of 43 days, and many were provided medications while hospitalized. We wondered why so many referred defendants were found competent, so we decided to contact the attorneys who had requested competency evaluations of their clients. Many admitted that they did not have a serious concern about their client's competence but nevertheless realized that they did have some mental health issues that needed attention. Rather than watch their clients deteriorate in jail, they motioned the court to remand them for competency evaluations.

The competency project was my first awareness of the impact of deinstitutionalization in terms of the manner in which those with mental health problems moved back and forth between jails and forensic hospital units. Many of these defendants had been prior patients at Dorothea Dix Hospital who, as part of deinstitutionalization, had been released only to be arrested and returned to the hospital, but this time to the forensic facility. The irony was startling to me. The forensic hospital was situated on the grounds of a mental hospital named after Dorothea Dix, the 1800s reformer who worked tirelessly to get individuals out of jails and provide them with more humane treatment in mental hospitals. Now it seemed we had come full circle.

While it was true that mental hospitals did provide better care than the jails, the hospitals soon became overcrowded and kept patients for years, turning them into chronic mental patients, as I had found in my experience at ASH. Deinstitutionalization shifted the patients back to the community, but many ended up homeless and community mental health services were seriously underfunded (Roesch & Golding, 1985). Many would get arrested, often for minor crimes, and the jails, of course, did not have the services to meet their needs. Attorneys began to see a referral for a competency evaluation as the only means to get them out of jail and into a setting where treatment would be available.

## BETTER WAYS TO MANAGE COMPETENCY TO STAND TRIAL EVALUATIONS

Observation during our study of inpatient forensic evaluations then led us to consider alternative assessment methods. North Carolina transported defendants from across the state to the central forensic hospital, and it seemed to us that the travel time and costs, and the average of 43 days for the evaluation itself, was a long time for assessing competence. To explore options, we trained eight members of a county mental health association to conduct interviews of 30 defendants, using one of the few competence-specific instruments available at the time, the Competency Assessment Instrument (McGarry & Curran, 1973), supplemented by some additional questions focusing on understanding of legal issues. The interviews lasted about 30 to 60 minutes, and we completed them within a day of a defendant's admission to the hospital.

We compared these decisions to those made by the regular competency evaluations done by its examiners, which required about six weeks and included interviews by psychiatrists, psychological testing, ward observations, and other background information collected by the forensic unit. Of course, these defendants spent most of the time simply sitting on the ward and were not seen by any staff. Overall, there was agreement on 27 of the 30 cases (25 agreements on competency and 2 on incompetency). So it seemed that the lengthy evaluation period did not add appreciably to the decision-making process for nearly all the cases. We suggested that the state should shift the focus of their competency evaluations to the community where short-term evaluations could be conducted, relying on the forensic hospital only for those cases in which incompetency seemed to be a real concern and for the short-term treatment of incompetent defendants and insanity defense cases.

One of the disturbing findings of my dissertation research was that there were many defendants found incompetent who were then held for extended periods of time under the indefinite treatment commitment statutes. We found a wide range of commitment lengths for competency restoration, with an average of about two years although many were held for 10 years or more. Interestingly, the U.S. Supreme Court had spoken to this issue a few years earlier, but I would not become aware of it until several years later when I was working on my dissertation. The case, *Jackson v. Indiana* (1972), addressed the constitutionality of automatic and indefinite commitment solely on the basis of a finding of incompetency. Justice Harry Blackmun wrote for the majority:

> A person charged by a State with a criminal offense who is committed solely on his incapacity to proceed with trial cannot be held more than a reasonable period of time necessary to determine whether there is a substantial probability that he will attain that capacity in the foreseeable future. (*Jackson v. Indiana*, 1972, p. 738)

Steve and I were interested in how the states interpreted *Jackson's* "reasonable period of time" and found enormous variability (Roesch & Golding, 1980). In 1979, six years after the *Jackson* decision, 19 states still allowed automatic indefinite commitments. Some states mandated release after six months, other states set 18 months as the limit, and still other states tied treatment length with the sentence that would have been given if the incompetent defendant had been convicted. Troubled by this, Steve and I wondered why Justice Blackman was not more specific in defining the length of time an incompetent defendant could be held. So we decided to call him and ask him about it. We worked at a federal agency at the time, with access to the federal directory of direct phone numbers. We dialed his number and were surprised when we actually got through to him. We introduced ourselves and we asked him what he meant by "reasonable period." He replied, "Well, you boys must not be lawyers." He then proceeded to give us a lesson on how Supreme Court decisions are made; we learned, of course, that this would be defined by each state, but ultimately a case could be brought to the Supreme Court challenging a state statute. Steve and I had the privilege of talking to Justice Blackman more than 10 years later at a reception in 1990 for the Distinguished Contribution to Psychology and Law award he received from the American Psychology-Law Society. We told him about our phone call, and he said he remembered it; the three of us had a good laugh about our legal naïveté.

Ed Seidman suggested I submit my dissertation to two award competitions sponsored by divisions of the American Psychological Association. One was a dissertation award sponsored by the Society for the Psychological Study of Social Issues, and the other was an award open to any research project sponsored by the Consulting Psychology division. I was fortunate to win both awards. The University of Illinois Press learned of the awards and asked if I would be interested in writing a book based on my dissertation. This book would be the first to focus solely on the topic of competency (Roesch & Golding, 1980). Steve and I were honored that the American Bar Association recognized the book with a Certificate of Merit award.

Steve and I continued our interest in developing competency assessment instruments. Thanks to Saleem Shah and a grant from the National Institute of Mental Health, we developed the Interdisciplinary Fitness Interview (Golding, Roesch, & Schreiber, 1984), a structured interview and rating scale designed to take into account both legal and mental health issues through the use of a joint interview by a mental health professional and a legal professional.

I took a faculty position at Simon Fraser University in Canada upon completing my PhD studies in 1977. There I collaborated with Christopher Webster and Derek Eaves to create an instrument for assessing fitness to stand trial. The Fitness Interview Test was designed to provide a brief screening assessment of competence to stand trial according to Canadian criteria (Roesch, Webster, & Eaves, 1984), later revised to be used in the United States as well (Roesch, Zapf, & Eaves, 2006).

## FORENSIC MENTAL HEALTH SERVICES AND ASSESSMENTS IN THE 21ST CENTURY

The areas of research that fascinated me early in my career have come a long way since the 1970s. Jails are recognizing the increased number of detainees with mental health issues and are implementing procedures for assessment and treatment (Nicholls, Roesch, Olley, Ogloff, & Hemphill, 2005). Diversion from legal processing has had a resurgence of attention during the past 20 years, so that now the formal processing of offenders has been reduced greatly in most states (Bilchik, 1999; Center for Health and Justice, 2013). Advances have been especially great regarding diversion of juveniles from legal processing (Models for Change Juvenile Diversion Workgroup, 2011) and with regard to the development of mental health courts (Wiener & Brank, 2013). Much research still needs to be done, however, to demonstrate how best to manage diversion systems to maximize their value.

Enormous progress has been made since the days when Steve and I recommended greater use of community alternatives to assess competency to stand trial and treat incompetent defendants. Beginning in the 1980s (Melton, Weithorn, & Slobogin, 1985), the use of community-based evaluations of competency has become more common (Grisso, Cocozza, Steadman, Greer, & Fisher, 1996; Melton, Petrila, Poythress, & Slobogin, 2007). The move away from the use of central institutions is also seen in the increased use of outpatient approaches for the treatment of incompetent defendants (Gowensmith, Frost, Speelman, & Therson, 2016). U.S. Supreme Court cases have shaped the way that the construct of competency is defined and incompetent defendants are treated (e.g., *Godinez v. Moran*, 1993; *Indiana v. Edwards*, 2008, *Sell v. United States*, 2003; *United States v. Duhon*, 2000).

Major progress has been made since the days when we were developing the first forensic assessment instruments. Such tools have increased both in number and in their reliability and validity for our assessments on a range of civil and criminal issues (Roesch & Zapf, 2013), and a series of books have provided forensic practitioners with best practices in forensic assessments (Heilbrun, Grisso, & Goldstein, 2009). Specific to competency to stand trial, a wide range of well-validated tools are now available (as reviewed in Grisso, 2003), as well as best-practices guides for evaluations of competence to stand trial (e.g., Zapf & Roesch, 2009; Zapf, Roesch, & Pirelli, 2013). Near the end of the 20th century, the law began applying competency to stand trial to juvenile proceedings, producing research and practice guides to employ developmentally relevant concepts and methods for their evaluation (Grisso, 2005; Kruh & Grisso, 2009; Viljoen & Roesch, 2005).

Despite these positive advances, the number of competency evaluations has increased dramatically over the past four decades. This likely reflects the fact that we have yet to provide the range of community services that would minimize the incarceration of individuals with mental health concerns. And despite the *Jackson* decision, many incompetent defendants continue to be held longer than is likely necessary due to the overcrowding of forensic and state hospitals (Gowensmith et al., 2016). Given that we now have a number of excellent assessment guides available, the field can now turn greater attention to treatment issues, both in terms of competence restoration (Zapf & Roesch, 2011) and community-based follow-up to minimize the cycle of arrests and hospitalizations of those offenders who have co-occurring disorders.

## REFERENCES

Bilchik, S. (1999). *Detention diversion advocacy: An evaluation.* OJJDP Juvenile Justice Bulletin, NCJ 171155.

Braginsky, B., Braginsky, D., & Ring, K. (1982). *Methods of madness: The mental hospital as a last resort.* Washington, DC: University Press of America.

Center for Health and Justice. (2013). *No entry: A national survey of criminal justice diversion programs and initiatives.* Chicago: Author.

*Godinez v. Moran,* 113 S. Ct. 2680 (1993).

Golding, S. L., Roesch, R., & Schreiber, J. (1984). Assessment and conceptualization of competency to stand trial: Preliminary data on the Interdisciplinary Fitness Interview. *Law and Human Behavior, 8,* 321–334.

Gottheil, D. (1979). Pretrial diversion: A response to the critics. *Crime & Delinquency, 25,* 65–75.

Gowensmith, W. N., Frost, L. E., Speelman, D. W., & Therson, D. E. (2016). Lookin' for beds in all the wrong places: Outpatient competency restoration as a promising approach to modern challenges. *Psychology, Public Policy, and Law, 22,* 293–305.

Grisso, T. (1986). *Evaluating competencies: Forensic assessments and instruments.* New York: Plenum.

Grisso, T. (2003). *Evaluating competencies: Forensic assessments and instruments* (2nd ed.). New York: Kluwer Academic/Plenum.

Grisso, T. (2005). *Evaluating juveniles' adjudicative competence: A guide for clinical practice.* Sarasota, FL: Professional Resource Press.

Grisso, T., Cocozza, J., Steadman, H., Greer, A., & Fisher, W. (1996). A national survey of hospital- and community-based approaches to pretrial mental health evaluations. *Psychiatric Services, 47,* 642–644.

Heilbrun, K., & Collins, S. (1995). Evaluations of trial competency and mental state at time of offense: Report characteristics. *Professional Psychology: Research and Practice, 26,* 61–67.

Heilbrun, K., Grisso, T., & Goldstein, A. M. (2009). *Foundations of forensic mental health assessment.* New York: Oxford University Press.

*Indiana v. Edwards,* 554 U.S. 164 (2008).

*Jackson v. Indiana,* 406 U.S. 715 (1972).

Kesey, K. (1962). *One flew over the cuckoo's nest.* New York: Viking.

Kruh, I., & Grisso, T. (2009). *Evaluation of juveniles' competence to stand trial.* New York: Oxford.

McGarry, A. L., & Curran, W. J. (1973). *Competency to stand trial and mental illness.* Rockville, MD: National Institute of Mental Health.

Melton, G., Petrila, J., Poythress, N., & Slobogin, C. (2007). *Psychological evaluations for the courts*. New York: Guilford.

Melton, G., Weithorn, L., & Slobogin, C. (1985). *Community mental health centers and the courts: An evaluation of community-based forensic services*. Lincoln: University of Nebraska Press.

Models for Change Juvenile Diversion Workgroup. (2011). *Juvenile diversion guidebook*. Chicago: John D. and Catherine T. MacArthur Foundation.

Moffitt, T. E., & Caspi, A. (2001). Childhood predictors differentiate life-course-persistent and adolescence-limited antisocial pathways, among males and females. *Development & Psychopathology*, *13*, 355–375.

Nicholls, T. L., Roesch, R., Olley, M. C., Ogloff, J. R. P., & Hemphill, J. F. (2005). *Jail Screening Assessment Tool (JSAT): Guidelines for mental health screening in jails*. Burnaby, BC: Mental Health, Law, and Policy Institute, Simon Fraser University.

Nicholson, R. A., & Norwood, S. (2000). The quality of forensic psychological assessments, reports, and testimony: Acknowledging the gap between promise and practice. *Law and Human Behavior*, *24*, 9–44.

Nietzel, M. T., & Dade, J. T. (1973). Bail reform as an example of a community psychology intervention in the criminal justice system. *American Journal of Community Psychology*, *1*, 238–247.

Roesch, R. (1976). Predicting the effects of pretrial intervention programs: A method for planning and decision-making. *Federal Probation*, *40*, 32–36.

Roesch, R. (1978). Does adult diversion work? The failure of research in criminal justice. *Crime and Delinquency*, *24*, 72–80.

Roesch, R. (1979). The evaluation of pretrial diversion programs: A response. *Crime & Delinquency*, *25*, 503–508.

Roesch, R., & Golding, S. L. (1980). *Competency to stand trial*. Urbana: University of Illinois Press.

Roesch, R., & Golding, S. L. (1985). The impact of deinstitutionalization. In D. P. Farrington & J. Gunn (Eds.), *Current research in forensic psychiatry and psychology: Aggression and dangerousness* (pp. 209–239). New York: Wiley.

Roesch, R., Webster, C. D., & Eaves, D. (1984). *The Fitness Interview Test: A method for assessing fitness to stand trial*. Toronto: University of Toronto Centre of Criminology.

Roesch, R., & Zapf, P. A. (Eds.). (2013). *Forensic assessments in criminal and civil law: A handbook for lawyers*. New York: Oxford University Press.

Roesch, R., Zapf, P. A., & Eaves, D. (2006). *Fitness Interview Test—Revised: A structured interview for assessing competency to stand trial*. Sarasota, FL: Professional Resource Press.

Rosenhan, D. (1973). On being sane in insane places. *Science*, *170*, 250–358.

*Sell v. United States*, 539 U. S 166 (2003).

*United States v. Duhon*, 104 F. Supp. 2d. 663 (2000).

Viljoen, J. L., & Roesch, R. (2005). Competency to waive interrogation rights and adjudicative competence in adolescent defendants: Cognitive development, attorney contact, and psychological symptoms. *Law and Human Behavior*, *29*, 723–742.

Wiener, R. L., & Brank, E. (Eds.). (2013). *Special problem solving courts: Social science and legal perspectives*. New York: Springer.

Zapf, P. A., & Roesch, R. (2009). *Evaluation of competence to stand trial*. New York: Oxford University Press.

Zapf, P. A., & Roesch, R. (2011). Future directions in the restoration of competence to stand trial. *Current Directions in Psychological Science, 2, 20,* 43–47.

Zapf, P. A., Roesch, R., & Pirelli, G. (2013). Assessing competency to stand trial. In I. B. Weiner & R. K. Otto (Eds.), *Handbook of forensic psychology* (pp. 281–314). New York: Wiley.

# 9

# Predictions of Violence

JOHN MONAHAN

Two defining elements of American political life in the 1960s set the stage for predictions of violence to emerge as an important concern in psychology and law during the following decade. The first element was the civil rights movement. Martin Luther King Jr. led the March on Washington in 1963. The Civil Rights Act introduced by President Kennedy that same year was signed by President Johnson in 1964. The second element was fear of violent crime. The violent crime rate reported by the FBI more than doubled over the decade of the 1960s. In 1968, Richard Nixon was elected president on a platform devoted to law and order. Shortly after his inauguration, the Safe Streets Act was passed, with a mandate to reduce violent crime.

The convergence of a heightened sensitivity to issues of civil rights and a heightened sensitivity to issues of public safety found expression—albeit in diametrically opposite ways—in the concept of predicting violence. Such predictions played a central role in what were portrayed by their advocates as reforms of the mental health and the criminal justice systems during the 1970s. The reconfiguration of the mental health system was driven primarily by political liberals who saw the rights of "mental patients" as a logical extension of the larger civil rights movement. The reconfiguration of the criminal justice system was propelled principally by political conservatives who saw violent crime as an existential threat.

Until writing this chapter, the irony here completely escaped me: Those who succeeded in changing the mental health system did so by moving that system to embrace predictions of violence, while those who succeeded in changing the criminal justice system did so by moving that system to abandon predictions of violence. How and why that happened—and how these two developments shaped my career—are described in the following discussion.

## MENTAL HEALTH LAW EMBRACES VIOLENCE RISK

Paul Appelbaum (1994, p. 12) noted in his authoritative history, *Almost a Revolution: Mental Health Law and the Limits of Social Change,* "By the end of the 1960s, the elements necessary to make mental health law a priority on the nation's legal agenda were at hand" (p. 12). Involuntary civil commitment was radically transformed in California by the enactment of the Lanterman–Petris–Short Act (Cal. Welf & Inst. Code, $5000 et seq.), which went into full effect in 1972. No more would people with a mental illness be subject to involuntary hospitalization merely if they were believed by a mental health professional to be in need of treatment. Now, civil commitment would be limited to people with a mental illness who were "dangerous"—that is, predicted to be at unacceptably high risk of violence, either to themselves or to others, or to be so "gravely disabled" that they were unable to meet their physical needs. The duration of time for which such people could be committed was also drastically limited.

A second major development in California law, this time initiated by the courts rather than the legislature, served to further heighten the salience of predictions of violence in mental health law. In *Tarasoff v. Regents of the*

*University of California* (1976), the California Supreme Court held that a psychologist or other mental health professional could be vicariously liable in tort for the violent acts of his or her patient if the psychologist "determines or, pursuant to the standards of his profession, should determine that his patient presents a serious danger of violence to another," and the psychologist fails to use "reasonable care to protect the intended victim against such danger" (p. 340). After *Tarasoff*, predictions of violence not only affected which patients could be involuntarily hospitalized, they also threatened to impact the very livelihood of the psychologists and other mental health professionals treating them. Within a few years, one national survey concluded that the only legal case better known among mental health professionals than *Tarasoff* was *Brown v. Board of Education* (Givelber, Bowers, & Blitch, 1984).

## CRIMINAL JUSTICE ABANDONS VIOLENCE RISK

Developments regarding the role of predictions of violence in the criminal justice system were as dramatic as they were in mental health. In California, indeterminate sentencing—whereby a convicted offender was given a short minimum sentence and a long maximum one, and released from prison whenever he or she was predicted to have an acceptably low risk of recidivism—was introduced in 1917. In 1976, however, indeterminate sentencing based on forward-looking predictions of an offender's likelihood of committing future crime was abolished in California, and shortly thereafter in many other states, in favor of fixed periods of confinement based entirely on backward-looking appraisals of an offender's perceived blameworthiness for crimes committed in the past. Only four years after predictions of violence became the lodestar for restructuring California's civil commitment standards in the Lanterman–Petris–Short Act, and only two months after vicarious tort liability for psychologists who negligently failed to predict their patients' violence became law in *Tarasoff*, risk assessment was banished from criminal sentencing (California Penal Code § 1170).

In *The Future of Imprisonment* (Morris, 1974, p. 29), Norval Morris, one of the most prominent law professors of his time, reflected the views of many of his contemporaries who viewed this abandonment with glee:

> So imprecise is the concept of dangerousness that the punitively minded will have no difficulty in classifying within it virtually all who currently find their miserable ways to prison and . . . probation or other community-based treatments. If one looks at the grist of the mill of city jails and state felony prisons it is hard not to drop these gnarled grains through the expansive hole of "dangerousness."

## VIOLENCE RISK AS A FOCAL TOPIC IN THE NASCENT FIELD OF PSYCHOLOGY AND LAW

In academia, interest in violence prediction grew along with interest in the broader psychology and law movement (Grisso, 1991). Stanley Brodsky published *Psychologists in the Criminal Justice System* in 1972. He concluded that "major questions arise about the overprediction of 'dangerousness' by mental health professionals as inappropriately restricting the liberty of many persons. Indeed, by some definitions, many mental health professionals themselves are dangerous" (p. 143).

Bruce Ennis and Thomas Litwack (1974) published "Psychiatry and the Presumption of Expertise: Flipping Coins in the Courtroom" in the *California Law Review*. They argued that "the perception of dangerousness is the single most important determinant of judicial decisions to commit individuals or to release patients requesting discharge from a hospital" (p. 711), despite the fact that psychologists and psychiatrists "have absolutely no expertise in predicting dangerous behavior—indeed, they may be less accurate predictors than laymen" (p. 735). That same year, sociologists Henry Steadman and Joseph Cocozza (1974) published *Careers of the Criminally Insane: Excessive Social Control of Deviance*, providing the study of violence prediction with what until that time was almost entirely lacking: actual empirical data on the predictive validity of these clinical assessments.

## RIGHT PLACE, RIGHT TIME

With the wisdom—and the biases—that only hindsight can provide, a number of things led me on the path to a career in psychology and law. For a long period in my childhood, I wanted to be a Catholic priest. Toward that end, I entered Maryknoll seminary in 1960, when I was 13 years old. Six years later, disillusioned with religion in general and Catholicism in particular, I left the seminary. I completed my BA at the State University of New York, Stony Brook—the only college I could walk to from my parents' home on Long Island, where my father was a local police officer. At the time I left the seminary, I had no idea what I would do with my life. I was moving away from something, not toward anything. Shortly after arriving at Stony Brook, and still without a college major, I happened upon the aptly titled book by Carl Rogers, *On Becoming a Person* (Rogers, 1961). Rogers had my number. He showed me a way to "help" other people that did not involve religion (or celibacy): I would become a clinical psychologist. Eighteen months later, I entered graduate school in clinical psychology at Indiana University.

At Indiana, my advisor was Kenneth Heller, one of the founders of the then-new field of community psychology. With Ken as my mentor, I became enthusiastic about working with social systems and not only with individual people (Heller & Monahan, 1977). For my PhD "minor," I chose to take several courses at the university's law school, rather than in another department within Arts and Sciences. I loved the much more unabashedly "applied" nature of legal education, as compared with the more intangible theorizing that, to my mind, characterized much of psychology. When it came time to choose my clinical internship, I opted for the Courts and Corrections Unit of the San Mateo, California, Department of Mental Health. There, under the tutelage of Leah McDonough, I learned how to do clinical evaluations for competence to stand trial and for the insanity defense—and how predictions of violence might be made for invoking California's new civil commitment statute. I was frustrated in regard to the latter task. While law reviews and sociology journals were teeming with analyses and data on the assessment of violence risk, no one in psychology or psychiatry was pulling these disparate sources together in a way that offered practical guidance to the clinicians who were making these assessments. I resolved to try to remedy this situation. I added "predictions of violence" to the bottom of my academic to-do list.

My first post-PhD job, in 1972, was in a new interdisciplinary program at the University of California (UC), Irvine, called Social Ecology. Working with psychologists of many different stripes (social, clinical, environmental), as well as criminologists, lawyers, and urban planners was a perfect fit for me. I wanted to keep true to my roots in clinical and community psychology, and—given the law enforcement household I had grown up in, the law school classes I had taken, and the forensic evaluations I had done—I chose the criminal justice and the mental health systems as the "community" settings to which I would devote my efforts. Shortly after arriving at UC Irvine, I met Henry Steadman at a meeting of the American Psychological Association. We immediately recognized one another as kindred spirits and began a series of collaborations, continuing to the present, on predictions of violence.

I thought that editing a book bringing together the various ways in which the mental health and the criminal justice systems had begun to interact would be a good way to jump-start an academic career. This turned out to be a humbling experience: 29 publishers in a row rejected my book proposal. But I was lucky on the thirtieth submission, and *Community Mental Health and the Criminal Justice System* was eventually published. I was even more fortunate that "predictions of violence" had by then risen to the top of my to-do list. I decided that my own chapter for the book would critically review all of the empirical research I could find on violence risk assessment (Monahan, 1976).

My professional life after that chapter appeared is a blur to me now. Only a few months later, the California Supreme Court cited the chapter in *Tarasoff*. Shortly after this, I was asked to testify before committees of the California legislature and before the U.S. Senate Judiciary Committee on the role of "dangerousness" in civil commitment and in criminal sentencing. I was also asked to be an expert witness in many *Tarasoff*-type cases around the country. The legal system's response to the chapter was dramatic, which convinced me that publishers do not always have a good read on the value of novel topics.

I learned more about the law by spending a year as a Fellow in Psychology and Law at Harvard Law School, in 1976, co-teaching a course with Alan Dershowitz and Alan Stone, and then another year at Stanford Law School, co-teaching a seminar with David Rosenhan. During these visits, I continued to work on the prediction of violence. An article I wrote with David Wexler, "A Definite Maybe: Proof and Probability in Civil Commitment" (Monahan & Wexler, 1978), was cited the following year by the U.S. Supreme Court in *Addington v. Texas* (1979), a case raising the burden of proof for "dangerousness" in civil commitment from "preponderance of the evidence" to "clear and convincing evidence." I chaired the Task Force on the Role of Psychology in the Criminal Justice System (1978) for the American Psychological Association. The final report of the Task Force stated that the validity of predictions of violence is

> extremely poor, so poor that one could oppose their use on the strictly empirical grounds that psychologists are not professionally competent to make such judgments. . . . Our position goes further. We hold that even in the unlikely event that substantial improvements in the prediction of criminal behavior were documented, there would still be reason to question the ethical appropriateness of extending an offender's confinement beyond the limits of what he or she morally "deserves" in order to achieve a utilitarian gain in public safety. (Task Force on the Role of Psychology in the Criminal Justice System, 1978, p. 1110)

Shortly after the work of the Task Force was completed, I received a call from Saleem Shah, the legendary chief of the Center for Studies of Crime and Delinquency at the National Institute of Mental Health. He told me that he read my work and thought what I had written about the prediction of violence was good, as far as it went. But it didn't go nearly far enough, he said, to have any real impact on violence predictions in either the mental health or the criminal justice systems. He wanted me to write an evidence-based book on the prediction of violence for his highly regarded National Institute of Mental Health monograph series (see Grisso, 1995). He would give me all the space and all the time I needed—plus a (very) small summer salary—but at the end of the day, he wanted a book that comprehensively addressed violence risk assessment, including its clinical, social, empirical, legal, and moral aspects.

I hesitated, fearing how much work this monograph would entail and fearing more that I was not intellectually up to the task. But Saleem Shah was not an easy person to say "no" to, and I eventually relented. Writing this book turned out to be an enormous challenge. It took a year to come up with a first draft, and a second year to rewrite that draft to take into account the line-by-line (and sometimes word-by-word) critique that Saleem provided. *The Clinical Prediction of Violent Behavior* finally came out in 1981. It began like this:

> At several points in its gestation, *The Clinical Prediction of Violent Behavior* had a working subtitle. When I was beginning the monograph, it was "Why You Can't Do It." About halfway through writing it, I changed the subtitle to "How to Do It and Why You Shouldn't." By the time I was finished, I was toying with "How to Do It and When to Do It." (Monahan, 1981, p. v).

The development of my thinking over the course of writing the book tracks these changes: from an empirical distaste for the prediction of violence, to an ethical aversion to engaging in it, to a concession that there may be circumstances in which prediction is both empirically possible and morally appropriate.

## FROM THE 1970S TO THE 1980S AND FROM A PSYCHOLOGY DEPARTMENT TO A LAW SCHOOL

In 1980, while the *Clinical Prediction of Violent Behavior* was in press, and through the intercession of my psychology and law friend Dick Reppucci,

I moved from the social sciences at UC Irvine to the School of Law at the University of Virginia. I continued to study predictions of violence, especially as they related to civil commitment and to criminal sentencing. But given my new employment setting, I wanted to put this work in a larger, more explicitly legal context.

As far as I could determine, I was only the second non-JD psychologist ever to join the full-time faculty at an American law school. The first was Donald Slesinger, who was hired by the Yale Law School in 1927. He planned to focus on the law of evidence. Slesinger resigned three years later, however, after finding that "little in the psychology literature was relevant to the evidentiary problems" in which he was interested (Schlegel, 1979, p. 481). I was determined to avoid his fate. Fortunately for me, there was a vastly larger body of psychology literature relevant to the law available in 1980 than Dr. Slesinger had as his disposal in 1927.

I found teaching law students to be much more challenging than teaching students in psychology. As I began preparing my first law school course, I asked a colleague how many teaching assistants I would be assigned. He stared at me and then began to laugh loudly. I had not known that teaching assistants were absent from legal education. From now on, I would be grading my own exams.

One of my new colleagues at the law school, Laurens Walker, had collaborated with psychologist John Thibaut in developing procedural justice, still one of the foundational concepts in psychology and law (Thibaut & Walker, 1975). Larry and I soon began work together on a law school casebook, *Social Science in Law* (Monahan & Walker, 1985), which is now in its ninth edition (Monahan & Walker, 2018) and has been translated into Chinese. We also began a series of law review articles on how law could benefit from the introduction of social science evidence. One of those articles, "Social Frameworks: A New Use of Social Science in Law" (Walker & Monahan, 1987), dealt directly with evidence in the form of predictions of violence.

In the mid-1980s, the John D. and Catherine T. MacArthur Foundation asked me to be the director of a newly created Research Network on Mental Health and the Law. Unlike the opportunity presented to me by

Saleem Shah in the late 1970s to write the *Clinical Prediction of Violent Behavior*—which I had struggled with—MacArthur was an opportunity that I threw myself into with abandon. The research agenda was ours to set, and the research support provided by the Foundation was more than sufficient to simultaneously launch several major initiatives.

The Network met several times over the course of a year to answer a single question posed by the Foundation: "In ten years, what are the central questions in mental health law likely to be, and what research can you undertake now to be able to have answers to those questions?" To no one's surprise, one of the questions the Network identified was how to improve the validity of predictions of violence.

Headed by Henry Steadman and Pamela Clark Robbins, the MacArthur Violence Risk Assessment Study identified a diverse array of 134 potential risk factors for violence, both static and dynamic. Where no instrument to adequately measure a potential risk factor was available, we commissioned the development of the necessary instrument (e.g., Novaco, 1994). Following Lidz, Mulvey, and Gardner (1993), we triangulated our outcome measure of violence, adding patient self-report and the report of a collateral informant to data from official police and hospital records. We studied both men and women, regardless of whether they had a history of violence. We conducted our one-year follow-up of a thousand patients at three short-term psychiatric facilities across the country. At one of the sites, we had a comparison group of 500 randomly chosen nonpatients who were assessed on the same risk factors (Monahan & Steadman, 1994). At its height, the study colloquially known as "MacRisk" had 20 full-time employees.

The software we ultimately developed to assist clinicians in predicting violence—the *Classification of Violence Risk (COVR)*; Monahan et al., 2001)—never received the widespread adoption that we had hoped for. Nevertheless, the data set for the study, which we posted on an open-access website,[1] has been downloaded over 1,000 times and continues to yield many original analyses (Monahan, Vesselinov, Robbins, &

1. http://www.macarthur.virginia.edu

Appelbaum, 2017; Skeem, Kennealy, Monahan, Peterson, & Appelbaum, 2016; Steadman, Monahan, Pinals, Vesselinov, & Robbins, 2015).

The MacArthur Foundation must have been pleased with the way the Research Network on Mental Health and the Law turned out, because they decided to fund a successor Research Network, which I also directed. This Research Network dealt with mandated community treatment, and it, too, came to address issues of violence risk (e.g., Swanson, Van Dorn, Monahan, & Swartz, 2006).

## ASSESSING THE FUTURE OF VIOLENCE RISK ASSESSMENT

Much of my current work—co-authored with Jennifer Skeem—continues to be focused on violence risk assessment but now more in the context of criminal sentencing than in the context of civil commitment (Monahan & Skeem, 2016; Monahan, Skeem, & Lowenkamp, 2017). Given the fiscal and human costs of mass incarceration, diverting offenders assessed as low risk for violent recidivism from jails and prisons to serve all or part of their sentences in community programs is now receiving bipartisan support. I have also expanded my interests to study the prediction of violent terrorism (Monahan, 2016).

In recent decades, the topic of violence risk assessment has gone global (Singh, Bjorkly, & Fazel, 2016). Numerous instruments have been published that are not adequately characterized by a simple clinical–actuarial dichotomy. Rather, the risk assessment process now exists on a continuum of rule-based structure, with completely unstructured (clinical) assessment occupying one pole of the continuum, completely structured (actuarial) assessment occupying the other pole, and various forms of partly structured and partly unstructured assessment lying between these poles. The recent release of the third version of the Historical-Clinical-Risk Management-20 (Version 3) "structured professional judgment" instrument (Douglas, Hart, Webster, Belfrage, Guy & Wilson, 2014)—revised on the basis of hundreds of studies conducted in dozens of countries—is a vivid indication of just how far, and how international, the field has come since its birth in the mid-1970s.

Violence risk assessment not only has gone international in recent decades, it has also gone developmental. A large number of violence risk assessment instruments have been developed for juveniles in the mental health or juvenile justice systems, modeled on instruments developed for adults (see Grisso, 2013). Three of the best-known and most studied are the Structured Assessment of Violence Risk in Youth (SAVRY; Borum, Lodewijks, Bartel, & Forth, 2010), the Youth Level of Service/Case Management Inventory (YLS/CMI; Hoge, 2010), and the Early Assessment Risk Lists for Boys (EARL-20B) and Girls (EARL-21G; Augimeri, Enebrink, Walsh, & Jiang, 2010).

Several issues concerning violence risk assessment remain to be resolved. Jennifer Skeem and I (Monahan & Skeem, 2016) focus on four of them. First, the choice among predictively valid risk factors as to which to include on risk assessment instruments is much easier in the mental health system, which is focused solely on forward-looking utilitarian concerns, than it is in criminal sentencing, which is jointly focused on forward-looking utilitarian concerns as well as on backward-looking considerations of moral blameworthiness. Second, the statistical appropriateness of making individual inferences from group data is seen by some as problematic (but not by Faigman, Monahan, & Slobogin, 2014). Third, risk is much more easily assessed than it is attenuated. Finally, the jury is still out on whether risk assessment contributes to the socio-economic and racial disparities that characterize populations involved in either the mental health or the criminal justice system (Skeem & Lowenkamp, 2016).

Progress in the field may depend on how these four issues get resolved. If only variables for which the person is perceived to be morally responsible can function as risk factors, if individual inferences cannot be informed by group data, if all risk factors must be "causal" and therefore pertinent to risk management, and if risk factors that correlate with social disadvantage are uniformly seen as taboo, then the future of violence risk assessment may well be dim. But if the orthogonal issues of forward-looking risk and backward-looking blame can be kept in their separate spheres, if group data can be seen to probabilistically influence estimates of individual risk, if risk assessment has uses independent of risk management, and if evidence-based violence risk assessment is compared to the likely alternatives to evidence-based violence risk assessment—such as unstructured and empirically uninformed judicial discretion—the future of the field looks bright.

## REFERENCES

*Addington v. Texas,* 441 U.S. 418 (1979).

Appelbaum, P. (1994). *Almost a revolution: Mental health law and the limits of social change.* New York: Oxford University Press.

Augimeri, L., Enebrink, P., Walsh, M., & Jiang, D. (2010). Gender-specific childhood risk assessment tools: Early Assessment Risk Lists for Boys (EARL-20B) and Girls (EARL-21G). In R. Otto & K. Douglas (Eds.), *Handbook of violence risk assessment* (pp. 43–62). New York: Routledge.

Borum, R., Lodewijks, H., Bartel, P., & Forth, A. (2010). Structured Assessment of Violence Risk in Youth (SAVRY). In R. Otto & K. Douglas (Eds.), *Handbook of violence risk assessment* (pp. 63–79). New York: Routledge.

Brodsky, S. (1972). *Psychologists in the criminal justice system.* Carbondale, IL: American Association of Correctional Psychologists.

Douglas, K., Hart, S., Webster, C., Belfrage, H., Guy, L., & Wilson, C. (2014). Historical-Clinical-Risk Management-20, Version 3 (HCR-20$^{V3}$): Development and overview. *International Journal of Forensic Mental Health, 13,* 93–108.

Ennis, B., & Litwack, T. (1974). Psychiatry and the presumption of expertise: Flipping coins in the courtroom. *California Law Review, 62,* 693–752.

Faigman, D., Monahan, J., & Slobogin, C. (2014). Group to individual (G2i) inference in scientific expert testimony. *University of Chicago Law Review, 81,* 417–480.

Givelber, D., Bowers, W., & Blitch, C. (1984). Tarasoff, myth and reality: An empirical study of private law in action. *Wisconsin Law Review, 1984,* 443–497.

Grisso, T. (1991). A developmental history of the American Psychology–Law Society. *Law and Human Behavior, 15,* 213–231.

Grisso, T. (1995). Saleem Shah's contributions to forensic clinical assessment. *Law and Human Behavior, 19,* 25–30.

Grisso, T. (2013). *Forensic evaluation for juveniles* (2nd ed.). Sarasota, FL: Professional Resource Press.

Hoge, R. (2010). Youth Level of Service/Case Management Inventory. In R. Otto & K. Douglas (Eds.), *Handbook of violence risk assessment* (pp. 81–95). New York: Routledge.

Heller, K., & Monahan, J. (1977). *Psychology and community change.* Homewood, IL: Dorsey.

Lidz, C., Mulvey, E., & Gardner, W. (1993). The accuracy of predictions of violence to others. *Journal of the American Medical Association, 269*, 1007–1011.

Monahan, J. (1976). The prevention of violence. In J. Monahan (Ed.), *Community mental health and the criminal justice system* (pp. 13–34). New York: Pergamon.

Monahan, J. (1981). *The clinical prediction of violent behavior.* DHHS Publication Number ADM 81–921. Washington, DC: Government Printing Office.

Monahan, J. (2016). The individual risk assessment of terrorism: Recent developments. In G. LaFree & J. Freilich (Eds.), *The handbook of the criminology of terrorism.* (pp. 520–534). Hoboken, NJ: Wiley.

Monahan, J., & Skeem, J. (2016). Risk assessment in criminal sentencing. *Annual Review of Clinical Psychology, 12*, 489–513.

Monahan, J., Skeem, J., & Lowenkamp, C. (2017). Age, risk assessment, and sanctioning: Overestimating the old, underestimating the young. *Law and Human Behavior, 41*, 191–201.

Monahan, J., & Steadman, H. (1994). Toward a rejuvenation of risk assessment research. In J. Monahan & H. Steadman (Eds.), *Violence and mental disorder: Developments in risk assessment* (pp. 1–17). Chicago: University of Chicago Press.

Monahan, J., Steadman, H., Silver, E., Appelbaum, P., Robbins, P., Mulvey, E. . . . Banks, S. (2001). *Rethinking risk assessment: The MacArthur study of mental disorder and violence.* New York: Oxford University Press.

Monahan, J., Vesselinov, R., Robbins, P. C., & Appelbaum, P. S. (2017). Violence to others, violent self-victimization, and violent victimization by others among persons with a mental illness. *Psychiatric Services, 68*, 516–519.

Monahan, J., & Walker, L. (1985). *Social science in law: Cases and materials.* Mineola, NY: Foundation.

Monahan, J., & Walker, L. (2018). *Social science in law: Cases and materials* (9th ed.). St. Paul, MN: Foundation.

Monahan, J., & Wexler, D. (1978). A definite maybe: Proof and probability in civil commitment. *Law and Human Behavior, 2*, 37–42.

Morris, N. (1974). *The future of imprisonment.* Chicago: University of Chicago Press.

Novaco, R. (1994). Anger as a risk factor for violence among the mentally disordered. In J. Monahan & H. Steadman (Eds.), *Violence and mental disorder: Developments in risk Assessment* (pp. 21–59). Chicago: University of Chicago Press.

Rogers, C. (1961). *On becoming a person.* Boston: Houghton Mifflin.

Schlegel, J. H. (1979) American legal realism and empirical social science: From the Yale experience. *Buffalo Law Review, 28*, 460–586.

Singh, J., Bjorkly, S., & Fazel, S. (Eds.). (2016). *International perspectives on violence risk assessment.* New York: Oxford University Press.

Skeem, J., Kennealy, P., Monahan, J., Peterson, J., & Appelbaum, P. (2016). Psychosis uncommonly and inconsistently precedes violence among high-risk individuals. *Clinical Psychological Sciences, 4*, 40–49.

Skeem, J. L., & Lowenkamp, C. T. (2016). Risk, race, and recidivism: Predictive bias and disparate impact. *Criminology, 54*, 680–712.

Steadman, H., & Cocozza, J. (1974). *Careers of the criminally insane: Excessive social control of deviance.* New York: Lexington.

Steadman, H., Monahan, J., Pinals, D., Vesselinov, R., & Robbins, P. C. (2015). Gun violence and stranger victims in the MacArthur Violence Risk Assessment Study. *Psychiatric Services, 66,* 1237–1241.

Swanson, J., Van Dorn, R., Monahan, J., & Swartz, M. (2006). Violence and leveraged community treatment for persons with mental disorder. *American Journal of Psychiatry, 163,* 1404–1411.

*Tarasoff v. Regents of the University of California,* 551 P.2d 334 (1976).

Task Force on the Role of Psychology in the Criminal Justice System, American Psychological Association. (1978). Report of the Task Force on the Role of Psychology in the Criminal Justice System (1978). *American Psychologist, 33,* 1099–1113.

Thibaut, J., & Walker, L. (1975). *Procedural justice: A psychological analysis.* Mahwah, NJ: Erlbaum.

Walker, L., & Monahan, J. (1987). Social frameworks: A new use of social science in law. *Virginia Law Review, 73,* 559–598.

# 10

# Developmental Psycholegal Capacities

**THOMAS GRISSO**

A merican society's conceptualization of children's needs and rights entered a period of reform in the mid-20th century. The reform arose in the context of changing perceptions of social justice, especially racial equality, gender equity, and protections for persons with disabilities. The decade of the 1960s began with the *UN Declaration of the Rights of the Child* (UN General Assembly, 1960) and ended with the creation of the federal Office of Child Development in 1969. Between those brackets came two White House Conferences on Children and Youth and the first two U.S. Supreme Court cases ever to consider the rights of youth in the juvenile justice system. It was in this historical context that psychologists began studying children's rights and children's legally relevant capacities, the topics through which I would eventually enter the field of psychology and law.[1]

---

1. This chapter uses two words in the title in the following ways. *Psycholegal* refers to characteristics of individuals that are relevant for defining legal (and sometimes ethical) questions about

## THE RISE OF CHILDREN'S RIGHTS

Reflecting on the children's rights movement, one commentator con-cluded in the mid-1970s that "for the first time [in history], children are being recognized as persons in their own right" (Takanishi, 1978, p. 20). That was a radical concept in those days. Legal rights are claims that an individual can make against others who owe them a duty or who unlaw-fully restrict their freedom, which implies autonomy to exercise those rights. Before mid-20th century, that notion when applied to children was a paradox in light of their dependency.

Legal and psychological analyses of the implications of children's new rights began to appear in the early 1970s. Among them was a *Harvard Educational Review* analysis by Hillary Rodham (1973), fresh out of law school, urging greater rights of self-determination for children and call-ing for clarification of the meaning of children's rights.[2] Within psychol-ogy, a first generation of treatises on children's rights appeared in two volumes, one edited by Gerald Koocher (1976) soon after his postdoc-toral clinical fellowship in Boston, the other a special issue of the *Journal of Social Issues* edited by Norma and Seymour Feshbach (Feshbach & Feshbach, 1978). The 36 chapters in these volumes focused primarily on clinical and family issues: for example, children's rights as therapy clients and research subjects, their rights to resist commitment and to refuse or accept medical treatment, their rights in divorce and custody cases, and their potential for suing their parents for neglect and abuse. None were reports of data-based research.

Despite the dramatic U.S. Supreme Court decisions of the 1960s, *Kent v. U.S.* (1966) and *In re Gault* (1967), only one of the treatises in those two volumes focused specifically on children's rights in juvenile justice. Juvenile courts had operated under a parens patriae doctrine, shielding adolescents

their abilities. *Capacities* refers to an individual's functional abilities, which themselves may vary depending on both the characteristics of the person and the situational context in which they are performed.

2. Years later, opponents used this article against her during her husband's U.S. presidential candidacy (Lindsay & Sarri, 1992) and again in her own recent presidential bid (Devoe, 2015).

from criminal penalties while allowing juvenile court judges to do whatever was in the best interests of the child. This judicial discretion eventually was the system's undoing. For decades, the Court said, delinquent youth had been provided "the worst of both worlds," receiving "neither the protections accorded to adults nor the solicitous care and regenerative treatment postulated for children" (*Kent v.* U.S., 1966, p. 556). The Court also stated, "Neither the 14th Amendment nor the Bill of Rights is for adults alone" (*In re Gault,* 1967, p. 13). *Gault* ordered that delinquency proceedings must include many of the same due process rights as for adult defendants—for example, the right to counsel, the right to challenge evidence offered against them, and safeguards against self-incrimination.

Nevertheless, the first generation of children's rights analyses by psychologists focused on clinical settings and custody disputes, taking only parenthetic note of the implications of *Kent* and *Gault* and leaving exploration of due process in juvenile courts to other disciplines. The 1970s did see important commentary by legal researchers on the confused state of the juvenile court in the wake of the new due process requirements (e.g., Rubin, 1976; Stapleton & Teitelbaum, 1972), and this era produced now-classic theories and research on delinquency, its prevention, and juvenile justice (e.g., Cicourel, 1968; Empey, 1976; Platt, 1969; Wolfgang, Figlio & Sellin, 1972). Yet almost all of these efforts were by criminology, sociology, and legal scholars, not psychologists.

In the mid- to late 1970s, however, a few psychologists began to engage in data-based studies about a uniquely psychological question raised by the children's rights reform: What are children's legally relevant capacities? How are children developmentally socialized to law and justice (Tapp & Kohlberg, 1977)? At what age do children develop a sense of intentionality consistent with legal responsibility (Keasey & Sales, 1977)? What factors influence children's reliability as witnesses (Dale, Loftus, & Rathbun, 1978)? What are children's capacities relevant for making medical decisions (Weithorn & Campbell, 1982)?

Some of the psychologists conducting these first empirical studies of children's psycholegal capacities were associated with the American Psychology–Law Society (AP–LS) during its inaugural years

(1969–1975). My early work would contribute as well. Yet, until the mid-1970s, five years beyond my University of Arizona clinical psychology PhD, I had read none of their works and was unaware of AP–LS itself. I had not even thought much about psychology's potential interactions with law.

## ALIENATION AND REDEMPTION

My first opportunity to apply psychology to a legal question came in 1975. I had taken a position at Saint Louis University that year, after five post-PhD years on the faculty at a small undergraduate college in Ohio. When I arrived in St. Louis, I introduced myself to the chief psychologist at the St. Louis County Juvenile Court Clinic, offering to do clinical evaluations if they occasionally needed someone from outside the court.

About a month later the chief juvenile court psychologist phoned with a request that went something like this.

> We have a problem here. The lawyers are starting to claim that their kids' confessions should not be admissible because they couldn't understand their *Miranda* warnings. We've never done evaluations for that sort of thing, there's nothing in the literature on it, and you're the only academic type who's shown your face in the door. We need some help! Can you study this?

I spent a couple of weeks thinking about this problem, and that set the stage for much of what I would do for the rest of my career. What evolved was one of the earliest demonstrations of a research logic and process that became common in later years when examining juveniles' and adults' psycholegal capacities. But personally, I found a reason for being a psychologist at a time when I was aimless. Let me explain that.

During my undergrad and graduate training throughout the 1960s, I had been somewhat like *The Uncommitted: Alienated Youth in American Society* about whom Kenneth Keniston (1965) had been writing. I felt estranged from society, uncomfortable with many of its mainstream values. I was no rebel. I simply didn't yet see a place for me anyplace. As an undergraduate I did not seriously consider law, medicine, business, education, or psychology as professions, because I resisted identifying with any profession. If people asked what I was planning to do, I said I was going to seminary. I'd been saying that since I was 10 (because that's what my father had done), but I had never quite believed it. I was uncommitted.

I adapted by trying to understand the two irreconcilable sides of the problem: society and myself. During my undergraduate years, I made deep dives into sociology, political theory, cultural anthropology, existentialist literature, and theology, trying to understand what was "wrong" with society. I tried to understand myself as well—the other side of the alienation equation—through creative writing (poetry), acting, choral music, and guitar. Society's undergraduate allowance to postpone commitment finally ended, so I committed without committing. I applied to a couple graduate schools in clinical psychology, not with any passion to become a psychologist, but to buy time to avoid an ultimate decision.

By that time I was inclined to believe that science might have potential for explaining social problems, but I felt certain about the inadequacy of either psychology (individuals) or sociology (social systems) to accomplish that independently. I seemed closest to finding insights at intersections—in those days only vaguely defined—between personality research, cross-cultural anthropological perspectives, and social psychology. A cross-disciplinary, person–environment interactive slant on questions was common among AP–LS scholars across the years, and much later that mindset would connect me with psychology and law.

Somewhere in the graduate school process I got hooked on clinical assessment. Not the clinical part (I had no passion to "work with patients"), but the method. I liked the process of creating and using assessment tools—operationalizing an abstract concept, turning ideas into measurable quantities, using them to test those ideas, and (the first glimmer of an aim) perhaps using them to test society's and clinicians' presumptions about people.

Receiving my PhD in 1969, I had no clear intentions about the next step. So I continued my noncommitment by taking a job at the same Midwestern college where I had been an undergraduate, splitting my time between student counseling and teaching. A colleague alerted me to a Thursday-afternoon consulting job at an Ohio juvenile corrections facility, and that became my first applied experience in juvenile justice.

The facility was not like the huge "reform schools" operated by most state juvenile corrections agencies of the time.[3] It was a collection of small buildings so deep in a forest that the security system was simply kids' fears of never making it home if they ran away. I evaluated youth upon admission and developed a strategy to match their developmental status with three different treatment milieus the place was using—behavior modification, positive peer culture, transactional analysis. I did some research (and published a few things) demonstrating that as kids neared their discharge dates they tended to mess up because of anxiety about going home (Grisso, 1975). Reading their records, I was struck by the inconsistent legal processes that sent them away and the terrible family conditions to which they were returning. I began trying out the idea of being a psychologist identified with juvenile justice, and about that time I read a book about psychologists in criminal justice. It was by Stan Brodsky (1973), and I was so grateful that I wrote a letter thanking him (see Brodsky, this volume). And in 1975, I got to Saint Louis University and in the door of the St. Louis County Juvenile Court.

Thinking about the juvenile court's *Miranda* dilemma was my redemption. The more I looked into it, the stranger it seemed that society (law and policy) would expect *Miranda* warnings ever to offer any actual protection of rights. And if it did for some kids, how could judges ever draw conclusions about which ones had the relevant capacities? After many years of industrious aimlessness, I had discovered a commitment, a redeeming possibility that I might do something useful by applying psychology's

3. The old reform schools were beginning to be dismantled in the 1970s, thanks to Massachusetts reformer Jerome Miller's experiment that replaced them with smaller residential programs (Miller, 1991).

developmental concepts and assessment methods to shape social policies. That enterprise of using psychology to change law was already afoot, as seen in this book's introductory chapter. But in 1975 I did not know that and, as described earlier, the first-generation essays on children and the law were not yet published.

## DISCOVERING JUVENILES' CAPACITIES (AND MINE)

Today, our approach to studying people's capacities relevant for legal competencies seems almost formulaic (Grisso, 2003): (a) dissect law to discover what functional abilities are legally relevant; (b) develop a set of psycholegal constructs by combining the law's intent with psychology's theoretical representations of similar abilities; (c) translate those into measurable operations to assess them; (d) form hypotheses by discovering what the law appears to believe about people's capacities as related to ages, disorders, and the like; (e) design the study so that it is demographically, ecologically, and procedurally relevant; and (f) frame and communicate the results to shape law and policy consistent with the findings.

Countless studies of the legally relevant capacities of children and persons with mental disabilities have followed this path across the past 40 years. But in the mid-1970s, as I began to search for studies to guide my research on kids' psycholegal capacities, I found no such model. Bits and pieces of the process were available. For example, a year earlier, Louis McGarry (1973), working with psychologist Paul Lipsitt, had published a functional analysis of abilities relevant for adults' competence to stand trial. Others were beginning to move in that direction, but their efforts were not in evidence at that time.

At some point it occurred to me that the *Miranda* problem might have grant-funding potential. This thought was extraordinarily naïve. I knew nothing about law or how to research it. I knew no one in the nascent field of psychology and law to consult, nor even that the field existed. My research experience included only a few small-n, nonfunded studies (how defense mechanisms manifested themselves on the Rorschach and the

Thematic Apperception Test; examining predictors of juveniles' adjustment to rehabilitation programs). I had never been mentored by anyone who had obtained a National Institute of Mental Health research grant, and my faculty colleagues, though supportive and encouraging, were primarily clinicians. The odds were dismal.

I found a Saint Louis University disabilities law professor, Jesse Goldner, who was willing to teach me how to Shepardize with the old, complex, pre-LexisNexis printed periodical index. I found patient tutors among a group of young juvenile-advocate lawyers just down the street at the very first National Juvenile Law Center, which the federal government had recently funded. (Sometimes you're just lucky.) The juvenile court from which the idea had arisen agreed to endure the practical inconvenience and ethical ambiguity of research on large numbers of juvenile detainees in its custody. A graduate student piloted our prototype measures in his dissertation research (Manoogian, 1978).

But most important, while seeking funding I discovered an emerging field of psychology and law and the people who were developing it. When you submitted a promising concept paper to Saleem Shah's Center for Studies of Crime and Delinquency at the National Institute of Mental Health, you got advice that shaped your idea toward the Center's missions. If your submission was funded, Saleem and his team became your mentors who guided, prodded, praised, scolded, and aggressively edited your efforts during the years of execution of the study (Grisso & Steadman, 1995).

Saleem recognized he was taking a chance when he funded someone who was far less than a journeyman researcher on legal issues. So he "assigned" Bruce Sales, one of the Center's study group members, to keep an eye on me and offer advice as I proceeded. It was through Sales, who had founded the University of Nebraska Psychology–Law Program a few years earlier, that I discovered AP–LS and the energetic young researchers who had assumed the organization's leadership in the mid-1970s about five years after its birth. And new books like Social Psychology in Court (Saks & Hastie, 1978) showed me that psychology and law had potential far beyond the narrow topic that had drawn me to it.

## THE *MIRANDA* WAIVER STUDY

The three-year study from 1976 to 1979 (Grisso, 1980, 1981) began with thorough statute and case law reviews that examined the context, process, and requirements of law regarding waiver of *Miranda* rights. I grappled with the law's "voluntary, knowing and intelligent" test for a valid waiver of rights (I am still struggling with that), the abilities the law considered relevant, and its apparent presumptions about juveniles' capacities to make a valid waiver.

I rounded up four bright graduate students—the first assistants I'd ever had—and set to work. Using a panel of juvenile court lawyers, judges, and psychologists, we constructed measures with objective scoring potential to assess people's comprehension ("understanding") of *Miranda* warnings, as well as their expectancies about how the rights worked in interrogation contexts (now called "appreciation" as a part of legal competence, but then I called it "perception of functions of rights"). After determining the basic psychometrics of those tools, we developed interviews to examine how juveniles thought when making waiver decisions by asking them how and why they would advise other youths in hypothetical *Miranda* waiver situations (which the legal competence world now calls the "reasoning" component). The study involved several hundred juveniles in detention as well as adults in criminal justice halfway houses, offering a comparison across ages, race, intelligence, and amount of experience with police and courts.

The heart of the project was the comparison of juveniles' and adults' capacities related to *Miranda* waiver (Grisso, 1980) and its implications for policy. A companion study used juvenile court archives to identify demographically the proportion of juveniles who waived or asserted their *Miranda* rights (Grisso & Pomicter, 1978). Two other studies examined the role of parents in their children's waiver decisions. One described the advice given by 390 parents to their children at the time of their actual arrests and questioning by police officers (Grisso, 1981). The other, a school-based study, examined over 700 parents' attitudes toward children's protective and self-determination rights (concepts we borrowed from Rogers & Wrightsman, 1978), and their reasons for hypothetical advice to their children if they were ever arrested (Grisso & Ring, 1979).

Those studies of the social and parental context had a special significance for me. I had long had a preference for a person–environment interactive view of the assessment of abilities. This matched with the law's "totality of circumstances" concept in *Miranda* cases, in which validity of waiver required weighing both the person's capacities and the situational context. Other researchers in later years would go much further to characterize situational variables in interrogation contexts (e.g., Feld, 2013; Kassin, 2005, 2008; Rogers, Hazelwood, Sewell, Shuman, & Blackwood, 2008, Rogers et al., 2012).

The results were translated for law and policy (Grisso, 1980, 1981), with emphasis on several key implications:

- The evidence that youths' understanding and appreciation of *Miranda* warnings was, on average, poorer than for adults.
- The empirical evidence showing the characteristics of youths (e.g., age, intelligence) related to understanding and appreciation of *Miranda* warning, offering guidance for judicial decisions about their legally relevant capacities.
- Empirical evidence that various judicial presumptions were wrong (e.g., their assumption that youth with more legal experience would understand their rights better).
- The evidence base for the apparent ineffectiveness of potential remedies for juveniles' diminished capacities to waive *Miranda* rights: for example, revising the warnings.
- Consideration of various potential legal remedies and their limits— requiring presence of parents, mandatory provision of legal counsel, creating a legal presumption of incapacity to waive *Miranda* rights at ages 14 and below.

The research measures were included in the appendices of the book reporting the study (Grisso, 1981), and some forensic clinicians began using them (stimulating me to publish them in a formal manual many years later: Grisso, 1998b). The 1981 report, though, offered no advice about forensic use of the measures. We did translate the results for use by clinicians in the juvenile court that had stimulated the study and patiently waited for us to complete it. Doing that translation sealed my interests for many years to come, leading eventually to a commitment to evidence-based forensic assessments for the broader range of legal competencies (Grisso, 1986) and juvenile forensic issues (Grisso, 1998a).

## THE EVOLUTION OF STUDIES OF JUVENILES' PSYCHOLEGAL CAPACITIES

Studies of youths' psycholegal abilities grew steadily in the 1980s as represented by two second-generation volumes, one edited by Reppucci, Weithorn, Mulvey, and Monahan (1984) and the other by Melton, Koocher, and Saks (1983). The first-generation volumes of the 1970s had framed the new children's rights issues and called for research. This second wave responded by examining, from a developmental perspective, the decisional capacities of children and adolescents to exercise their rights, especially their comprehension, reasoning, and autonomy. Most of the focus still was on children's decisions in medical, psychiatric, child custody, and research settings, with the notable exception of work on children's capacities as witnesses (e.g., Goodman, Golding, & Haith, 1984; for general reviews, see Ceci & Bruck, 1993; Goodman & Bottoms, 1993).

Only 2 of the 29 authors for the 1980s volumes had written chapters for the first-generation volumes in the 1970s. Fresh out of graduate school, Gary Melton convened a meeting of young researchers to collect the chapters for one of those volumes. This was the first time I had met those who would become leaders in this field as it began to mature. More authors in the second-generation volumes based their chapters on their empirical research results. Psychologists' studies of adolescents' capacities to make healthcare decisions were fueled by a series of U.S. Supreme Court cases (beginning with *Planned Parenthood of Central Missouri v. Danforth*, 1976) on the rights of adolescents to make decisions about abortions. By the late 1980s, enough research had been done to inform American Psychological Association amicus briefs on this question (*Hartigan v. Zbaraz* 1987; *Hodgson v. State of Minnesota*, 1990).

Thus, for two decades (1970–1990), the emerging field of children's psycholegal capacities was driven primarily by questions about civil legal issues: children's decisions regarding healthcare, research participation, and family custody issues. My studies on capacities of youths related to due process in juvenile court were the exception. The next 20 years (1990–2010), however, saw a dramatic shift toward studying juvenile's capacities in delinquency and criminal law contexts. This redirection of the field likely was stimulated by a nationwide reform in juvenile justice in the late 1980s and early 1990s, emphasizing punishment of juvenile offenders as though they were adults (Grisso, 1996). This increased the stakes associated with defense of juvenile offenders. It also drew reactive attention to the developmental capacities of adolescents associated with the law's presumptions about their culpability and (returning to the theme of my research 20 years earlier) their legal competencies—that is, their capacities for decision-making in legal contexts. Thus, a third generation of work during the 1990s began to provide developmental and clinical perspectives, both theoretical and empirical, on those questions:

- adolescents' risk-taking and legally relevant decision-making in light of their relative developmental immaturity (e.g., Abramovitch, Peterson-Badali, & Rohan, 1995; Arnett, 1992; Furby & Beyth-Marom, 1992; Grisso & Schwartz, 2000; Scott, Reppucci, & Woolard, 1995; Steinberg & Cauffman, 1996)
- prevalence of mental disorders among juvenile justice youth (Cocozza, 1992; Otto, Greenstein, Johnson, & Friedman 1992), relevant when examining their psycholegal capacities
- various forensic assessment issues specific to juvenile justice (e.g., Grisso, 1997; Kruh & Brodsky, 1997; Rogers, Hinds, & Sewell, 1996), including the first book devoted entirely to specialized psychological forensic assessments in delinquency cases (Grisso, 1998a).

These contributions were a prelude to an outpouring of reports—a 21st-century fourth generation—describing studies of juveniles' capacities in delinquency and criminal proceedings. For example, research on juveniles' competence to stand trial, of which there had been almost none before the late 1990s, soared during 2001–2010 (for reviews, see Fogel, Schiffman, Mumley, Tillbrook, & Grisso, 2013; Viljoen, Penner, & Roesch, 2012), and new projects reexamined juveniles' waiver of *Miranda* rights (e.g., Goldstein, Condie, Kalbeitzer, Osman, & Geier, 2003; Rogers et al., 2008; Viljoen & Roesch, 2005).

A prominent contributor to this surge in studies of juveniles' capacities was the MacArthur Foundation's Research Network on Adolescent Development and Juvenile Justice, chaired by Laurence Steinberg. Its programs of research examined (a) adolescents' decisional capacities relevant for culpability mitigation (for reviews, see Scott & Steinberg, 2008; Steinberg & Scott, 2003), (b) their capacities relevant for competence to stand trial (Grisso et al., 2003; using a design patterned after my original *Miranda* studies), and (c) desistance from delinquency (reviewed by Mulvey, 2011; for studies focusing on youths' perceptions of the threat of sanctions as a risk-taking deterrent, see Anwar & Loughran, 2011; Loughran et al., 2015). Some of these efforts built on the serendipitous rise of neuroscience research in the late 1990s, demonstrating adolescents' relative immaturity in brain development (for reviews, see Luna & Wright, 2016; Steinberg, 2008).

Meanwhile, significant advances were being made in two other domains that informed research on juveniles' psycholegal capacities. New evidence identified the prevalence of behavioral health needs of youths in juvenile justice settings, adding disability to developmental immaturity when explaining youths' decisional capacities (for reviews, see Grisso, 2004; Nagel, Guarnera, & Reppucci, 2016). The past two decades saw extraordinary advances in research on juvenile recidivism and risk assessment (for reviews, see Hoge, 2016; Russell & Odgers, 2016), as well as research on developmental trajectories for offending (for reviews, see, e.g., Mulvey, 2014; Vincent, Kimonis, & Clark, 2016; Woolard & Fountain, 2016).

The new studies of adolescents' normative immaturity in risk-taking, self-regulation, and decision-making created a powerful message for policy and practice in juvenile justice. The results were cited by the U.S. Supreme Court in its series of cases declaring that the developmental immaturity of adolescents created constitutional limits on sentencing for serious offenses by juveniles (*Graham v. Florida*, 2010; *Miller v. Alabama*, 2012; *Montgomery v. Louisiana*, 2016; *Roper v. Simmons*, 2005). Regarding practice, the field began offering tools and evidence-based guidelines for assessing youths' legally relevant capacities in delinquency cases (e.g., Goldstein, Zelle, & Grisso, 2012; Grisso, 2005, 2013; Heilbrun, DeMatteo, & Goldstein, 2016; Kruh & Grisso, 2009; Rogers et al., 2008; Salekin, 2004, 2015; Sharf, Rogers, Williams, & Drogin, 2017).

## THE FUTURE OF RESEARCH ON DEVELOPMENTAL PSYCHOLEGAL CAPACITIES

At AP–LS conventions, symposia on children and legal issues have risen from less than 5% of the program in the late 1990s to about 25% in recent years. Research in this area has far exceeded anything I would have imagined when it was launched 40 years ago. With hesitance, then, I will hazard some guesses about three directions that seem to be emerging in this field.

Our earliest questions about children's and adolescents' capacities for consent to treatment and research participation have never been satisfactorily addressed. Might we now return to those questions, using the developmental science and research methods that have matured in our efforts to examine youths' capacities in juvenile justice contexts? There is evidence in Europe of a potential resurgence in studies of youths' competence to consent in healthcare contexts (e.g., Hein et al., 2015; World Health Organization, 2015).

Global migration and refugee placement are moving our nation rapidly toward cultural diversity that may be unlike any other time in our history. At least in theory, cultural background matters with regard to knowledge and expectancies that young people bring to risky decisions on the street and in legal contexts (Grisso, 2012). Might we begin to include cultural background as a variable in our database for developmental studies of children's psycholegal capacities?

Finally, the new neuroscience and behavioral research on youths' abilities has begun to identify the young adult years as developmentally beyond adolescence but not yet adultlike in potentially legally relevant ways (e.g., Cohen et al., 2016). This is opening up new terrain for developmental studies relevant for law and policy.

Predictions are risky, but those who use psychology to study legally relevant capacities are richly imaginative. They will continue to find new ways to provide important information for law and policy regarding developmental psycholegal capacities.

## REFERENCES

Abramovitch, R., Peterson-Badali, M., & Rohan, M. (1995). Young people's understanding and assertion of rights to silence and legal counsel. *Canadian Journal of Criminology, 37,* 1–18.

Anwar, S., & Loughran, T. A. (2011). Testing a Bayesian learning theory of deterrence among serious juvenile offenders. *Criminology, 49,* 667–698.

Arnett, J. (1992). Reckless behavior in adolescence: A developmental perspective. *Developmental Review, 12,* 339–373.

Brodsky, S. L. (1973). *Psychologists in the criminal justice system.* Urbana: University of Illinois Press.

Ceci, S., & Bruck, M. (1993). Suggestibility of the child witness: A historical review and synthesis. *Psychological Bulletin, 113,* 403–439.

Cicourel, A. (1968). *The social organization of juvenile justice.* New York: Wiley.

Cocozza, J. (Ed.). (1992). *Responding to the mental health needs of youth in the juvenile justice system.* Seattle, WA: National Coalition for the Mentally Ill in the Criminal Justice System.

Cohen, A., Breiner, K., Steinberg, L., Bonnie, R., Scott, E., Taylor-Thompson, K. . . . Casey, B. (2016). When is an adolescent an adult? Assessment cognitive control in emotional and nonemotional contexts. *Psychological Science, 27,* 549–562.

Dale, P., Loftus, E., & Rathbun, L. (1978). The influence of the form of the question on the eyewitness testimony of preschool children. *Journal of Psycholinguistic Research, 7,* 269–277.

Devoe, P. (2015). Flashback: Hillary compared marriage, childhood to slavery. *The Daily Caller,* June 9. Retrieved from http://dailycaller.com/2015/06/09/flashback-hillary-compared-marriage-childhood-to-slavery/

Empey, L. (1976). The social construction of childhood, delinquency and social reform. In M. Klein (Ed.), *The juvenile justice system* (pp. 27–54). Berverly Hills, CA: Sage.

Feld, B. (2013). *Kids, cops and confessions: Inside the interrogation room.* New York: New York University Press.

Feshbach, N., & Feshbach, S. (Eds.). (1978). *Special issue: The changing status of children: Rights, roles and responsibilities. Journal of Social Issues, 34*(2).

Fogel, M., Schiffman, W., Mumley, D., Tillbrook, C., & Grisso, T. (2013). Ten-year research update (2001–2010): Evaluations for competence to stand trial (adjudicative competence). *Behavioral Sciences and the Law, 31,* 165–191.

Furby, L., & Beyth-Marom, R. (1992). Risk taking in adolescence: A decision-making perspective. *Developmental Review, 12,* 1–44.

Goldstein, N., Condie, L., Kalbeitzer, R., Osman, D., & Geier, J. (2003). Juvenile offenders' Miranda rights comprehension and self-reported likelihood of false confessions. *Assessment, 10,* 359–368.

Goldstein, N., Zelle, H., & Grisso, T. (2012). Miranda *Rights Comprehension Instruments.* Sarasota, FL: Professional Resource Press.

Goodman, C., & Bottoms, B. (Eds.). (1993). *Child victims, child witnesses: Understanding and improving testimony.* New York: Guilford.

Goodman, G., Golding, J., & Haith, M. (1984). Jurors' reactions to child witnesses. *Journal of Social Issues, 40,* 139–156.

*Graham v. Florida,* 130 S.Ct. 2011 (2010).

Grisso, T. (1975). Conflict about release: Environmental and personal correlates among institutionalized delinquents. *Journal of Community Psychology, 3,* 396–399.

Grisso, T. (1980). Juveniles' capacities to waive Miranda rights: An empirical analysis. *California Law Review, 68,* 1134–1166.

Grisso, T. (1981). *Juveniles' waiver of rights: Legal and psychological competence.* New York: Plenum.

Grisso, T. (1986). *Evaluating competencies: Forensic assessments and instruments.* New York: Kluwer/Plenum.

Grisso, T. (1996). Society's retributive response to juvenile violence: A developmental perspective. *Law and Human Behavior, 20,* 229–247.

Grisso, T. (1997). Juvenile competency to stand trial: Questions in an era of punitive reform. *Criminal Justice, 12,* 4–11.

Grisso, T. (1998a). *Forensic evaluation of juveniles.* Sarasota, FL: Professional Resource Press.

Grisso, T. (1998b). *Instruments for Assessing Understanding and Appreciation of Miranda Rights: Manual.* Sarasota, FL: Professional Resource Press.

Grisso, T. (2003). *Evaluating competencies: Forensic assessments and instruments* (2nd ed.). New York: Kluwer/Plenum.

Grisso, T. (2004). *Double jeopardy: Adolescent offenders with mental disorders.* Chicago: University of Chicago Press.

Grisso, T. (2005). *Evaluating juveniles' adjudicative competence: A manual for clinical practice.* Sarasota, FL: Professional Resource Press.

Grisso, T. (2012). *Exploring the potential for culture-based research on psychopathology and assessment of delinquent youth.* Keynote presentation at the 2012 Conference of European Forensic Child and Adolescent Psychiatry and Psychology, Berlin.

Grisso, T. (2013). *Forensic evaluation of juveniles* (2nd ed.). Sarasota, FL: Professional Resource Press.

Grisso, T., & Pomicter, C. (1978). Interrogation of juveniles: An empirical study of procedures, safeguards, and rights waiver. *Law and Human Behavior, 1,* 321–342.

Grisso, T., & Ring, M. (1979). Parents' attitudes toward juveniles' rights in interrogation. *Criminal Justice and Behavior, 6,* 221–226.

Grisso, T., & Schwartz, R. (Eds.). (2000). *Youth on trial: A developmental perspective on juvenile justice.* Chicago: University of Chicago Press.

Grisso, T., & Steadman, H. (1995). Saleem A. Shah: The man and his imperative. *Law and Human Behavior, 19,* 1–3.

Grisso, T., Steinberg, L., Woolard, J., Cauffman, E., Scott, E., Graham, S. . . . Schwartz, R. (2003). Juveniles' competence to stand trial: A comparison of adolescents' and adults' capacities as trial defendants. *Law and Human Behavior, 27,* 333–363.

*Hartigan v. Zbaraz,* 481 U.S. 1008 (1987).

Heilbrun, K., DeMatteo, D., & Goldstein, N. (Eds.). (2016). *APA handbook of psychology and juvenile justice.* Washington, DC: American Psychological Association.

Hein, I., Troost, P., Lindeboom, R., Christiaans, I., Grisso, T., van Goudoever, J., & Lindauer, R. (2015). Assessing children's competence to consent to treatment. In I. Hein (Ed.), *Children's competence to consent to medical treatment or research* (pp. 91–101). Amsterdam: Amsterdam University Press.

*Hodgson v. State of Minnesota,* 853 F.2d 1452 (1990).

Hoge, R. (2016). Risk, need, and responsivity in juveniles. In K. Heilbrun, D. DeMatteo, & N. Goldstein (Eds.), *APA handbook of psychology and juvenile justice* (pp. 179–196). Washington, DC: American Psychological Association.

*In re Gault,* 387 U.S. 1 (1967).

Kassin, S. (2005). On the psychology of confessions: Does innocence put innocents at risk? *American Psychologist, 60,* 215–228.

Kassin, S. (2008). The psychology of confessions. *Annual Review of Law and Social Science, 4,* 193–217.

Keasey, C., & Sales, B. (1977). Children's conception of intentionality and the criminal law. In B. Sales (Ed.), *Psychology in the legal process* (pp. 127–146). New York: Plenum.

Keniston, K. (1965). *The uncommitted: Alienated youth in American society.* New York: Harcourt, Brace.

*Kent v. U.S.,* 383 U.S. 541(1966).

Koocher, G. (Ed.). (1976). *Children's rights and the mental health professions.* New York: Wiley.

Kruh, I., & Brodsky, S. (1997). Clinical evaluations for transfer to criminal court: Current practices and future research *Behavioral Sciences and the Law, 15,* 151–165.

Kruh, I., & Grisso, T. (2009). *Evaluations of juveniles' competence to stand trial.* New York: Oxford University Press.

Lindsay, D., & Sarri, R. (1992). What Hillary Rodham Clinton really said about children's rights and child policy. *Youth Services Review, 14,* 473–483.

Loughran, T., Brame, R., Fagan, J., Piquero, A., Mulvey, E., & Schubert, C. (2015). *Studying deterrence among high-risk adolescents.* Washington, DC: Office of Juvenile Justice and Delinquency Prevention.

Luna, B., & Wright, C. (2016). Adolescent brain development: Implications for the juvenile criminal justice system. In K. Heilbrun, D. DeMatteo, & N. Goldstein (Eds.), *APA handbook of psychology and juvenile justice* (pp. 91–116). Washington, DC: American Psychological Association.

Manoogian, S. (1978). *Factors affecting juveniles' comprehension of* Miranda *rights.* Unpublished doctoral dissertation, Saint Louis University.

McGarry, A. L. (1973). *Competency to stand trial and mental illness.* Publication no. ADM-77-103. Rockville, MD: National Institute of Mental Health, Department of Health, Education and Welfare.

Melton, G., Koocher, G., & Saks, M. (Ed.). (1983). *Children's competence to consent.* New York: Plenum.

Miller, J. (1991). *Last one over the wall: The Massachusetts experiment in closing reform schools.* Columbus, OH: Ohio State University Press.

*Miller v. Alabama,* 132 S.Ct. 2455 (2012).

*Montgomery v. Louisiana,* 577 U.S. ___ (2016).

Mulvey, E. (2011). *Highlights from Pathways to Desistance: A longitudinal study of serious adolescent offenders.* Washington, DC: U.S. Department of Justice, Office of Justice Programs, Office of Juvenile Justice and Delinquency Prevention.

Mulvey, E. (2014). Using developmental science to reorient our thinking about criminal offending in adolescence. *Journal of Research in Crime and Delinquency, 51,* 467–479.

Nagel, A., Guarnera, L., & Reppucci, N. (2016). Adolescent development, mental disorder, and decision making in delinquent youths. In K. Heilbrun, D. DeMatteo, & N. Goldstein (Eds.), *APA handbook of psychology and juvenile justice* (pp. 117–138). Washington, DC: American Psychological Association.

Otto, R., Greenstein, J., Johnson, M., & Friedman, R. (1992). Prevalence of mental disorders among youth in the juvenile justice system. In J. Cocozza (Ed.), *Responding to the mental health needs of youth in the juvenile justice system* (pp. 7–48). Seattle, WA: National Coalition for the Mentally Ill in the Criminal Justice System.

*Planned Parenthood of Central Missouri v. Danforth,* 428 U.S. 52 (1976).

Platt, A. (1969). *The child savers.* Chicago: University of Chicago Press.

Reppucci, N., Weithorn, L., Mulvey, E., & Monahan, J. (Eds.). (1984). *Children, mental health, and the law.* Berverly Hills, CA: Sage.

Rodham, H. (1973). Children under the law. *Harvard Educational Review, 43,* 487–514.

Rogers, C., & Wrightsman, L. (1978). Attitudes toward children's rights:Nurturance or self-determination? *Journal of Social Issues, 34,* 59–68.

Rogers, R., Blackwood, H., Fiduccia, C., Steadham, J., Drogin, E., & Rogstad, J. (2012). Juvenile *Miranda* warnings: Perfunctory rituals or procedural safeguards? *Criminal Justice and Behavior, 39,* 229–249.

Rogers, R., Hazelwood, L., Sewell, K., Shuman, D., & Blackwood, H. (2008). The comprehensibility and content of juvenile Miranda warnings. *Psychology, Public Policy and Law, 14,* 63–87.

Rogers, R., Hinds, J., & Sewell, K. (1996). Feigning psychopathology among adolescent offenders: Validation of the SIRS, MMPI-A, and SIMS. *Journal of Personality Assessment, 67,* 244–257.

*Roper v. Simmons,* 543 U.S. 551 (2005).

Rubin, T. (1976). The eye of the juvenile court judge: A one-step-up view of the juvenile justice system. In M. Klein (Ed.), *The juvenile justice system* (pp. 133–159). Beverly Hills, CA: Sage.

Russell, M., & Odgers, C. (2016). Desistance and life-course persistence: Findings from longitudinal studies using group-based trajectory modeling of antisocial behavior. In K. Heilbrun, D. DeMatteo, & N. Goldstein (Eds.), *APA handbook of psychology and juvenile justice* (pp. 149–175). Washington, DC: American Psychological Association.

Saks, M. J. & Hastie, R. (1978). *Social psychology in court.* New York: Van Nostrand.

Salekin, R. (2004). *Risk-Sophistication-Treatment Inventory.* Lutz, FL: Psychological Assessment Resources.

Salekin, R. (2015). *Forensic evaluation and treatment of juveniles: Innovation and best practice.* Washington, DC: American Psychological Association.

Scott, E., Reppucci, N., & Woolard, J. (1995). Evaluating adolescent decision-making in legal contexts. *Law and Human Behavior, 19,* 221–244.

Scott, E., & Steinberg, L. (2008). *Rethinking juvenile justice.* Cambridge, MA: Harvard University Press.

Sharf, A., Rogers, R., Williams, M., & Drogin, E. (2017). Evaluating juvenile detainees' *Miranda* misconceptions: The discriminant validity of the Juvenile Miranda Quiz. *Psychological Assessment, 29,* 556–567.

Stapleton, W., & Teitelbaum, L. (1972). *In defense of youth: A study of the role of counsel in American juvenile courts.* New York: Russell Sage Foundation.

Steinberg, L. (2008). A social neuroscience perspective on adolescent risk-taking. *Developmental Review, 28,* 78–106.

Steinberg, L., & Cauffman, E. (1996). Maturity of judgment in adolescence: Psychosocial factors in adolescent decision making. *Law and Human Behavior, 20,* 249–272.

Steinberg, L., & Scott, E. (2003). Less guilty by reason of adolescence: Developmental immaturity, diminished responsibility, and the juvenile death penalty. *American Psychologist, 58,* 1009–1018.

Takanishi, R. (1978). Childhood as a social issue: Historical roots of contemporary child advocacy movements. *Journal of Social Issues, 34,* 8–28.

Tapp, J., & Kohlberg, L. (1977). Developing senses of law and legal justice. In J. Tapp & F. Levine (Eds.), *Law, justice, and the individual in society: Psychological and legal issues* (pp. 89–105). New York: Holt, Rinehart and Winston.

UN General Assembly (1960). *Declaration of the Rights of the Child, 20 November 1959, A/RES/1386(XIV).* London, H. M. Stationery Office.

Viljoen, J., Penner, E., & Roesch, R. (2012). Competence and criminal responsibility in adolescent defendants: The role of mental illness and adolescent development. In B. Feld & D. Bishop (Eds.), *The Oxford handbook on juvenile crime and juvenile justice* (pp. 526–548). New York: Oxford University Press.

Viljoen, J., & Roesch, R. (2005). Competence to waive interrogation rights and adjudicative competence in adolescent defendants: Cognitive development, attorney contact, and psychological symptoms. *Law and Human Behavior, 29,* 723–742.

Vincent, G., Kimonis, E., & Clark, A. (2016). Juvenile psychopathy: Appropriate and inappropriate uses in legal proceedings. In K. Heilbrun, D. DeMatteo, & N. Goldstein (Eds.), *APA handbook of psychology and juvenile justice* (pp. 197–232). Washington, DC: American Psychological Association.

Weithorn, L., & Campbell, S. (1982). The competency of children and adolescents to make informed treatment decisions. *Child Development, 53,* 1589–1598.

Wolfgang, M., Figlio, R., & Sellin, T. (1972). *Delinquency in a birth cohort.* Chicago: University of Chicago Press.

Woolard, J., & Fountain, E. (2016). Serious questions about serious juvenile offenders: Patterns of offending and offenses. In K. Heilbrun, D. DeMatteo, & N. Goldstein (Eds.), *APA handbook of psychology and juvenile justice* (pp. 141–157). Washington, DC: American Psychological Association.

World Health Organization. (2015). *Core competencies in adolescent health and development for primary care providers, including a tool to assess the adolescent health and development component in pre-service education.* Geneva, Switzerland: Author.

# 11

# Correctional Psychology

**STANLEY L. BRODSKY**

A s the date for my court martial drew closer in December 1967, I pretended nothing special was happening and went about my daily duties at the maximum-security military prison at Fort Leavenworth, Kansas. As a 27-year-old captain in the Army Medical Service Corps, I had spent the last two and a half years assessing and treating prisoners, supervising the 15 enlisted men with MA degrees who worked with me, and struggling with institutional practices that corroded my heart and fueled my indignation.

I had never been in a prison before. My closest experience was as a college student picketing the New Hampshire State Prison in protest of the incarceration of lay Methodist minister Willard Uphaus.[1] Uphaus held retreats in New Hampshire and refused to reveal the names of people

1. The state's position was eventually upheld by the U.S. Supreme Court in *Willard Uphaus v. Louis C. Wyman, Attorney General* (1960).

attending, whom the attorney general of New Hampshire suspected were Communist sympathizers. My second related experience was working full time for a few weeks one summer at the New Hampshire State Hospital in Concord. I was alone on the 11:00 PM to 7:00 AM shift prior to the days of psychotropic drugs, and occasionally I was startled by the screaming of a few of the 70 patients for whom I was responsible. Every hour, as instructed, I pulled out my ring of skeleton keys, entered the wards, and ran a key along the bottom of the bare feet of patients to see if they were alive. It was a dispiriting experience.

Assigned to Fort Leavenworth, I found myself head of psychology, working with my wife Annette Brodsky (not yet having received her PhD). It was a trying time. The psychiatrist captain in charge of the mental health unit would eavesdrop on phone calls of mental health staff and break into our offices at night to go through our files. If there was a hint of negativity toward him—for most of us, it was antagonism and fear—he would seek to ship us off to Vietnam.

While I cared deeply about what was wrong at Fort Leavenworth, I had no sense that my activities would reflect a scintilla of my participation as an evaluation expert in later class action suits against prison conditions. As an officer, I was assigned to a regular rotating duty as officer of the day, which meant every 10 days I would be solely in charge of the prison from 5:00 PM until 8:00 AM the next day. The correctional personnel on duty were accustomed to severely punishing problem prisoners as well as those who showed silent insubordination (i.e., the dirty look).[2] Prisoners were sent arbitrarily to disciplinary segregation. Segregation was miserable: barren cells, concrete slabs for beds, a hole in the floor for toilet purposes that was flushed from the outside if the guards felt like it, a minimal diet, little clothing, and a single bright exposed light bulb on all day and night.

I sought to make the case to the senior officers in charge that segregation conditions were inhumane, morally wrong, and needed to be changed.

2. This was not long before the book came out titled *Military Justice Is to Justice as Military Music Is to Music* (Sherrill, 1970).

Nobody listened. Finally, I tried a different path. The Army had a program in which personnel were encouraged to write directly to Washington to submit suggestions to improve the Army achieving its goals and mission, with the potential to get possible incentive bonuses. I explained how the improper and harmful conditions in disciplinary segregation were inconsistent with the stated mission. A team from the Inspector General's Office came to our institution, inspected the facilities, and ordered that mattresses, toilets, reading matter, clothing, and adequate food be provided. They denied a financial payoff for me, explaining the changes were already stated in the regulations. That didn't matter.

The senior officers were furious. They started assigning me to inventory all of the pens and pencils in prison. I complied. Then they ordered me to inventory all of the toothbrushes and toothpaste. I did that too. Then the big push came. I was ordered to inventory all of the stored grain and farm implements on the prison farm, about a two-week job. I declined, saying they were doing this just to punish me. They said it was a direct order; because I disobeyed a direct order, they initiated the procedural steps toward a court martial. My main antagonist contacted psychologists around the country, seeking without success to locate someone who would affirm that I was irresponsible and incompetent. As the court martial date approached, they offered me a deal. If they assigned enlisted men to conduct the prison inventory, would I sign off on it? Oh, yes, I agreed. And the harassment stopped. In retrospect, I was both foolish and brave. I had the idea of trying to make a difference. And this is what it led to, starting with the place of psychology in systems and institutions of criminal justice.

## CORRECTIONAL PSYCHOLOGY AND THE CRIMINAL JUSTICE SYSTEM

On the grounds of what is now known as the Bok Tower Gardens at Lake Wales, Florida, among rolling acres of ferns, camellias, and jasmine designed by Fredrick Laws Olmstead Jr., are the 60-bell Bok Tower Carillion and a 20-room Mediterranean design mansion. Through 1970 and 1971, that mansion was periodically occupied by up to 30 of us, mostly psychologists, but also psychiatrists, correctional administrators, and prominent figures from the bench. Our main Lake Wales Conference of 1971 was held in the mansion overlooking the Olmstead landscape, and it was a marking point in the development of modern correctional psychology. The Lake Wales Conference and the book that followed portrayed what mental health professionals were and should be doing in corrections.

A humility disclaimer is in order: The conference was not my idea. I was influenced by Saleem Shah, as were many of the other contributors. Saleem, along with Art Kandel, pointed me down the path to this project, and they helped coordinate the funding from the three federal agencies that supported it. A few years earlier I had been awarded a National Institute of Mental Health (NIMH) grant to study the interpersonal relationships of prisoners at the Menard, Illinois, state prison. I arranged to have photocopied all the letters inmates wrote and received and audio recorded all their visits[3] for their first 18 months of incarceration (Brodsky, 1975). Saleem was the NIMH project officer.

In contrast to Saleem's thoughtful and measured way of approaching issues, Art Kandel was the buoyantly extroverted, treatment-focused chief psychologist at the Patuxent Maryland Institution for Defective Delinquents—really: defective delinquents. It was a psychology-run prison in which most decisions were made by mental health staff based on behavioral and psychodynamic treatment programs. Patuxent was later fiercely attacked for its reliance on treatment outcomes, its use of indeterminate sentencing, and its use of the indefensible, unscientific, and pejorative concept of defective delinquency (Coldren, 2004).

I was president of the American Association of Correctional Psychologist (Art was president before me), and I received the grant for the conference. I had learned something important at Ft. Leavenworth—that it was

---

3. In those naïve days before Institutional Review Boards, such research had an occasional and improvised *laissez-faire* quality to it. When I found that I was turned down by 8 of the first 10 men I had asked to volunteer to participate for $5 a month, I shifted the request. I told the next potential participants that some prisoners would be given the opportunity to earn $5 a month by agreeing to have their letters copied and visits recorded. Then almost everybody agreed.

possible to make a difference in the lives of some prisoners who were treated harmfully.

The Lake Wales Conference and its three follow-up meetings led me to the conclusion that psychologists' work may be divided into that of system professionals who seek to help prisons do their jobs better and system challengers who struggle against injustices and unfair punishment and who consider it proper to shake up the system. I was skeptical of the mental health prisons, like the component of the Marion, Illinois, federal prison, which ran on transactional analysis principles, and other variations of the Patuxent model, and I liked the few therapeutic communities in prisons.

No mental health professionals working in corrections had been educated or trained for the job. Most were on a steep learning curve, and frequently we did not know much about the professional or scholarly foundations of what we were doing. At Lake Wales, we declared the need for university-based training models for psychology graduate education to prepare psychologists to work in the justice system in general and in corrections.

It was not just prisons that were at issue. Behavioral scientists were needed to engage in formulating public policy to aim at decriminalization and to promote just outcomes of trials, sentencing, and confinement. Correctional psychology was portrayed as simplistic. It had not attained the professional maturity and specialized training that already was widespread in forensic psychology. Tess Neal (2016) has described the Lake Wales Conference as ushering in the modern era of correctional psychology, as well as helping to define clear boundaries between forensic and correctional psychology.

*Psychologists in the Criminal Justice System* was my book that came from the Lake Wales Conferences, and it was widely read. Saleem had encouraged me to put money in the budget for distribution, and 5,000 copies were privately printed and given away in 1972. The next year the University of Illinois Press commercially published the book (Brodsky, 1973). I had no special expectations for the book, but it became a resource and stimulus for psychologists interested in the field. I have a copy of a letter that Tom Grisso wrote me in 1974 (before he was *the* Tom Grisso) describing how the book got him thinking.

## CRIMINAL JUSTICE AND BEHAVIOR (THE JOURNAL)

At the same time *Psychologists in the Criminal Justice System* came out, I was starting up the journal *Criminal Justice & Behavior*; it was not straightforward. The American Association of Correctional Psychologists had been publishing a nonrefereed, mimeographed or prisoner-printed journal called *The Correctional Psychologist*, and intermittently titled *The Journal of Correctional Psychology* (American Association of Correctional Psychologists, 1975), distributed only to association members and not to libraries. This collection of mostly discursive essays and casual research studies was far from being uniformly respectable. Still, as I now review dozens of issues from the 1960s and early 1970s, there were substantive articles by Saleem Shah, Asher Pacht, and Robert Levinson, as well as some of my own.

The roles that led me into the Lake Wales Conference also led me to initiate a search for a legitimate replacement for *The Correctional Psychologist* to publish research in correctional and offender psychology. The broad challenge was how to make psychological work in corrections more scientific and more accountable. The plan was to establish a scholarly journal as the cornerstone for scientific correctional psychology, although some observers would have considered the phrase *scientific correctional psychology* an oxymoron.

Sage Publications and I titled the journal *Criminal Justice & Behavior* to draw a large subscribing audience. The subtitle, *An International Journal*, was added for the same reason, even though there was nothing international about it, unless one counted the Sage offices in London where I played table tennis with the staff. In those precomputer days of hard copy submissions, most of the early submitted manuscripts were tatty, dog-eared papers that probably had been rejected multiple times elsewhere. The early issues depended on me calling on friends to submit their quality manuscripts to an unknown journal. They agreed. Thus, the first issue in March 1974 included articles by Ned Megargee, Philip Ash, and Marguerite Warren. In the editor's introduction, I declared that the purpose of *Criminal Justice & Behavior* was to publish reports of how "behavioral sciences seek to understand and influence agencies, clients, and processes related to criminal justice." Newly enchanted with the writings of Ambrose Bierce, I drew on his satirical definitions in describing birthing the new journal by quoting him: "Birth is the first and direst of all disasters." I asserted the goal of objectivity, stating that we would avoid accepting manuscripts based on "a polite recognition of another's resemblance to ourselves" (Brodsky, 1974, pp. 3–4).

After my eight years as first (and unpaid) editor, the editorship passed on to a variety of committed editors. It evolved from a corrections and psychology journal to one that covered criminology and psychology–justice topics except for forensic psychology. *Criminal Justice & Behavior* flourished and now publishes articles examining psychological and behavioral aspects of the juvenile and criminal justice systems, including offender treatment and classification.

## GRADUATE TRAINING IN CORRECTIONAL PSYCHOLOGY IN THE LAND OF COTTON

Two of the participants in the Lake Wales conference and the follow-up meetings were Ray Fowler, head of the Psychology Department and Carl Clements, then a new assistant professor at the University of Alabama. Ray was an MMPI maven who developed the first computer-mediated MMPI interpretation program for assessing prisoners. At about the same time as the Lake Wales Conference, Ray had gone fishing in the Gulf of Mexico with the then-head of the Law Enforcement Assistance Administration. Between baiting their hooks, the conversation drifted to why psychologists were not doing more to make a difference in the abysmal state of prisons and treatment of inmates. As a consequence, Ray and the University of Alabama received a large grant to offer undergraduate and graduate training in correctional psychology. Ray sought me out to shepherd the program and made me an offer I could not refuse. He created a position that did not exist for my wife who had finally finished her PhD in 1970; soon we were lugging our two kids with us to Tuscaloosa. One of earliest hires was the first African-American faculty member in the Psychology Department, Charles Owens, and we were off and running. In our description of the Correctional–Clinical Psychology Program (Fowler & Brodsky, 1978), Ray and I noted that our particular emphasis was on psychology applied to correctional and offender populations. But we also observed that the concerns encompassed a broader range of psychological applications to legal problems.

We identified eight major areas of our correctional psychology program. Some were garden variety: consultation, training, serving as an information clearinghouse, and issuing of a series of publications by center personnel. One less common activity was testifying in class action suits, including the marker cases of *Wyatt v. Stickney* (1971; rights of institutionalized psychiatric patients), *Pugh v. Locke* (1972, and *Newman v. State of Alabama* (1972; adequate medical and mental healthcare for Alabama prisoners; see Gormally, Clements, Brodsky, & Fowler, 1972, and *Donaldson v. O'Connor*, 1975, right to treatment).

I learned soon that the first fully integrated restaurant in Tuscaloosa had replaced its glass windows with plywood because locals would throw bricks at the windows. I had not known that this small, then very ordinary southern university, its psychology department, and I would soon be enmeshed in many major mental hospital and prison class actions in the context of a correctional psychology academic-action focus. At the beginning Ray was the major player. I was involved.

The correctional emphasis diminished over time. Ray and Carl retired, and Chuck Owens left. We continued to place many of our students in American Psychological Association–approved correctional internships, mostly with the Federal Bureau of Prisons, but we accepted fewer students interested in corrections. As we filled faculty openings, the bright, productive applicants were mostly invested in forensic topics. The core correctional psychology graduate class was taught less often. Like most (but not all) other psych–law clinical programs, we metamorphosed into a forensic rather than correctional psychology, despite the history of correctional education, research, and activism.

## THE PSYCHOLOGY DEPARTMENT THAT (SORT OF) TOOK OVER A PRISON SYSTEM

For more than two decades, Judge Frank M. Johnson of the Middle District of Alabama had federal marshals offering protection to him. Some of his early rulings supported Rosa Parks, were against his former college classmate George C. Wallace, and denied the effort to ban the Selma-to-Montgomery civil rights march. Johnson ordered the desegregation of Alabama schools. He issued the landmark *Wyatt v. Stickney* (1971) order against the Alabama Department of Mental Health, spelling out the constitutional rights of institutionalized psychiatric patients.

By 1971, Johnson had found the correctional facilities of Alabama to be unconstitutionally barbaric, and in January 1976 he described cruel and unusual punishment in the Alabama prison system. These court rulings were the beginning of my long, protracted involvements in legal actions challenging practices in prison and jails in Alabama and elsewhere. In the *Pugh v. Locke* decision in January 1976, Judge Frank Johnson designated our Center to reclassify all inmates in the Alabama Prison System. In one five-month period, our faculty and graduate students interviewed, assessed, and reclassified 3,192 inmates within an openly hostile and resistant prison system (Brodsky, 1977).

In that first summer after the court order, 30 faculty and graduate students from our psychology department, accompanied by a university police officer for our safety, spent a summer living in Slapout, Alabama. It was the beginning of efforts to reclassify the prisoners at the nearby Draper Correctional Center. Few men were classified as needing maximum security by our teams. Over 20% were seen as appropriate for community custody, over 30% for minimum custody, and a large proportion of the remaining men for medium custody.

When I wrote about this lawsuit and the subsequent events (Brodsky, 1986), I observed how it was both promising and frustrating in terms of attaining the goals we had set. In his detailed analysis of both the legal issues and the voluminous daily notes that Ray Fowler and I had kept, Larry Yackle (1989) offered a dour conclusion. He observed that repeated conflicts between the psychology department and the Department of Corrections commissioner, his chief consulting psychologist, and the primary warden resulted in little permanent change and minimal follow-through. Despite repeated hearings and court orders and successful reclassification of all of the targeted inmates, most of the existing problems remained. From my perspective, it was a legal, institutional version of Whac-A-Mole, in which once one apparent problem was resolved, another popped up. In 1979, Judge Johnson left the U.S. District Court to take a position on the Fifth Circuit Court of Appeals, reportedly in part to be rid of the persistent problems in the prison cases.

## PRISON CLASS ACTION SUITS

Starting in the early 1970s and for the next three decades, I found myself regularly serving as an evaluating expert, usually retained by the plaintiffs, in prison, jail, and mental hospital class action suits around the country. I was not the only person doing this work, but I was doing a lot of it along with Craig Haney (Haney & Lynch, 1997). I inspected all the Alabama men's prisons and many in Mississippi, Michigan, Ohio, Illinois, Maryland, Alaska, South Carolina, Puerto Rico, and elsewhere (Brodsky, 1985). Then-President Clinton signed both the Prison Litigation Reform Act in 1996 and subsequent legislation in 1999 to protect prospective defendants in class actions[4] (Hammond, Hill, & Ekstein, 2000), and many fewer attorneys filed mental health- or prison-related suits.

4. Pub. L. No. 106-37; 113 Stat. 185 (20 July 1999); 15 USC 6601 et seq. See more at http://corporate.findlaw.com/law-library/clinton-congress-compromise-y2k-legislation-to-muffle-litigation.html#sthash.rQGcPmw5.dpuf

When Kent Miller and I wrote about prison class actions (Brodsky & Miller, 1981), we noted that the initial positive attitudes to lawsuits of some state defendants had shifted and that "reform cannot be rammed down the throat" (p. 211). In addition to the Alabama litigation, we discussed a project in which we concluded that 7 of 10 men in solitary confinement on death row were moderately or serious disturbed as a result of their treatment.

Examining individual units and organizational structures in prisons seemed a useful path. When Forrest Scogin and I reported on the inmates in protective custody at three large southwestern prisons (Scogin & Brodsky, 1988), we found that two of the prison units appeared to cause major psychological harm. These prisoners were mostly restricted to their cells and not allowed to participate in institutional programs. A third prison had adequate space and programs.

When one is asked to inspect jails, prisons, and occasionally mental hospitals with physically and psychologically toxic living conditions, a particular effort is needed to maintain objectivity. The attorneys are often dedicated and engaging. The despair of prisoners and attorneys alike can be substantial. Part of my continuing effort had been to stay objective and speak to what I knew. Within the standard criteria for these lawsuits, I have usually been asked on the stand if the conditions and treatment shocked my conscience, with the plaintiff attorneys fully expecting an affirmative answer. Many of the conditions were truly dreadful. But my answer was that nothing shocked me after years of making these evaluations.

I spent more time in Alabama prisons than anywhere else. In this poor state, prisons have been underfunded, overcrowded, and dangerous, but that has been true in most states. At the 1985 Nebraska Symposium on Motivation (Brodsky, 1986) I observed the contrast between about 2 million individual psychological assessments of prisoners a year and the close to 100 evaluations of total institutions for lawsuits. Moreover, I concluded the Heisenberg principle applied to these evaluations, in which the act of observing often changed how the institutions worked.

In some of the inspected prisons in Alabama, triple bunk beds filled all of the space in small rooms with narrow spaces between the rows of bunks. The men there spent 23 hours a day in these non-air-conditioned dormitories in semitropical south Alabama. There have been some improvements over time, but the conditions remain bad. For every apparent success by suits, there are often delaying tactics, appeals, superficial compliance, and continuing problems. The attorneys think about victories and losses; the typical victory in court is not necessarily followed by actual changes in jails and prisons.

## SEGUES INTO COURT TESTIMONY AND FORENSIC PSYCHOLOGY

Ames Robey was one of the psychiatric pioneers for three decades in assessing competency to stand trial following *Dusky v. United States* (1960), as well as one of the most dramatic, brilliant, and controversial forensic psychiatrists. When I went to the Center for Forensic Psychiatry headed by Ames in Ypsilanti, Michigan, for the summer of 1970, it was on a hunch that I would learn much more about forensic psychology from Ames. Up to that time, much of my work had been focused on correctional psychology. With Ames, that summer I co-authored my first article about testifying in court (Brodsky & Robey, 1972), and I watched Ames testify in court. I learned what to do: Be clear, be confident about my conclusions, stay on target, and engage with the audience. As inspections from prison lawsuits and other civil court cases filled more of my time, I often found myself on the stand.

Within the next few years I started testifying often and giving talks about testifying. In the aftermath of my divorce in 1981, I paid for setting up a series of expert witness workshops. They were financially disastrous but professionally wonderful, led to paying workshops, and I slipped more into the businesses of testifying and of leading workshops. They started me in the active business of talking and writing about testifying in court.

A few events led me to think that this was where I belonged. I twice evaluated the Mayaguez Boys Industrial School in Puerto Rico after a class action suit was filed in the name of the lead plaintiff, Angel Figueroa

Santana. When he was 12 years old, Santana had been sent to the school for three charges of malicious mischief. He had constant epileptic attacks, had been assessed as having an IQ of 61, and was in need of medical treatment. For the next four years, he was in solitary confinement most of the time. My review of his medical records indicated that before Santana died at the age 16 on the floor of his isolation cell, he was regularly beaten, and his physical and mental health deterioration were ignored: "He is thin and hardly eats, a social worker technician reported. He is weak and can hardly speak. He vomits. He finds that his tongue sticks out of his mouth and he cannot put it back in. He has a tic and begins to shake" (Brodsky, 1982, p. 128).

In that culture, characterized by exuberant emotional display, I found the boys to be depressed, to have trouble sleeping, and most to have blunted affect. While outside the high concrete walls a lovely view overlooked the confluence of the Atlantic Ocean and the Caribbean Sea, inside were barbed wire barriers, crowded dormitories, toilets chronically stopped up, and dirt or concrete floors. While in isolation, the boys had no access to educational or other services. The most common reported experience was feeling emotionally strangled or asphyxiated. I testified in federal court about the intolerable living conditions and how toxic the setting was to the residents. Nevertheless, change was slow, in part because the federal judge refused to accept the negotiated settlement conditions.

Sometimes it went better. In a wrongful death suit against one state correctional system, I testified for two and a half days that the psychiatrist in charge had erred. He was a problem, having had his license suspended for unethical practices in two other states, and then currently practicing under the supervisory umbrella of somebody else's license. To save money under the contract from the state, the psychiatrist severely cut back on all of the psychotropic medications for inmates, and one inmate hung himself. My testimony seemed to go well, but I became sure of it when a junior attorney from the defense firm came to me during a break and asked if I would autograph her copy of one of my books. There was no cross-examination. The eventual settlement was in part satisfactory—a mixed outcome that was common in such suits unless the defense was already ready to make a difference.

During expert witness workshops starting in the 1970s and right up to the present, I played the role of an attorney conducting aggressive, clever, or challenging cross-examinations, often demanding to know what the experts had published, how they knew what they knew, and what the scientific bases were for their testimony. It was exciting. Testimony itself became one of my favorite professional activities, and I was enchanted with the give and take and the task of being professional and, at the same time, trying to be comfortable and positive in the face of tough questioning. In the workshops and in working as consultant with individual expert witnesses, I raised questions and offered answers on topics like what to do when one has a panic attack on the stand, how to respond when one's mind goes blank, and possible solutions when one feels trapped. Some mental health forensic professionals offered horror stories of crying or passing out or contradicting themselves on the stand or being verbally beaten up, sometimes just because they were women experts (see Larson & Brodsky, 2014; Neal, Guadagno, Eno, & Brodsky, 2012).

I started writing books about testimony. Norm Poythress suggested that I organize the books much like his favorite resource for playing duplicate bridge, that is, short, how-to chapters in alphabetical order. Thus, I took a title from a little-known book (book titles cannot be copyrighted) of *Testifying in Court*, and wrote it in 1991, followed by four more testifying books (Brodsky, 1999, 2005, 2013; Brodsky & Gutheil, 2016).

## CORRECTIONAL PSYCHOLOGY STRUGGLES AND SUCCESSES

Psychology has a long-standing ambivalence toward correctional psychology. Many parties have been disillusioned by the limitations of the mental health professions working with and in prisons. Instead of throwing major resources into training, higher education, and development of the subdiscipline of correctional psychology, psychology–law has been instead drawn to forensic psychology, with its attendant drama, pretrial evaluations, and possibilities of high income in independent practice. Despite Texas Tech University offering a major PhD program heavily devoted to correctional psychology, and other graduate programs in clinical psychology having some components, correctional psychology has not flourished. The Federal Bureau of Prisons and a few states have developed professional, skilled, and valued mental health staff and services, but these few bright spots shine in an otherwise drab and discouraging professional landscape. In my own university I have seen (and assume some responsibility for) the emphasis on correctional psychology as a major focus fade into a relatively small piece of psych–law graduate education.

Yet bright spots have emerged in contemporary correctional psychology. A sea change has occurred in the specifics of treatment efforts in prisons. Psychodynamic treatments prevailed in the 1960s and 1970s, but now therapists frequently draw on cognitive behavior therapy and evidence-based approaches. Mental health professionals have discarded prevention of recidivism and "cures for criminality" as treatment goals. Instead, a variety of treatment options for disordered and distressed offenders have prevailed (e.g., on targeted interventions with coerced clients, see Brodsky, 2011). Furthermore, almost all prison systems have housing units or institutions exclusively for disordered prisoners.

Is the situation better now than it was over 50 years ago when I started at Ft. Leavenworth? Absolutely. Is it anywhere near okay in most states in the country? It is not: The typical set of practices is far from okay. My conclusion may seem overly negative. The good news is that class action suits have illuminated many of the failings in mental health services and living conditions in prisons. Graduate education in clinical and forensic psychology has had halo effects that spill into corrections. Psychologists and other mental health professionals are attending more to what is happening and what they can do. A body of useful knowledge has emerged. Those are reasonable starts.

# REFERENCES

American Association of Correctional Psychologists. (1975). *The Journal of Correctional Psychology.* Millwood, NY: Kraus Reprint.

Brodsky, S. L. (1973). *Psychologists in the criminal justice system.* Urbana: University of Illinois Press, 1973.

Brodsky, S. L. (1975). *Families and friends of men in prison: The uncertain relationship.* Lexington, MA: Lexington Books (D.C. Heath Company).

Brodsky, S. L. (1982). Correctional change and the social scientist: A case study. *Journal of Community Psychology, 10,* 128–132.

Brodsky, S. L. (1977). Psychology at the interface of law and corrections: The Alabama correctional psychology experience. *Law and Psychology Review, 3,* 1–13.

Brodsky, S. L. (1986). Empirical assessment and civil actions. In G. Melton (Ed.), *Nebraska Symposium on Motivation 1985: The law as a behavioral instrument.* Lincoln: University of Nebraska Press.

Brodsky, S. L., & Gutheil, T. G. (2016). *The expert expert witness, Revised edition.* Washington, DC: American Psychological Association Books.

Brodsky, S. L. (2013). *Testifying in court: Second edition.* Washington, DC: American Psychological Association Books.

Brodsky, S. L. (2004). *Coping with cross-examination and other pathways to effective testimony.* Washington, DC: American Psychological Association Books.

Brodsky, S. L. (1999). *The expert expert witness: More maxims and guidelines for testifying in court.* Washington, DC: American Psychological Association Books.

Brodsky, S. L. (2011). *Therapy with coerced and reluctant clients.* Washington, DC: American Psychological Association.

Brodsky, S. L., & Robey, A. (1972). On becoming an expert witness: Issues of orientation and effectiveness. *Professional Psychology, 3,* 173–176.

Brodsky, S. L., & Fowler, R. D. (1978). Development of a correctional–clinical psychology program, *Professional Psychology, 9,* 440–447.

Brodsky, S. L., & Miller, K. S. (1981). Coercing change in prisons and mental hospitals: The social scientist and class action suit. In J. M. Joffe & G. W. Albee (Eds.), *Prevention through political action and social change.* Hanover, NH: University Press of New England.

Coldren, J. R., Jr. (2004). *Patuxent institution: An experiment in corrections.* New York: Lang.

*Donaldson v. O'Connor,* 422 U.S. 563 (1975).

*Dusky v. United States,* 362, U.S. 402 (1960).

Gormally, J. F., Brodsky, S. L., Clements, C. B., & Fowler, R. D., Jr. (1972). *Minimum mental health standards for Alabama prisons.* Tuscaloosa, AL: Center for Correctional Psychology.

Hammond, L., Hill, D. A., & Ekstein, T. (2000). Aiding the incarcerated A hard job made harder. *Litigation, 26*(2), 44–46.

Haney, C., & Lynch, M. (1997). Regulating prisons of the future: Psychological analyses if supermax and solitary confinement. *NYU Review of Law & Social Change, 23,* 477–562.

Larson, B. S., & Brodsky, S. L. (2014). Assertive women as expert witnesses: A study of assertive and defensive responses in male and female experts. *Behavioral sciences and the Law, 32,* 149–163.

Neal, T. M. S. (2016). Forensic psychology and correctional psychology: Distinct but related subfields of psychological science and practice. Unpublished and privately distributed paper.

Neal, T. M., Guadagno, R., Eno, C., & Brodsky, S. L. (2012). Warmth and competence on the witness stand: Implications for credibility of male and female expert witnesses. *Journal of American Academy of Psychiatry and Law, 40*(4), 488–497.

*Newman v. State of Alabama,* 349 F. Supp. 278 (M.D. Ala. 1972).

*Pugh v. Locke,* 406 F. Supp. 318 (M.D. Ala. 1976).

Sherrill, R. (1970). *Military justice is to justice as military music is to music.* New York: Harper & Row.

*Willard Uphaus v. Louis C. Wyman, Attorney General,* 364 U.S. 388 (81 S.Ct. 153, 5 L.Ed.2d 148 1960).

*Wyatt v. Stickney,* 325 F. Supp. 781 (M.D. Ala. 1971).

Yackle, L. W. (1989). *Reform and regret: The story of federal judicial involvement in the Alabama prison system.* New York: Oxford University Press.

# 12

# The Founding and Early Years of the American Board of Forensic Psychology

FLORENCE W. KASLOW

I t is deceptively easy to think of medical specialties like pediatrics, obstetrics, gynecology, and nephrology as having a very long-standing practice of certification. In actuality, board certification in a medical specialty was only introduced in 1933 by the American Board of Medical Specialties. There are currently 24 general board certifications, within which there are as many as four specialties in some, specifically within psychiatry and neurology, plus 14 subspecialties, including forensic psychiatry. Being board certified in a specialty is close to routine in medical practice, with about 85% of physicians within the United States being certified (Sutherland & Leatherman, 2006). Psychiatry was one of the earliest specialties, dating back to 1935.

Professional psychology was slower to develop. While incorporated in 1947, the American Board of Professional Psychology (ABPP) did not take its present form until 60 years after medicine, in 1993 (ABPP, n.d.). With 15 specialties, among them psychoanalysis, rehabilitation psychology, couple and family psychology, school psychology, and neuropsychology, much of the content covered by direct service is represented. Unlike with physicians, only a minority of professional psychologists are board certified, largely because it is unusual for work environments or careers to require such certification. In this chapter, I write about the start of board certification by the American Board of Forensic Psychology and its allied partner, the American Academy of Forensic Psychology (AAFP). This chapter describes the beginnings.

## HOW I GOT THERE

In 1972 and 1973, I served as a consultant to the Pennsylvania Law and Justice Institute. The then-commissioner of the Pennsylvania Bureau of Corrections, Stewart Werner, approached me at a conference and asked if I would be willing to work out an arrangement to place psychology doctoral students from an American Psychological Association (APA) approved psychology program in the Pennsylvania prison system under my supervision for their internships. He offered to fund my salary and the internships. A few weeks later, Jules Abrams, chair of the psychology program at Hahnemann Medical College (now University), asked if he could interest me in leaving my teaching appointment at another medical college and joining the faculty at Hahnemann. I told him about the offer from Commission Werner, and everything moved swiftly after that.

In September of 1973, I began teaching in the Department of Mental Health Sciences at Hahnemann, primarily in psychology but also in psychiatry and in the family therapy program. A student unit of three was sent to Graterford Maximum Security Prison. My simultaneous appointment to the Bureau of Corrections was as consultant for training and treatment. I learned what it was to walk a cellblock, to always have an honor prisoner accompany me, to make sure our students were well protected and cautious, and how to do (and did) hostage negotiations. I always experienced a great sense of relief when I exited the prison, and the gates clanged shut behind me.

A year later, Israel Zwerling, the chair of the Department of Mental Health Sciences at Hahnemann and himself a clinical and forensic psychiatrist, asked if I would co-teach a course he was introducing in forensic psychiatry. Honored, thrilled, and a bit naïve, I accepted and began reading avidly. He asked me to run several day-long forensic programs, and I invited the best-known and most respected people I could over a period of a few years to offer panels and solo presentations. I chaired the programs and let the acknowledged experts do the presenting. This provided me various excellent opportunities to continue learning from the best and brightest. I also attended workshops outside of the Philadelphia area to get an exposure to different speakers and domains. It all was intriguing, challenging, and exciting. I also joined the American Psychology–Law Society.

Zwerling created a Forensic Psychology and Psychiatry section within the department in 1975 and asked me to chair it. He appointed mostly psychiatrist members from the department along with two other psychologists to be members. When I told lawyers and judges what we were doing, several prominent judges asked if they might apply for adjunct teaching appointments in the department and serve in the Forensic Section. Zwerling and I were surprised and liked the idea, and he rapidly had all their credentials checked. Voila! We soon had four well-respected judges on board.

In the meantime, PhD–JD programs had been started at the University of Nebraska–Lincoln under Bruce Sales, one at Stanford University headed by David Rosenhan, and one combining the resources of the University of Maryland Psychology Department and John Hopkins University Law School with Donald Bersoff as its director. I began thinking we had an excellent department in which to also begin a combined program. Therefore, I contacted the dean of Villanova Law School, Charles O'Brien, with whom I had worked when I was consultant to the Pennsylvania Law and Justice Institute, with Dr. Zwerling's permission. We agreed we could and should try to develop a joint PsyD (the degree Hahnemann awarded)–JD program between Hahnemann and Villanova (Kaslow, 1976).

We moved quickly through the administrative structures of both universities to get the program approved. In 1979, we admitted the first class of five ultra-bright students into a program projected to run six years. Students were to spend years one, three, and five in the Psychology Department, and years two, four, and six at the Law School. All had to meet the entrance requirements of both programs and fulfill all regular curriculum requirements, plus spend summers in practica and internships that incorporated the interface of psychology and law, such as the *guardian ad litem* unit at the Philadelphia Juvenile Court. I co-directed the joint program for several years with Associate Dean Gerald Abraham at Villanova. I sometimes attended and/or taught classes at the law school. The program was greeted with excitement and enthusiasm, and it flourished for many years (Kaslow, 2000).

## PROFESSIONAL RIVALRY

One day in 1976, a psychiatrist colleague asked me, "Have you heard that psychiatry is moving toward board certification in forensics?" I had not. I was friendly with a local academic psychiatrist at another university, a valued colleague who was active in the American Academy of Psychiatry and Law, an influential national forensic psychiatry organization. I called him, and he responded that any such development was years away. I suggested we consider a joint credentialing process of forensic psychologists and psychiatrists; his response was, "Sounds like a good idea; when the time draws closer, let's discuss it."

At the next monthly meeting of our forensic section, one of our psychiatrist members announced that they had received their applications for applying for board certification. I was appalled at the "deception." It was clear some action had to be taken to ensure that psychologists did not lose the foothold we had gained in the forensic world, particularly since the *Jenkins v. U.S.* (1961) decision (Kaslow, 2000) in which psychologists were identified as belonging to a learned science and profession and therefore qualified to give expert opinions on issues of mental disease.

I wrote to Bruce Sales, the president of AP–LS in 1976–1977, to inform him about this development and my misgivings. He suggested that I set up a committee to study the matter. The reception to my inquiries was mixed. A few forensic psychologists thought preoccupation with additional credentialing was unnecessary. Others did not respond. Nevertheless, I moved forward and placed a notice in the AP–LS bulletin indicating that we were creating a committee to study the need for establishing a diplomate (the term current then) in forensic psychology. We met on a Sunday afternoon at Hahnemann Medical College. A hearty band of pioneers came at their own expense, and we designated ourselves the initial committee. The members who first served with me were Leonard Paul from Pennsylvania; Martin Kurke and David Shapiro from Washington, DC; Hirsch Silverman from New Jersey; and Charlton S. Stanley from Mississippi.

We started out as strangers and quickly bonded with one another. We immediately recognized that forensic psychology had many applications outside the clinical realm. Although most of us were clinical or counseling psychologists, our original sextet also agreed it was essential to include nonclinical concerns involving human factors, industrial/organizational psychology, and the interface with legal, judicial, and correctional systems in roles such as serving as expert witnesses. We used the term *forensic psychology* to encompass the application of many aspects of psychology that interfaced with numerous aspects of law, legal systems, correctional systems, and family systems. Having arrived at a common understanding as to the multifaceted meaning of forensic psychology, we agreed that board certification should be pursued immediately. Forensic psychology constituted a specialty area within psychology that has its own body of knowledge and many specific skills for competent practice, and our expertise needed to be publicized and showcased.

We reported back to AP–LS. Our self-selected group was ambivalent about the action we had taken and reluctant to move ahead swiftly. Nevertheless, we did not want to appear in court as expert witnesses and find in the credentialing process that we were perceived to be unqualified because, unlike the psychiatrists, we were not board certified. They were moving full-speed ahead; their first date for administering examinations already had been set for 1977.

We turned to the Board of Professional Affairs of the APA for information about the process for becoming recognized as a specialty area. APA responded, albeit slowly, that they were not ready to consider new specialties. It is now several decades later, and they still do not accredit doctoral programs in specialties beyond the original ones of clinical, counseling, industrial/organization, and school psychology. This inaction persists despite the knowledge and activity explosion that has occurred in forensic psychology and other specialty areas clamoring for such recognition such as neuropsychology and family psychology.

The response from the ABPP was initially neutral. They were not ready to help us organize, but they did send us material on the ABPP diplomating process, and we followed it closely.

We believed that our mission warranted rapid movement. United by our shared purpose, we decided at our second meeting that we would go it alone if we received no positive sanction from any official bastion of organized psychology. We each contributed $100 to a start-up fund for initial expenses; this was to be applicable against our application fees.

By 1977 Paul Lipsitt had become AP–LS president (after Bruce Sales) and decided to attend our meeting in a liaison role. Impressed by what we wanted to do, he became the seventh member of our committee and arranged for us to receive a loan of $1,000 from AP–LS, which we repaid in 1978. Later presidents of AP–LS, including John Monahan and Len Bickman, were also most cooperative.

## THE FORENSIC BOARD WAS FOUNDED

Some of the AP–LS board remained unconvinced about the necessity of certification. Many of the leaders of AP–LS were academics and researchers who were interested in investigating and teaching about law and psychology. They were not on the forensic firing line providing reports and testimony to lawyers and the courts and thus were not being driven by our sense our urgency. Therefore, we decided to spin off from being a committee of AP–LS. We sent AP–LS our report and resigned en masse as a committee, but most of us retained our personal membership in it. We reconstituted as a self-created independent board to which the AP–LS president would have a liaison role.

We elected officers at this second historic meeting in 1977. I was president; Hirsch Silverman, vice-president; David Shapiro, secretary; and Martin Kurke, treasurer. As a follow-up to our second meeting, Marty, Paul, and I drafted the first set of bylaws. We thought that we should have independent legal counsel to handle the incorporation and to double check the bylaws. With the board's approval, I asked Richard Bazelon, who had become a member of the forensic section at Hahnemann, to serve in this capacity. He was well respected in mental health law circles, a member of the University of Pennsylvania Law School faculty, and the Bazelon name was held in high esteem. He was easy to work with and was pleased to be asked. With our incorporation, we became a viable corporate entity (Kaslow, 2000).

I remember long nights of sitting up organizing, writing, and typing up what was to constitute the credentialing process, the guidelines for work samples, and the basic bibliography. In the next stage, various board members contributed to the initial core knowledge document. We decided that at the diplomate level individuals should have a solid knowledge of the core areas, not just of a narrow spectrum, and spent countless hours hammering away at what should be included as core. We overspent our meager funds. I contributed thousands of dollars out of my personal account to keep the board afloat until examination fees began coming in.

## STANDARDS AND EXAMINATIONS

We agreed that our standards should be set very high, and there should be no exceptions. No one would be grandfathered. This was the advice of Hirsch Silverman, who was already board certified in clinical psychology and had been one of the psychologists involved in the infamous Boston Strangler trial in 1967. From the first, we agreed everyone would have to pass all three stages of the ABPP process: credentials review, work sample review, and the oral examination. We knew that we wanted to affiliate with ABPP as soon as possible. We were also aware that rigor in our standards would mean that we would not have to undo what had already been accomplished.

Hirsch carefully instructed us on the requisite format for the conduct of exams. The board decided that I should be the first one examined when we were ready in 1978. Hirsch chaired the exam with the other five board members comprising my committee. Since one of my work samples was on the teaching of forensic psychology, which I was doing at Hahnemann, I was interrogated on just about every item on the syllabus. I was awarded certificate #001 and hung it proudly in my office (certificate numbers changed when we became an official ABPP board).

All of the other board members were examined by three- or four-person committees; we were very demanding of each other. Next, we decided that it was imperative that we not be just an East Coast organization and that it was time to go national. I recommended Arthur Bodin and David Rosenhan, stars in the forensic firmament whom I knew and who were both active in forensic psychology work in California. They were approached and accepted, and this brought us up to our full contingent of nine members.

Soon we shifted to comply with our new bylaws, and when vacancies occurred, any diplomate could nominate a possible board member. In 1978 we began to publicize the existence of ABFP and our diplomating process. To our surprise and pleasure, mixed with some dismay, some of the first applications came from very well-known psychologists who already held other diplomates and had fine reputations. It quickly became obvious that we had identified a need in the larger field. Some of the work samples reflected aspects of the field we had not included in our original core knowledge document. Each month we learned that the broad umbrella phrase *forensic psychology* subsumed much more than our early vision encompassed. We revised and expanded the document accordingly.

As we formed the first dozen-and-a-half committees, we read avidly to augment our own knowledge base to be well-informed examiners. After the original first seven exams, everyone serving on an examining committee had to be a diplomate. Thus, we all put many hours into reviewing credentials and work samples and in serving on exam committees until the pool of qualified examiners increased.

I served as liaison to the ABPP Board of Trustees. Melvin Gravitz was then ABPP board president and was responsive to our needs, encouraging us in our undertaking. The linkages set up at that time helped create a basis for our later affiliation with ABPP.

Dr. Gravitz became one of the early applicants for certification in forensic psychology. I read diligently about forensic hypnosis, the subject of his work sample, to be a well-informed examiner, as did the other committee members. Other APA notables including Ted Blau, Gary VandenBos, Pat DeLeon, and Stephen Morse also took and passed the exam early on. They were positively impressed with what we were doing and with our diplomating process. Several of them later became involved as board members. Ted Blau, an APA recent past president and a diplomate in clinical psychology, quickly became an involved, influential, and valued board member and was especially helpful in a guiding role. Dr. VandenBos became the APA liaison to ABFP for a few years.

To publicize our existence, we began making presentations at the Eastern Psychological Association and other regional and state meetings. Board members and other diplomates wrote articles describing the concerns that ABFP was established to address, like the need for recognition of forensics as a specialty area of psychology (Kaslow & Abrams, 1976; Kurke, 1980, Kaslow, 1989) and books on the role of the forensic psychologist (Cooke, 1980). These efforts led to an increase in the flow of diplomate applications.

## THE AMERICAN ACADEMY OF FORENSIC PSYCHOLOGY

In the late 1970s, APA had asked different groups to work on specialty guidelines for practice in their arena. Paul Lipsitt and I drew up and submitted the first specialty guidelines for the practice of forensic psychology. We truly felt that we were accomplishing a great deal.

Since some of the early diplomates wanted to be involved with ABFP beyond the time when they received the board's imprimatur, I suggested we establish the AAFP as our membership, continuing education, and fundraising arm. It was formed in 1978. I was elected first president of the AAFP. Since then, these two boards have remained separate, yet collaborative, an arrangement that has evolved favorably for both—with the Academy running very successful workshops in forensic topics several times a year and fulfilling both their educational and fund raising missions to advance the field of forensic psychology.

Our first award for distinguished contribution to forensic psychology was given to Margaret Ives in 1980 at the APA convention in Montreal at the first meeting of ABFP. Ives was then executive director of ABPP and had encouraged us from the very start. She had a long-standing interest in forensics and had been the expert witness in the precedent-setting *Jenkins* decision already mentioned (*Jenkins v. U.S.*, 1961; Kaslow, 2000).

In 1985, the Academy initiated an annual award, the Distinguished Contribution to Forensic Psychology award, to recognize outstanding contributions. In addition, it decided to award dissertation grants annually to doctoral students proposing meritorious studies. In 1995, shortly after the tragic death of Saleem Shah in an auto accident, the Saleem Shah Award for Early Career Excellence in Psychology and Law was established, in conjunction with AP–LS.

The AAFP workshop series that has become the model for successful Academy continuing education efforts was initially chaired by Arthur Bodin, then by David Shaprio, followed by Curtis Barrett. Alan Goldstein took over as chairperson for many years, followed by Randy Otto. These intense workshops essentially provide a major avenue for specialization in forensic psychology. Presented several times a year, these remarkable programs offer training in a broad range of forensic areas, including the intersections of psychology with civil, criminal, mental health, and family law.

## WHAT IT WAS LIKE PERSONALLY

Those first three or four years when I was at the helm were a heady time of good esprit de corps, high energy, much mutual affection, and great productivity. We took many risks and usually succeeded. The next chapter in the story belongs to my successors: David Rosenhan, Robert Howell, Newton "Bud" Jackson, Herbert Weissman, Melvin Rudov, and others who followed. In retrospect, I am proud to have been the "birth mother" of ABFP and AAFP.

To those who helped create the ABFP, I have deep gratitude for their cooperation and belief in our joint venture and for always being there when needed from the very beginning. Their vigorous intellectual perspectives and their extensive backgrounds enabled us to expand our horizons and to become a national rather than an East Coast organization. Gerry Cooke, Bob Strochak, and Bud Jackson, and other early diplomates also generously gave of their time on numerous committees—I don't know how we could have managed without their excellent input. Many people made themselves available to serve on examining committees and shared in this ambitious enterprise energetically. We also acknowledge the excellent input of our legal counsel Richard Bazelon and his colleagues for steering us through the legal incorporation process and seeing that everything was set up properly.

I appreciated the honor and privilege of being elected first president of both the Board and the Academy and the opportunity to serve with fellow forensic psychologists in creating this board and doing the work it entailed in the formative years. It was often an almost overwhelming task, the magnitude of which none of us comprehended in advance. It was a challenging and rewarding experience. I tried to pilot us through the critical formative years with as much tact, energy, courage, diligence, and humor as I could. The greatest unanticipated byproduct was the very special friendships and collegial relationships we formed; it was the most "loving" and cohesive board I have ever served on. I shall treasure the rich friendships almost as much as my diploma and the continuity of the Board. (Kaslow, 1980).

In 1984 Herb Weismann and Paul Lipsitt, president and vice-president of ABFP, respectively, were invited to meet with the ABPP Board in St. Louis (they later called it the Spirit of St. Louis). There they were queried about our bylaws and examination process. ABFP was accepted as meeting the high standards of ABPP. Our careful preparation toward this goal paid off. In 1985 ABPP accepted our application to become its sixth approved specialty board, and ABFP has remained in good standing and an active member board of the ABPP Board of Trustees since being recognized. All of our diplomates were approved and their board certifications were converted by ABPP, which is what we had originally intended. After we were invited to join ABPP, Paul Lipsitt, then the president of ABFP, and Paul King, ABPP president, formalized in the signing of a document our official designation as an ABPP specialty. Dr. Lipsitt was elected to the ABPP board as the first forensic psychology representative (Personal communication, P. Lipsitt, June 22, 2017).

ABFP has a dignified heritage and many accomplishments to its credit. I believe its mission should continue to expand in the next decades as the role of forensic psychologists continues to increase in many realms of our society.

## REFERENCES

American Board of Professional Psychology. (n.d.). Academic history. Retrieved from https://www.abpp.org/i4a/pages/index.cfm?pageID=3909

Cooke, G. (1980). *The role of the forensic psychologist.* Springfield, IL: Thomas.

*Jenkins v. United States*, 307F.2d 631, 651—652 (DC Circuit 1961).

Kaslow, F. (1976). Forensic psychology: An evolving subspecialty at Hahnemann Medical College. *Professional Psychology, 11,* 72–77.

Kaslow, F. (1980). Perspective from the president. *Bulletin of the American Academy of Forensic Psychologists, 1,* 1.

Kaslow, F. (1989). Early history of the American Board of Forensic Psychology: A retropective account. *Forensic Reports, 2,* 206–311.

Kaslow, F. W. (2000). Preparation for forensic family therapy practice. In F. W. Kaslow (Ed.), *Handbook of couple and family forensics: A sourcebook for mental health and legal professionals.* New York: Wiley.

Kaslow, F., & Abrams, J. C. (1976). Forensic psychology and criminal justice: An evolving subspecialty at Hahnemann Medical College. *Professional Psychology, 7,* 445–452.

Kurke, M. I. (1980). Forensic psychology: A threat and a response. *Professional Psychology, 11,* 72–77.

Sutherland, A., & Leathrman, S. (2006). Does certification improve medical standards? *BJM, 333,* 439–441.

# 13

# Community Psychology, Public Policy, and Children

N. DICKON REPPUCCI

Fifty years ago, the field of clinical psychology was dominated by psychoanalytic theory with its focus on the individual and "intra-psychic supremacy." There was little or no emphasis on social context. Several social events of the 1950s and 1960s—for example, the 1954 Supreme Court desegregation case, President Kennedy's 1963 message to Congress on the need for a focus on community mental health and President Johnson's War on Poverty (Sarason, 1974, pp. 22–23)—began to have a major impact on some clinical psychologists. Among them were Jim Kelly, Ira Iscoe, Emory Cowen, and Seymour Sarason, who had become aware of the need to think in terms of person and environment fit.

Several of these psychologists gathered in Swampscott, Massachusetts, in 1965 and produced documents that led to the formal creation of the field of community psychology (Bennett et al., 1966). The most essential goal was to develop an activist prevention-oriented psychology that could deliver services in the community. The predominant societal events of the

1960s and 1970s were the civil rights movement and the ever-expanding involvement in the Vietnam War that brought rage and violence to our cities. I became a psychologist during this era.

Fifteen years ago, I wrote a chapter (Reppucci, 2004) titled "The Accidental Community Psychologist" for a book edited by James Kelly and Anna Song (Kelly & Song, 2004). They had asked a few of us to use personal biography as a mechanism for understanding how each of us became involved with the field of community psychology that literally did not exist when I had entered graduate school. The editors of the current volume have made a similar request. My assignment is to focus on the early rise of community psychology research, how my own research at the time sought to change juvenile corrections by providing an alternative focus to intervening with adolescents, and how these endeavors led to an increased effort to influence public and legal policy regarding youth.

## DISCOVERING A COMMUNITY PSYCHOLOGY APPROACH

In September 1968, I arrived as an assistant professor at the Yale University Psychology Department. I had just completed a PhD in clinical psychology from Harvard's interdisciplinary Social Relations Department (now defunct) for which my dissertation topic, supervised by developmental psychologist Jerome Kagan, was *Antecedents of Conceptual Tempo in the Two-Year-Old Child.* (Reppucci, 1968). This research (Reppucci, 1970, 1971) provided me with a focus on development and the importance of longitudinal research. I had completed a clinical internship in 1965–1966 at the Palo Alto Veterans Administration Hospital where I mainly treated young Vietnam War casualties, first on an open ward and then on the maximum security ward for "dangerous patients" that had been the inspiration for Ken Kesey's 1962 novel, *One Flew Over the Cuckoo's Nest.* Although the usual expectation is that an assistant professor's dissertation will be a launching pad for his research agenda, I had not been hired at Yale with such an expectation. Rather I planned to pursue teaching and research on behavioral interventions and psychopathology with an emphasis on adolescents. However, as a result of interviewing with Seymour Sarason, I also became excited about an involvement at his university-based, community-oriented Psycho-Educational Clinic.

Sarason's clinic was vastly different from other clinical psychology venues of the time as it had an ecological emphasis on psychology in community settings (see Sarason, Levine, Goldenberg, Cherlin, & Bennett, 1966), not on one-to-one psychotherapy. It was based on a culture of exploration into the mores and organizational regularities of helping settings in our society, with the goal of understanding these regularities to bring about changes in their policies and actions. In fact, my enthusiasm for accepting the job was to work with Seymour and to be centered in learning about and using this new community perspective to inform applied endeavors. Thus, at Seymour's behest, although unprepared, I had readily agreed to become a school consultant to a high school in a local working-class suburb of New Haven that had contracted with the clinic for services. Seymour also suggested (in the form of an "offer I could not refuse") that I consult with one of the town's elementary schools.

Both were stretches in terms of my background, although the high school less so because I had some experience working with troubled adolescents and young adults; in comparison, the last time I had been involved with elementary school children was when I was one myself. My anxieties were high and only slightly alleviated when Seymour said, "Don't worry. You will figure out what to do once you are in the settings! Just read our book!" (see Sarason et al., 1966).

My academic teaching assignments were uncomfortable in other ways. My graduate school background prepared me to teach psychopathology, but upon arriving I learned that a senior faculty member was teaching the psychopathology courses. Thus, I ended up teaching seminars on both adolescence and behavior modification, heavily influenced by Albert Bandura's social learning theories (Bandura, 1969), as well as co-teaching with Seymour a seminar on community psychology, about which I knew little. I was overwhelmed with new explorations and preparations, but at that time I did not know where my teaching of adolescence and community psychology would lead me.

Every Friday morning, Seymour masterfully orchestrated a weekly two-hour, freewheeling seminar for all affiliated Clinic faculty and graduate students. Topics focused on preventive interventions in helping institutions (e.g., centers for persons with mental retardation and public schools) with the goal of changing them in ways that would enhance the lives of individual kids, staff members, and teachers. The implications of current societal issues, such as racism and urban violence, usually neglected by psychologists at that time, were also a focal point.

These discussions were some of the most exciting intellectual experiences of my life. Seminar leaders ranged from Clinic faculty (e.g., Ira Goldenberg, Ed Trickett, and Seymour) and graduate students to invited guests. For example, Warren Bennis, the president of the University of Buffalo (Sarason, 1988), was asked by Seymour "to tell it exactly like it is" from an administrator's perspective, while Commissioner Ellis MacDougall discussed his plans and policies for the newly established Connecticut Department of Corrections. Our goal was to learn how these settings actually operated (Sarason, 1972) and, with this understanding, to determine what, if anything, psychologists could do regarding the creation and change of these settings and the communities in which they existed.

One of these seminars provided the initial impetus for me to focus on psychology's potential to improve juvenile justice and led me to engage in much of the research that I have pursued over the past five decades. Specifically, the aforementioned Commissioner MacDougall asked if any of us would join with him and his staff to help develop a new system of corrections. I took the request seriously and, at the end of his talk, volunteered my services. He seemed pleased but immediately turned me over to the person who had accompanied him to the Clinic meeting, Dr. Charles Dean, his Director of Research and Development. Dean was a PhD sociologist, who had left a university faculty position to gain a first-hand appreciation for why the changes being advocated by academics were so often not being implemented or, if implemented, failed to deliver the promised positive changes in the "real world" of corrections. Over the next six years,

Dean and I became collaborators and worked closely together on several projects.

## DISCOVERING PSYCHOLOGY'S POTENTIAL FOR JUVENILE JUSTICE

To appreciate psychology's potential for intervening in and improving juvenile justice, a brief historical overview of the system and the programs that were being practiced at the time provides a social context. The initial juvenile court began in Illinois in 1899 as a result of social reformers lobbying for legislation to create an entity with rehabilitative intent rather than punishment and was rapidly emulated in most states (Levine & Levine, 1970). The goal was individualized justice using the indeterminant sentence and parole as vehicles for rehabilitation. Born in optimism, the juvenile court espoused a medical model that would bring psychiatry and law together by means of court-connected child guidance clinics. For the next 60 years or so, the courts were largely deemed a success. However, by the second half of the century, the court was widely viewed as having slipped back to punishment as its primary goal. As Justice Fortas stated in *Kent v. U.S.* (1966): "The child receives the worst of both worlds; that he gets neither the protections accorded to adults nor the solicitous care and regenerative treatment postulated for children." In the following year, the landmark *In re Gault* (1967) decision altered the legal landscape for youth by granting them several due process rights and ushering in the children's rights movement. With recidivism rates hovering around 60% to 70%, the failure of juvenile justice was widely recognized.

Correctional treatment programs fell roughly into three major categories: (a) the guided group interaction tradition that focused on peer group dynamics (e.g., positive peer culture; Dean & Reppucci, 1974; Empey & Erickson, 1972); (b) the community approach as seen in the correctional halfway house movement (Keller & Alper, 1970) and the California Youth Authority Community Treatment Project (e.g., Warren, 1969); and (c) the behavior modification approach with its emphasis on overt behaviors and the systematic manipulation of the environment to change these behaviors (Cohen & Filipczak, 1971; U.S. Bureau of Prisons, 1970). Unfortunately, even the sparse data presented to back up the claims of success made by correctional administrators of the few evaluated programs were relatively inconclusive (Dean & Reppucci, 1974). The situation in juvenile corrections had become so bad that the most-watched intervention was the approach taken by Jerome Miller, the commissioner of Juvenile Corrections in Massachusetts, who systematically closed down and eliminated these institutions as the only way to reform them (Bakal, 1973).

When I look back on my projects with Dean, I am struck by how naïve I was about how settings actually function and how certain parameters exist even before an organizational setting opens its doors (Sarason, 1972). The first collaborative venture that we pursued was focused on creating a therapeutic setting for adolescent delinquents that would facilitate reintegration with their families. The fact that the new facility was located on top of a mountain, miles from the population centers from which the vast majority of the boys had come, was ignored, even though our central goal was reintegration of the boys to their local communities and families. Suffice it to say that the paper we published on that intervention was titled: "We Bombed in Mountview" (Reppucci, Sarata, Saunders, McArthur, & Michlin, 1973). We did in fact learn a lot but were unsuccessful in establishing the therapeutic setting that was our goal. Not only did several structural features (e.g., distance and isolation) negate the goal of change and reintegration, but also using individual therapy as the change method was doomed from the start. As one youth put it: "I'd rather be bad than mad!" And for many of these inner-city youth, being arrested and sentenced to time in a juvenile correctional facility was a typical rite of passage, and therefore not the "big thing" that it tended to be for the few middle-class kids in the facility.

The next project involved conducting groups at a reformatory for incarcerated male youth between the ages of 17 and 21 who had been convicted of drug crimes. Verne McArthur's doctoral dissertation, which was published as the book *Coming Out Cold* (McArthur, 1974), evolved from this endeavor. It described the transition of youth from the reformatory back into the community. Again, we learned a lot about process and pitfalls, especially about youth and substance abuse, but were unable to facilitate a more positive transition to the community.

Then, an event in the spring of 1970 forever changed my life and those working with me. In the wake of a shooting incident at the Connecticut School for Boys (CSB), Dean was asked to become its superintendent to facilitate significant institutional change. The CSB was the sole state facility for adjudicated juveniles between the ages of 12 and 16 years. It had been in operation for more than 100 years but had recently been placed under the auspices of a newly created Department of Children and Youth Services. Dean met with Seymour and me to discuss whether he should accept the position. We agreed that this assignment would be exciting but unpredictable. Nevertheless, we encouraged Dean to accept the offer and promised that, if he did, we would work closely with him for the foreseeable future. As it turned out, Seymour was not able to stay the course other than as a sounding board, but I and several graduate students (Terry Saunders, Brian Sarata, Leland Wilkinson) became active participants, with most of us spending a minimum of a day a week at the facility for the next four years.

Unlike other projects at the time, our focus was not to change the behavior of the boys alone but rather to change the institutional culture of the CSB from punishment to rehabilitation while simultaneously reducing the number of boys incarcerated (approximately 200 in eight residential cottages when the intervention started). This change effort was to be accomplished using current staff with little or no increased financial resources, because the goal was to develop a system that could last after the Yale consultants and Dean were gone and could be a model for other financially strapped institutions.

After extensive input from multiple staff focus groups (Sarason, 1974), a quasi-experimental, longitudinal design was implemented. Two cottages were designated to implement a social learning system that included many organizational changes and the development of a behavioral system with clear and consistent guidelines for both staff and youth. Boys admitted to these units were not hand-picked as less aggressive. The goal was to focus on these experimental units first and then gradually convert the entire institution within a few years. This change strategy also allowed for a systematic evaluation of experimental and control groups of both staff and residents.

At the end of three years (see Dean & Reppucci, 1974; Reppucci, Dean, & Saunders, 1975; Reppucci & Saunders, 1982; Wilkinson & Reppucci, 1973), we considered the project successful. Staff job satisfaction and perceived social climate were not different in the social-learning and nonsocial learning cottages at the onset (Time 1). Significant positive increases appeared only in the social learning cottages at Time 2, and increases then appeared in the nonsocial learning cottages at Time 3 after they had been converted to a social learning approach. For youth, measures of social climate were more positive over time, and recidivism rates were decreased for the social learning cottages in contrast to youth in the nonsocial learning cottages. Likewise, for social learning cottage staff, both social climate and job satisfaction measures increased and absenteeism decreased as compared to the nonsocial learning cottage staff. Perhaps most important, the average length of stay at the CSB for youth had been cut in half.

A subsequent integration of the CSB and the equivalent girls' facility provided more learning experiences for me because Dean became the superintendent for the newly combined institution. Shortly thereafter, he asked me to assume the part-time position of Director of Clinical Services. Thus, for a year, along with being a full-time Yale faculty member, I oversaw the clinical services department until a qualified person was trained in the social learning program.

The bottom line is that this project (e.g., Reppucci, 1973; Reppucci & Saunders, 1974) established my credentials as a community psychologist with an expertise in institutional change, consultation, juvenile justice, and behavior modification in natural settings. In addition, I realized how much I did not know about the law as a framework for the operation of such facilities. This realization was crystalized by a judge in a small town explicitly sending one of our released boys back to the CSB. Even though the boy had not committed a new offense, the judge ordered that the boy not be released for at least a year. Such an order meant the treatment system itself could not function properly as the entire social learning program was called into question. It also was an explicit stimulus for my intensive involvement in the study of children, law, and public policy.

## INTEGRATING COMMUNITY PSYCHOLOGY AND LAW

I have been a professor in the Psychology Department at the University of Virginia since 1976. As part of my being hired as Director of Clinical Training, I negotiated the establishment of a freestanding community psychology program that would focus on research and intervention linked to community and policy change in human service settings, especially those providing services to children, youth, and families. Moreover, I was lucky that a former Yale undergraduate student, Edward Mulvey, whose senior thesis I had supervised and who had worked at the CSB after graduation, decided to join me as a graduate student in this new program. I promised Ed an experience that would facilitate his becoming an expert in developmental and community psychology with a focus on law and kids. Ed, a born risk-taker, accepted the challenge. Our partnership worked, and by the time Ed earned his PhD six years later, there was a coterie of community and clinical graduate students interested in studying law and youth. I emphasize this because my impact on law and psychology has in large part been the result of these collaborations with graduate students, many of whom are now leaders in the field.

During my first eight years at Virginia, my growth in law and public policy was greatly increased by my involvement in Law Professor Richard Bonnie's Institute of Law, Psychiatry and Public Policy and my interaction with John Monahan and Elizabeth Scott who joined the Institute's faculty during that time. Over the years, Scott and I have collaborated on numerous projects related to law and children (e.g., Scott, Reppucci, & Aber, 1988; Scott, Reppucci, Antonishak, & DeGennaro, 2006; Scott, Reppucci, & Woolard, 1995). I also chaired an American Psychological Association (APA) Task Force on Public Policy from 1980 to 1984 to explore the use of psychological research in the service of public and legal policy initiatives, an activity that was not commonly encouraged in that era. The report of that Task Force (1984, 1986), as well as an invited APA G. Stanley Hall Lecture entitled "Psychology in the Public Interest" (Reppucci, 1985), encouraged such activities as important to psychology and society and cemented my commitment to such endeavors. In addition, being a member of Saleem Shah's National Institute of Mental Health Grant Review Committee on Violence and Aggression in the early 1980s provided me with an appreciation of how little developmental and clinical psychological research was being done in juvenile justice and the law and an opportunity to interact with leading researchers from a number of disciplines (e.g., Tom Grisso, Stan Brodsky, Delbert Eliot, Malcolm Klein, Loren Roth) who greatly broadened my perspective.

At about this same time, my colleagues and I (Reppucci, Weithorn, Mulvey, & Monahan, 1984) provided a series of integrative, critical summaries of several of the most salient issues that link mental health, law and children in the family, the healthcare system, the juvenile justice system, and the educational system. This edited book was meant as an initial step to explicate several areas where a marriage of legal principles and social science was beginning to come together. At the time, no such volume existed. In the first chapter, we (Mulvey, Reppucci, & Weithorn, 1984) provided a general framework of the parent–child–state triad that was familiar to legal scholars but not psychologists. What became most evident from this work was the need to attend to the complex web of interests between state, parent, and child in public policies for children and families. For the past four decades, my students and I have used this framework to study multiple issues of importance to psychologists and attorneys invested in children and youth, always keeping in mind that for research to be meaningful to the law, psychologists must formulate and conceptualize questions that are directly relevant to the law.

Just as we were finishing that book, earlier work I had done on child abuse and neglect (e.g., Rosenberg & Reppucci, 1983, 1985) re-engaged my attention as I became focused on the issue of child sexual abuse. In 1983, the McMartin Day Care Sexual Abuse Case in Los Angeles made the headlines of every newspaper and news magazine in the country. The day care owners and the teachers were all charged with committing sexual acts with their young charges. Although the resulting investigation and trial lasted for several years, it ended in the exoneration of all alleged perpetrators. One critical reason for dismissal of charges was that mental health professionals who conducted the assessment interviews with the children and the accused adults often used inappropriate techniques such as leading questions that made much of the information obtained unusable in court. Clearly, the assessments would have been conducted differently if only the psychologists had understood the legal framework in which they were operating. This realization was the final powerful stimulus that my future research and teaching should focus on the interface between law, psychology, and children.

At approximately this same time, I became aware that there was no serious overview of what psychologists knew and did not know about the sexual abuse of children. Robert Cohen, the director of the Virginia Treatment Center for Children, provided funds for me to compile a comprehensive report on the topic that the Center could distribute to the clinicians of Virginia to use for training, practice, and prevention. Jeffrey Haugaard, a graduate student in my research laboratory, and I produced the requested report and subsequently expanded it into a book, *The Sexual Abuse of Children* (Haugaard & Reppucci, 1988), and an *American Psychologist* article, "Sexual Abuse of Children: Myth or Reality" (Reppucci & Haugaard, 1989). Both of these publications received widespread readership.

During this same period, the result of the McMartin trial and a controversial developmental question ("Do children lie?") led Haugaard and me to begin exploring children's lying about their sexual abuse in legal contexts. The controversy had gained widespread attention with two opposing psychological groups, one led by Gail Goodman (children never lie in abuse situations) and the other by Steven Ceci (children do lie some of the time), embarking on numerous research endeavors to answer the question (Haugaard & Reppucci, 1992). Haugaard's (1990) doctoral dissertation, *Children's Definitions of the Truth and Their Competence as Witnesses in Legal Proceedings*, was a first attempt to study the potential impact of parental figures on influencing children's testimony (Haugaard, Reppucci, Laird, & Nauful, 1991). The nature of this controversy increased the attention on the linkage of psychology, law, and children and helped draw more students into the field.

## THE FUTURE OF COMMUNITY PSYCHOLOGY, CHILDREN, AND THE LAW

In summary, my training in the interdisciplinary Social Relations Department in the 1960s and my newly found identity as a community psychologist in the 1970s at the Psycho-Educational Clinic coalesced in the 1980s. My overriding goal was to develop a coalition of child–psychology–law researchers who could provide a more empirical basis for legal and social policy. The most important impact I have had on the field of psychology and law has been through the integrative work of several of my former graduate students (e.g., Ed Mulvey, Jeffrey Haugaard, Preston Britner, Sharon Portwood, Jennifer Woolard, Sarah Cook, Candice Odgers, Carrie Fried Mulford, Preeti Chauhan, Barbara Oudekerk) who have used the lens of community, clinical, and developmental psychology to advance public policy. Over the past 40 years, numerous psychologists have pursued this goal, both in their research and their training. Many psychology and law training programs now exist and are the source of new researchers who continue to provide insights based on empirical data and theory that should lead to more positive settings and policies for youth and families.

Finally, I am happy to report that the field of psychology and law has blossomed, specifically in regard to children. A great many psychologists and lawyers are now pursuing research and action projects in this area (for reviews, see Bottoms, Reppucci, Tweed, & Nysse-Carris, 2002; Owen-Kostelnik, Reppucci, & Meyer, 2006; Scott & Steinberg, 2008). The increase in juvenile justice research, especially around culpability and children's decision-making in legal contexts, received a tremendous boost in the mid-1990s from the creation of the MacArthur Foundation's Research Network on Adolescent Development and Juvenile Justice. Its large-scale efforts have focused on children's competence to stand trial (Grisso et al., 2003), its longitudinal study of youths' delinquency trajectories (Mulvey, 2011), and its numerous studies of fundamental psychological differences between youth and adults (e.g., Scott & Steinberg, 2008; Steinberg & Cauffman, 1996). In addition, research on psychology, law, and children has expanded greatly in the civil issues arena, especially around decision-making capabilities relating to medical, educational, and family issues. The field is vibrant, creative, and exciting, and there is every indication that it will remain so for the foreseeable future.

## REFERENCES

American Psychological Association Task Force on Psychology and Public Policy. (1984). *The final report of the APA Task Force on Psychology and Public Policy.* Washington, DC: American Psychological Association

American Psychological Association Task Force on Psychology and Public Policy. (1986). Psychology and public policy. *American Psychologist, 46,* 914–921.

Bakal, Y. (1973). *Closing correctional institutions.* Lexington, MA: D.C. Heath.

Bandura, A. (1969). *Principles of behavior modification.* New York: Holt, Rinehart & Winston.

Bennett, C., Anderson, L., Cooper, S., Hassol, D., Klein, D., & Rosenblum, G. (1966). *Community psychology: A report of the Boston Conference on the Education of Psychologists in Community Mental health.* Boston: Boston University.

Bottoms, B., Reppucci, N. D., Tweed, J., & Nysse-Carris, K. (2002). Children, psychology and the law: Reflections on past and future contributions to science and policy. In J. Ogloff (Ed.), *Taking psychology and law into the twenty-first century* (pp. 61–117). New York: Kluwer Academic/Plenum.

Cohen, H., & Filipczak, J. (1971). *A new learning environment.* San Francisco: Jossey-Bass.

Dean, C., & Reppucci, N. D. (1974). Juvenile correctional institutions. In D. Glaser (Ed.), *The handbook of criminology* (pp. 865–895). Chicago: Rand McNally,

Empey, L., & Erickson, M. (1972). *The Provo Experiment.* Lexington, MA: D.C. Heath.

Grisso, T., Steinberg, L., Woolard, J., Cauffman, E., Scott, E., Graham, S. . . . Schwartz, R. (2003). Juveniles' competence to stand trial: A comparison of adolescents' and adults' capacities as trial defendants. *Law and Human Behavior, 27,* 333–364.

Haugaard, J. (1990). *Children's definitions of the truth and their competency as witnesses in legal proceedings.* Unpublished doctoral dissertation, University of Virginia.

Haugaard, J., & Reppucci, N. D. (1988). *The sexual abuse of children: A comprehensive guide to current knowledge and intervention strategies.* San Francisco: Jossey-Bass.

Haugaard, J., & Reppucci, N. D. (1992). Children and the truth. In S. Ceci, M. DeSimone Leitchtman, & M. Putnick (Eds.), *Social and cognitive factors in early deception* (pp. 29–46). New York: Erlbaum.

Haugaard, J., Reppucci, N. D., Laird, J., & Nauful, T. (1991). Children's definitions of the truth and their competency as witnesses in legal proceedings. *Law and Human Behavior, 15*, 253–272.

*In re Gault*, 387 U.S. 1 (1967).

Keller, O., & Alper, B. (1970). *Halfway houses: Community-centered correction and treatment*. Lexington, MA: D.C. Heath.

Kelly, J., & Song, A. (Eds.). *Six psychologists tell their stories*. Binghamton, NY: Haworth.

*Kent v. U.S.*, 383 U.S. 541 (1966).

Kesey, K. (1962). *One flew over the cuckoo's nest*. New York: Viking.

Levine, M., & Levine, A. (1970). *Social history of helping services.* New York: Appleton-Century-Crofts.

McArthur, A. V. (1974) *Coming out cold: Community reentry from a state reformatory.* Lexington, MA: D.C. Heath.

Mulvey, E. (2011). *Highlights from Pathways to Desistance: A longitudinal study of serious adolescent offenders.* Washington, DC: U.S. Department of Justice, Office of Justice Programs, Office of Juvenile Justice and Delinquency Prevention.

Mulvey, E., Reppucci, N. D., & Weithorn, L. (1984). Mental health, law, and children. In N. D. Reppucci, L. Weithorn, E. Mulvey, & J. Monahan (Eds.), *Children, mental health and the law* (pp. 15–24). Beverly Hills, CA: Sage.

Owen-Kostelnik, J., Reppucci, N. D., & Meyer, J. (2006). Testimony and interrogation of minors: Assumptions of maturity and immorality, *American Psychologist, 61*, 286–304.

Reppucci, N. D. (1968). *Antecedents of conceptual tempo in two-year old children.* Unpublished doctoral dissertation, Harvard University.

Reppucci, N. D. (1970). Individual differences in the consideration of information among two-year old children. *Developmental Psychology, 2*, 240–246.

Reppucci, N. D. (1971). Parental education, sex differences, and performance on cognitive tasks among two-year old children. *Developmental Psychology, 4*, 19–23.

Reppucci, N. D. (1973). The social psychology of institutional change: General principles for intervention. *American Journal of Community Psychology, 1*, 330–341.

Reppucci, N. D. (1985). Psychology in the public interest. In A. Rogers & C. Scheier (Eds.), *The G. Stanley Hall Lecture Series*. Vol. 5. Washington, DC: American Psychological Association.

Reppucci, N. D. (2004). An accidental community psychologist. In J. Kelly & A. Song (Eds.), *Six psychologists tell their stories* (pp. 41–62). Binghamton, NY: Haworth.

Reppucci, N. D., Dean, C., & Saunders, J. T. (1975). Job design variables as change measures in a correctional facility. *American Journal of Community Psychology, 3*, 315–325.

Reppucci, N. D., & Haugaard, J. (1989). The prevention of child sexual abuse: Myth or reality. *American Psychologist, 44*, 1266–1274.

Reppucci, N. D., Sarata, B., Saunders, J. T., McArthur, A. V., & Michlin, L. (1973). We bombed in Mountville: Lessons learned in consultation to a correctional institution for adolescent offenders. In I. I. Goldenberg (Ed.), *The helping professions in the world of action* (pp. 145–164). Lexington, MA: D.C. Heath.

Reppucci, N. D., & Saunders, J. T. (1974). The social psychology of behavior modification: Problems of implementation in natural settings. *American Psychologist, 29*, 649–660.

Reppucci, N. D., & Saunders, J. T. (1982). Measures of staff morale and organizational environment as indicators of program change in an institution for youthful offenders. In A. Jeger & R. Slotnick (Eds.), *Community mental health and behavioral ecology: A handbook of theory, research and practice* (pp. 171–186). New York: Plenum.

Reppucci, N. D., Weithorn, L., Mulvey, E., & Monahan, J. (1984). *Children, mental health and the law.* Beverly Hills, CA: Sage.

Rosenberg, M., & Reppucci, N. D. (1983). Abusive mothers: Perceptions of their own and their children's behavior. *Journal of Consulting and clinical Psychology, 51,* 674–682.

Rosenberg, M., & Reppucci, N. D. (1985). Primary prevention of child abuse. *Journal of Consulting and Clinical Psychology, 53,* 576–585.

Sarason, S. B. (1972). *The creation of settings and the future societies.* San Francisco: Jossey-Bass.

Sarason, S. B. (1974). *The psychological sense of community: Prospects for a community psychology.* San Francisco: Jossey-Bass.

Sarason, S. B. (1988). *The making of an American psychologist: An autobiography.* San Francisco: Jossey-Bass.

Sarason, S. B., Levine, M., Goldenberg, I., Cherlin, D., & Bennett, E. (1966). *Psychology in community settings: Clinical, educational, vocational, social aspects.* New York: Wiley.

Scott, E., Reppucci, N. D., & Aber, M. (1988). The role of the child's preference in custody proceedings. *Georgia Law Review, 22,* 1035–1078.

Scott, E., Reppucci, N. D., Antonishak, J., & DeGennaro, J. (2006). Public attitudes about the culpability and punishment of young offenders. *Behavioral Sciences and the Law, 24,* 815–832.

Scott, E., Reppucci, N. D., & Wollard, J. (1995). Evaluating adolescent decision making in legal contexts. *Law and Human Behavior, 19,* 221–244.

Scott, E., & Steinberg, L. (2008). *Rethinking juvenile justice.* Cambridge, MA: Harvard University Press.

Steinberg, L., & Cauffman, E. (1996). Maturity of judgment in adolescence: Psychological factors in adolescent decision-making. *Law and Human Behavior. 20,* 249–272.

U.S. Bureau of Prisons. (1970). *Differential treatment: —A way to begin.* Washington, DC: U.S. Department of Justice.

Warren, M. (1969). The case for differential treatment of delinquents. *Annals of the American Academy of Political and Social Science, 381,* 47–59.

Wilkinson, L., & Reppucci, N. D. (1973). Perceptions of social climate among participants in token economy and non-token economy cottages in a juvenile correctional institution. *American Journal of Community Psychology, 1,* 36–43.

THOMAS GRISSO AND STANLEY L. BRODSKY

Epilogue or overture? Every ending is a beginning. Every event shapes our future. So it is with this book, with the anniversary of the Society that it commemorates, and with the roots of the field of psychology and law that it describes and celebrates.

As editors, we have been changed by working with the chapter authors, and we have heard the same from the authors themselves. Several of them have commented that the assignment to reflect on their early professional years that shaped the field affected them in ways they had not anticipated. Some discovered ways to conceptualize the field and found explanations for how it evolved, understandings they had not entertained before looking back and trying to make sense of it. And some discovered things about themselves—aspects of their early motivations and strivings. Viewing the beginnings from a later developmental stage in your life can do that.

The process of writing this book turned into a virtual conversation among us—a reflection on who we were, who we are, and what we did that blossomed in those who followed us. We came to know our earliest colleagues in new ways, despite working alongside them for 50 years.

We are not done. The authors and editors of this book represent the first cohort in modem psychology and law to retire or to be near that decision. Yet our CVs are not archived. We all continue to be active scholars, consultants, and advisors, contributing to the field's evolution. You don't quit doing something you love. You find creative ways to do it differently, freed from the demands of employers.

Speaking now as editors, what do we see for modem psychology and law as it moves past its first 50 years? One of us once wrote a developmental history of psychology and law as it reached "adulthood" in its twenty-first year (Grisso, 1991). The modern field of psychology and law manifests the maturity and wisdom associated with mid-life. Its level of sophistication makes our early contributions seem almost naïve but also prescient. We look at the field now in a generational sense, recognizing those who we have trained, who have gone on to train others, who will soon be training yet others entering the field. We view this with the pride of an older generation secure in its knowledge that those whom they nurtured will exceed their own accomplishments.

And like most elders, we worry. We do not worry about the abilities of those who follow us. We worry about changing times and about how the demands of the world will challenge our successors.

For example, we worry about the challenges of increasing diversity in the world that we serve. Racial and ethnic minorities will soon constitute the majority of citizens of the country. That population increasingly will be unlike the population on which our foundational psychology and law research has been based and on which many of our forensic assessment methods have been normed. Our psychology and law researchers and forensic clinicians themselves, as a Society, will not reflect the nation's diversity unless we witness an accelerated trend in the diversity of ethnic backgrounds of those entering the field.

We worry also about divisiveness within the field. Differentiation is a basic principle of development. As our field develops further, differentiation upon differentiation offers multiple risks for fracturing the broader field of psychology and law. At some point, the differentiated parts may become so complex and disparate, developing separate identities, that they may lose sight of the value of unity. Can the American Psychology–Law Society (AP–LS) meet the interests of those who study juries and those who study psychopathy? Those whose interests are in criminal law and those in juvenile law? Those who perform forensic assessments and those who engage in treatment in correctional settings? How do such disparate interests fit in a single psychology and law tent?

But we are consoled by history. Fifty years have taught us the resilience of the field of psychology and law. In the face of evolutionary differentiation of the field, AP–LS continues to thrive despite threats of possible dissolution over the disparate interests of researchers and forensic practitioners. In addition, we see trends that offer a trajectory toward unity. For example, we have witnessed an increasing demand in the training and expectations for forensic practitioners regarding scholarly and data-based foundations for practice. If we were able to construct a 50-year graph of forensic practitioners' perceived value of a science base for their work, it would show a markedly rising slope, bringing practitioners and researchers closer together in their support of the focus on science.

The field will surmount individual interests in favor of the excitement and tension at its core—the dynamic relation between science and advocacy. Moreover, we have confidence in the wisdom of the field to recognize the advantages of unity. Break-away organizations with very specific and narrow foci would sacrifice the political impact and credibility of a Society that represents all of psychology and law to the public and the legal system. We are certain of one more thing that promises to sustain the field and its vitality, and it is demonstrated in every chapter of this book: The law will always make assumptions about human behavior, and it will always be in need of applied psychological research and those who can interpret it to guide legal decisions, advise legal processes, and improve legal systems. After 50 years, almost daily we still witness new questions to which we can apply our knowledge base, research methods, and courtroom testimony. The field continues to attract young researchers, practitioners, and legal scholars with extraordinary creativity and perseverance.

Epilogue or overture? Endings are beginnings. For those who will be witnessing the seventy-fifth and one-hundredth anniversaries of the field of modern psychology and law, we leave this book as a bench mark and time capsule. Remember the roots it describes and use it to measure how much you have accomplished since these first 50 years.

*Addington v. Texas*, 98, 149
Alfini, James, 111
American Academy of Forensic
 Psychology, 196–206
American Board of Forensic Psychology,
 196–206
*The American Jury* (Kalven/Zeisel),
 61–63, 73
American Psychology– Law Society
 (AP–LS), 10–21, 11nn5–6, 13n7,
 14n8, 119–122
*Apodaca v. Oregon*, 46
Ares, Charles, 81
Arizona Jury Project, 73
Arizona State Hospital, 128–130
*Arizona v. Chapple*, 37
Aspen, Marvin, 71
*Atkins v. Virginia*, 106

*Ballew v. Georgia*, 47, 50, 67–68
Bandura, Albert, 209
Baron, Charles, 47–48, 50
Barrows, Sydney Biddle, 52
Bazelon, David, 9
Bazelon, Richard, 201
Bennis, Warren, 210
Bersoff, Donald, 13
Blackmun, Harry, 9, 67–68, 136–137
Blau, Ted, 203
Bodin, Arthur, 202

Bok Tower Gardens, 180–181
Bonnie, Richard, 103, 105, 215
Brain Overclaim Syndrome, 106
Brodsky, Stanley, 146, 178–192, 223–225
*Brown v. Board of Education*, 7, 9, 145
Buckhout, Robert, 36, 45
*Buck v. Bell*, 5, 5n3
Burtt, Harold, 3–5, 4n2

Campbell, Donald, 63
"Case of the Mayflower Madame," 52
Causal theory of excuse, 100, 104
Champaign County diversion program,
 131–132
Chapple, Dolan, 37
Charlton, D., 55
Chicago Jury Project, 45
*Children's Definitions of the Truth and
 Their Competence as Witnesses
 in Legal Proceedings* (Haugaard),
 217–218
Children's rights, capacities. *See also*
 community psychology
 autonomy, 159, 168–169
 clinical evaluations, 161–164
 competency to stand trial, 139
 cultural background, 171–172
 decision-making, 169–170
 due process, 159–160
 historical context, 158–161

Children's rights, capacities (*cont.*)
  *Miranda* problem, 163–165
  *Miranda* waiver study, 166–168
  parens patriae doctrine, 159–160
  predictions of violence, 154
  reform schools, 163, 163n3
  research studies, 164–165, 168–171
  sentencing, limits on, 171
  sexual abuse, 216–218
  terminology, 158n1
  testimony of, in legal contexts, 217–218
Christie, Richard, 113
Civil Rights Act of 1964, 143
*Clark v. Arizona,* 105
*Classification of Violence Risk (COVR),*
  152–153
Clements, Carl, 184
Clinical assessments
  community psychology, 217
  forensic, 138–140
  predictive validity, 146, 149
  tools, 149–150, 152–155
*Clinical Prediction of Violent Behavior*
  (Monahan), 150
Clinical psychology development, 7
Cocozza, Joseph, 146
Cohen, Ned, 103
Cohen, Robert, 217
*Colgrove v. Battin,* 67
*Coming Out Cold* (McArthur), 212
*Community Mental Health and*
  *the Criminal Justice System*
  (Monahan), 148
Community psychology. *See also* children's
  rights, capacities
  approach, discovery of, 208–211
  background, 207–208
  child sexual abuse, 216–218
  clinical assessments, 217
  parent–child–state triad, 216
  public policy, 215–216
  seminars, 210–211
  training, 215
Competency Assessment Instrument, 135
Competency to stand trial, 136–137

cash bail system, 131–132
community-based evaluations, 135–136,
  138–139
defendants found IST, 84–85, 134
deinstitutionalization movement,
  128–130, 134–135
forensic evaluations in, 133–139
functional definition of
  competency, 134
indefinite treatment commitment,
  136–137
juvenile proceedings, 139
Connecticut School for Boys, 213–215
Contract Buyers League case, 63
Conyers, John, 104
*The Correctional Psychologist,* 183
Correctional psychology
  Alabama prisoner reclassification,
    186–187
  class actions lawsuits, 187–189
  criminal justice system and,
    180–183, 181n3
  expert witnesses, 185, 189–191
  graduate training in, 184–186
  jail/diversion reform, 130–133, 138
  journal publications, 183–184
  prison conditions, 178–180, 186,
    188, 190
  prisoners interpersonal relationships
    study, 181, 181n3
  prison-to-hospital transfers, 82n2, 85
  reforms, 191–192
Cowen, Emory, 207
*Criminal Commitments and Dangerous*
  *Mental Patients* (Wexler), 84
*Criminal Justice/Behavior,* 183–184
Criminal responsibility
  case law, 96–98, 97n1
  causal theory of excuse, 100, 104
  compatibilism, 100
  death penalty application, 105–106
  determinism/free will in, 99–101, 99n2
  diminished capacity doctrine, 97–98,
    101–104, 121
  evidence exclusion, 105

expertise role in predictive reliability,
   98–99, 101, 103
fundamental psycholegal error,
   99–101, 99n2
insanity defense, 97, 97n1, 104–106
mitigating conditions in, 99–101, 99n2
sexual predators, 106

Dangerousness, burden of proof, 149
*Daubert* standards, 22
*Daubert v. Merrill Dow
   Pharmaceuticals,* 55
Davis, Angela, 36
Dean, Charles, 210–214
Death penalty application, 105–106
Defendants found NGRI, 85–86, 134
Deinstitutionalization movement, 128–130,
   134–135
DeLeon, Patrick, 120, 203
*Delling v. Idaho,* 105
Denbeaux, Mark, 52
Dershowitz, Alan, 95, 149
Determinism/free will, 99–101, 99n2
Devine, D. J., 65
Diamond, Shari S., 61–74
Diminished capacity doctrine, 97–98,
   101–104, 121
Dix, Dorothea, 128, 135
DNA typing, 54–55
*Donaldson v. O'Connor,* 185
Dror, I. E., 55
*Dusky v. United States,* 9, 189
Duty of reasonable care to third parties,
   86–88, 144–145

Early Assessment Risk Lists for Boys
   (EARL-20B)/Girls (EARL-21G), 154
Ebbesen, Ebbe, 44
Education. *See* training
Elwork, Amiram, 112
Ennis, Bruce, 146
*Essays in Therapeutic Jurisprudence*
   (Wexler/Winick), 90
Eugenics movement, 5, 5n3
Expert witnesses

correctional psychology, 185, 189–191
eyewitness testimony, 36–42
predictions of violence, 148–149
social psychology, 51, 55
Eyewitness testimony
expert witnesses, 36–42
as field of research, 35
history of, 32–33
leading questions effects on, 34–35
legal standards for, 42
memory distortion effects,
   31–34, 38–42
repressed memory cases, 38–40
research, evolution of, 38–39
social psychology, 45, 53

Faigman, David, 55
Fernald, Grace, 3
Feshbach, Norma, 159
Feshbach, Seymour, 159
Forensic psychology
in competency to stand trial
   evaluations, 133–139
development of, 20
in social psychology, 51–52,
   54–56, 55n1
*Specialty Guidelines for Forensic
   Psychologists,* 15–16, 20
training in, 196–206
Fowler, Ray, 184, 187
Franklin, George, 38
Free, James, 71
Freedman, Jonathan, 33
*Frye v. United States,* 3

*Gault, In re,* 9, 80, 159–160, 211
Goldenberg, Ira, 210
Golding, Stephen, 15, 131, 133–138
Goldner, Jesse, 165
Gooding, William, 127–128, 132
Gravitz, Melvin, 203
Grisso, Thomas, 116, 158–172, 183,
   223–225
*Griswold v. Connecticut,* 9
Group decision research, 45–52

Haber, Ralph, 106
Hallisey, Robert, 51–52
Haney, Craig, 187
Hargrove, David, 117
Hart, Stephen, 130
Haugaard, Jeffrey, 217
Healy, William, 3
Heller, Kenneth, 147
Hinckley, John W., 97n1, 104
Holler, Ron, 130

Insanity defense
  criminal responsibility, 97, 97n1,
    104–106
  defendants found NGRI, 85–86
Insanity Defense Reform Act of 1984,
    97n1, 102, 104
Institute of Law, Psychiatry and Public
  Policy, 215
*International Journal of Forensic Mental
  Health,* 130
Involuntary commitment. *See* civil
  commitment
Iscoe, Ira, 207
Ives, Margaret, 204

*Jackson v. Indiana,* 136
Jail/diversion reform, 130–133, 138
*Jenkins v. U.S.,* 9, 204
Johnson, Frank M., 121, 186, 187
*Johnson v. Louisiana,* 46
*Judging in a Therapeutic Key*
  (Wexler/Winick), 90–91
Jury behavior
  active jury studies, 71–73
  group decision research, 45–52
  judge/jury research, 68–69
  jury selection, 63–64, 112–114
  legal instructions to, 70–71, 73, 111–112
  research, history of, 61–66
  sampling procedures, 63
  sentencing studies, 68–69
  simulation research, 69–70
  size studies, 66–68
Juvenile justice, 211–219

Juvenile Psychopathic Institute, 3
Juveniles. *See* children's rights, capacities;
  community psychology

Kagan, Jerome, 208
Kalven, Harry, 45, 49, 61–62, 73
Kandel, Art, 181
*Kansas v. Crane,* 106
*Kansas v. Hendricks,* 106
*Karsjens v. Jesson,* 106
Kaslow, Florence W., 195–206
Kelly, James, 207, 208
Kenneth Kuumba Shackleford Community
  Institute, 131–132
*Kent v. U. S.,* 159–160, 211
King, Paul, 206
Konecni, Vladimir, 44
Koocher, Gerald, 159
Kurke, Martin, 199, 201

*Lake v. Cameron,* 9
Lake Wales Conference, 181–184
Lanterman–Petris–Short Act, 98, 144, 145
*Law and Human Behavior,* 11–12,
  11nn5–6, 65, 118
*Law and Psychology in Conflict*
  (Marshall), 8
*Law in a Therapeutic Key* (Wexler/
  Winick), 90
*Legal and Criminal Psychology* (Toch), 8
*Legal Psychology* (Burtt), 3–5, 4n2, 8
Lempert, R. O., 69
*Lessard v. Schmidt,* 96
Levi, Judith, 71
Levinson, Robert, 183
Libby, Scooter, 41
Lipsitt, Paul, 200, 203, 205–206
Litwack, Thomas, 146
*Lockhart v. McCree,* 70
Loftus, Elizabeth, 33–42

MacArthur Violence Risk Assessment
  Study, 152
MacDougall, Ellis, 210
Mainstream project, 91–92

Marshall, James, 8
Marston, William, 3, 3n1
McArthur, Verne, 212
McDonald, Eddy Bobby, 37
McDonough, Leah, 147
McGarry, A. Louis, 133, 164
McMartin Day Care Sexual Abuse Case, 216–218
Melton, Gary, 19
Mental health law, 114–115
*Mental Health Law: Major Issues* (Wexler), 81
Mental Hygiene Law, 98
Miller, Jerome, 212
Miller, Kent, 188
Miller, Michael, 116
*Miranda* waiver study, 166–168
Moffitt, Terrie, 128
Monahan, John, 143–155, 215
Morris, Norval, 118, 146
Morse, Stephen J., 94–107
Morse, Steve, 203
Mulvey, Edward, 215
Munsterberg, Hugo, 2, 4–6, 32, 45

Nason, Susan, 38
*Natanson v. Kline*, 9
National Jury Project, 114
Neal, Tess, 182
*Newman v. State of Alabama*, 185
Niemi, Janice, 36

O'Brien, Charles, 197
*O'Connor v. Donaldson*, 98
Ogloff, James, 19
*On the Witness Stand* (Munsterberg), 2, 32
Ostrom, Tom, 46, 47
Otto, Randy, 16
Owens, Charles, 185

Pacht, Asher, 183
Palmer, John, 34
Patuxent Maryland Institution for Defective Delinquents, 181
Paul, Leonard, 199

Perlin, Michael, 80
Perlman, Harvey, 110, 117–118
Péron, A. E., 55
Pilpel, M. E., 2–3
*Planned Parenthood of Central Missouri v. Danforth*, 168–169
*Plessy v. Ferguson*, 5
*Powell v. Texas*, 96
Poythress, Norman, 103, 191
*Practicing Therapeutic Jurisprudence* (Wexler/Winick), 90
Predictions of violence
    clinical assessments predictive validity, 146, 149
    criminal justice system, 145–146
    expert witnesses, 148–149
    indeterminate sentencing, 145–146
    juveniles, 154
    mental health system reforms, 143–144
    outcome measures, 152–153
    research agenda, 150–153
    risk assessment resources, 149–150, 152–155
    tort liability, 86–88, 144–145
Prison Litigation Reform Act of 1996, 187
*Psychologists in the Criminal Justice System* (Brodsky), 182–183
*Psychology, Public Policy, and Law*, 119
Psychology and law
    conferences, 12
    demographics, degrees, 16–20
    dormant era, 6–7
    expert opinion focus of, 21–23
    federal initiatives in, 9–10
    human rights, 9
    identity, professional interests, 18–21
    interorganizational relations, 14–16, 14n8
    law affecting psychology, 115–116
    legal psychology era, 2–5, 3n1, 4n2, 5nn3–4
    maturation, identity of, 13–14, 119–121, 223–225
    mental health law, 114–116
    modern era, 8

Psychology and law (*cont.*)
  postwar law, 9
  psycholegal interventions, 116–117
  psychological science on, 111–113
  psychologists aiding law, 113–115
  publication resources, 11–12, 11nn5–6,
     118–119
  science/advocacy focus of, 21–23
  standards in, 12, 15–16, 22–23, 161,
     201–203
  training in (*See* training)
Publication resources, 11–12, 11nn5–6,
     118–119
*Pugh v. Locke,* 185, 186

Racial discrimination, 5, 5n4, 7
Rappaport, Julian, 131
Reasonable period of time, 137
Reppucci, N. Dickon, 150, 207–219
Risinger, Michael, 52
Roberti, David, 103
Robey, Ames, 189
*Robinson v. California,* 96
Rodham, Hillary, 159, 159n2
Roesch, Ronald, 65, 127–140
Rosenhan, David, 149, 197, 202

Safe Streets Act, 143
Saks, Michael J., 45–57, 67–68
Sales, Bruce, 84, 109–122, 165, 197–199
Santana, Angel Figueroa, 189–190
Sarason, Seymour, 207–210
Sarata, Brian, 213
Saunders, Terry, 213
Schopp, Robert, 89–90
Scogin, Forrest, 188
Scott, Elizabeth, 215
Seidman, Edward, 131, 137
Sexual predators, 106
Shah, Saleem, 10, 84, 118, 138, 149, 165,
     181, 183
Shapiro, David, 199, 201
Shulman, Jay, 113–114
Shuman, Dan, 81
Silverman, Hirsch, 199, 201–202

Skeem, Jennifer, 153, 154
Slesinger, Donald, 2–3, 151
Slobogin, Christopher, 103
Social psychology
  applications to law, 44–46
  context effects, 55
  development, 6–7
  expert witnesses, 51, 55
  eyewitness identification, 45, 53
  forensic sciences, 51–52, 54–56, 55n1
  group decision research (jury
     behaviors), 45–52
  jury research, 52
  law, potential for, 48–50
  procedural justice, 53–54
  psychological evidence, court's use
     of, 50–52
  tort system, 56–57, 56n2
*Social Psychology in Court* (Saks/Hastie),
     48–50, 165
*Social Science in Law* (Monahan/
     Walker), 151
Society for the Psychological Study of
     Social Issues, 6–7
Song, Anna, 208
*Specialty Guidelines for Forensic
     Psychologists,* 15–16, 20
Spellman, Barbara, 54
St. Louis County Juvenile Court Clinic, 161
Standards, 12, 15–16, 22–23, 161, 201–203
Stanley, Charlton S., 199
Steadman, Henry, 146, 148
Steinberg, Laurence, 170
Stinchcombe, Arthur, 111
Stone, Alan, 95, 149
Strachan, Roger, 128
Structured Assessment of Violence Risk in
     Youth (SAVRY), 154
Suggs, David, 114

Tapp, June Louin, 6, 119
*Tarasoff v. Regents of the University of
     California,* 86–88, 144–145
"The Administration of Psychiatric
     Justice," 81–82, 82n2

Therapeutic jurisprudence, 81–82, 82n2
  criminal commitment contingency
    structures, 84–86
  defendants found IST, 84–85, 134
  defendants found NGRI, 85–86, 134
  duty of reasonable care to third parties,
    86–88, 144–145
  early history of, 79–81
  family reintegration, 212
  indeterminate confinement, 84
  involuntary commitment, 81–82, 82n2
  law as therapy, 88–90
  Mainstream project, 91–92
  prison-to-hospital transfers, 82n2, 85
  therapeutic application of the law,
    82, 82n2
  "Token and Taboo," 83–84
  token economies, 83–84
Therapeutic Jurisprudence: The Law as a
    Therapeutic Agent (Wexler), 89
Thibaut, John, 44, 49, 53, 151
Third parties, duty of reasonable care to,
    86–88, 144–145
Tinker v. Des Moines, 9
Toch, Hans, 8
Tort liability, 86–88, 144–145
Tort system, 56–57, 56n2
Training
  board certification, 195–199
  community psychology, 215
  correctional psychology, 182,
    184–186
  forensic psychology, 196–206
  publication resources, 117–118
  standards in, 12–13, 13n7, 22–23,
    201–203
Trickett, Ed, 210

United States v. Brawner, 97
Uphaus, Willard, 178, 178n1
The Use/Nonuse/Misuse of Applied Social
    Research (Saks), 50

VandenBos, Gary, 203
Villanova Training Conference, 13
Violence predictions. See predictions of
    violence

Walker, Laurens, 44, 49, 53, 151
Weismann, Herb, 205
Weiten, W., 65, 70
Wells, Gary, 35
Werner, Stewart, 196
Wexler, David B., 78–92, 117, 149
Whetstone, Charles, 46–47
White, Dan, 102, 103
Wigmore, John Henry, 6, 32, 69
Wilkinson, Leland, 213
Willard Uphaus v. Louis C. Wyman,
    Attorney General, 178, 178n1
Williams v. Florida, 46, 50, 63, 66–67
Winick, Bruce, 80, 90–91
Wounded Knee Trials, 113–114
Wundt, Wilhelm, 2
Wyatt v. Aderholt, 121
Wyatt v. Stickney, 9, 83, 121, 185, 186

Yackle, Larry, 187
Youngberg v. Romeo, 98
Youth Level of Service/Case Management
    Inventory (YLS/ CMI), 154

Zeisel, Hans, 45, 49, 61–64, 66–67, 71, 73
Ziskin, Jay, 10, 18
Zwerling, Israel, 197